The Decade of Letting Things Go

The Decade of Letting Things Go

A POSTMENOPAUSE MEMOIR

Cris Mazza

The University of Georgia Press

ATHENS

Published by the University of Georgia Press
Athens, Georgia 30602
www.ugapress.org
© 2024 by Cris Mazza
All rights reserved
Designed by Kaelin Chappell Broaddus
Set in 10.25/13 Minion 3 Regular by Kaelin Chappell Broaddus
Printed and bound by Sheridan Books, Inc.
The paper in this book meets the guidelines for permanence
and durability of the Committee on Production Guidelines for
Book Longevity of the Council on Library Resources.

Most University of Georgia Press titles are
available from popular e-book vendors.

Printed in the United States of America
28 27 26 25 24 P 5 4 3 2 1

Library of Congress Cataloging-in-Publication Data
Names: Mazza, Cris, author.
Title: The decade of letting things go : a postmenopause memoir / Cris Mazza.
Description: Athens : The University of Georgia Press, 2024. |
    Series: Crux : the Georgia series in literary nonfiction
Identifiers: LCCN 2024008384 | ISBN 9780820367545 (paperback) |
    ISBN 9780820367552 (epub) | ISBN 9780820367569 (pdf)
Subjects: LCSH: Mazza, Cris. | Women authors, American—Biography. |
    Older women—United States—Biography.
Classification: LCC PS3563.A988 Z46 2024 | DDC 814/.54 [B]—dc23/eng/20240618
LC record available at https://lccn.loc.gov/2024008384

To Mark and Jim.
Some things do not need to be let go.

And

To my sisters and brothers,
fellow residents and caretakers
of the house on the hill.

There are few things this country is less interested in than aging women. . . . Once they've passed the age of facile objectification and commodification, they're supposed to disappear. How dare they not cooperate with our national insistence that older women become invisible?

—Leslie Bennetts, "Go Away? Why Should She?" *Los Angeles Times*, March 9, 2008

Contents

Author's Foreword (Written Afterward)   xiii

Acknowledgments   xv

Fear Itself   1

Like a Boyfriend   7

Brutality of the Hunt (for Serenity)   11

House (What Things Are Called)   23

How Substandard Closet Design Inflamed
My Chronic Dread   33

Feral   44

Camp (An Unruly Word)   56

Oneiric (Another Word I've Never Said)   64

Neighborhood (Taking It to the Grass)   77

Northwoods Nap (Classically Conditioned)   104

A Finished Brain   113

Intercourse in Absentia   133

Friend, Partner, Boyfriend   139

Condom Races   146

Nothing to Offer   161

I Work, Therefore I Am:
A(n Incomplete) Conversation about Identity
(with Footnoted Asides)   181

Dark Money   198

The Summer of Letting Things Go   206

Day of Reckoning   225

Author's Foreword (Written Afterward)

Let me be the first to remark: the decade in question had to be expanded to include the years it took to finish this book.

Originally titled *Faulty Logic*. B follows A; therefore A caused B. Because menopause happened, and then life changed. But "the change" didn't cause the life changes. This book is not *about* menopause.

True, menopause *allowed* me to finally admit my dysfunctional sex life was not going to improve, that anorgasmia was permanent. At the very least, menopause put the period at the end of that sentence. Wasn't there more to life than sex? I had to believe so.

But menopause—which is the body's decay, not the character or persona—completes a passage to near invisibility. So at one time this book was titled *Invisibility*.

Yet the majority of essays here aren't about becoming or being made to feel invisible. Still I couldn't help but wonder, If life events take place after a person becomes invisible, did they really happen?

Acknowledgments

Acknowledgments made to the following publications in which these essays appeared in earlier versions:

Anomaly for "Nothing to Offer"

Ascent for "How Substandard Closet Design Inflamed My Constant Dread"

Brevity for "Feeding Time" in "The Summer of Letting Things Go"

Crab Creek Review for "Plumbing" in "The Summer of Letting Things Go"

Eckleberg Review for "Condom Races"

Essay Daily for "Neighborhood"

Lit at the End of the World (Moria Books) for "Camp"

LitBreak for "Touched" in "The Summer of Letting Things Go"

Literary Orphans for "Still Early" in "The Summer of Letting Things Go"

Packingtown Review for "I Work, Therefore I Am"

Ragazine for "Intercourse in Absentia"

Nervous Breakdown for "Like a Boyfriend," "Feral," "House," and "Brutality of the Hunt (for Serenity)"

Rumpus for "A Finished Brain" and "Oneiric"

Western Humanities Review for "Northwoods Nap"

The Decade of Letting Things Go

Fear Itself

2010

In fifth or sixth grade, I found some crudely produced porn—a magazine page folded up, dropped on the dirt-road shoulder where I walked home from school. There were no women in the thumbnail photos, approximately nine on the page. They were all penises. I believe they were semi-erect, or even recently erect but semiflaccid. Even in this phase of arousal, these penises were enormous. I think I could barely even stare—perhaps glanced quickly, but over and over and over.

I had only recently learned what intercourse was. Now I was facing (even if obliquely) the mammoth objects that were supposed to go inside me. Instantly fear burgeoned. Fear that had already been germinating due to how sex had been described to me on the playground the year before as being "stuck together" butt to butt like the silkworm moths in our classroom terrarium. Maybe I'd have been better off seeing real ones on boys my age. Because Franklin Roosevelt was right: fear is the greatest enemy. It can cause reactions more harmful than the object of fear itself, even when it comes to sex.

Ten-plus secretly fearful years later, a mentor said to me, "Obsessing is like overcooking an egg. The cell breaks down, corrodes, and gets really ugly."

Because there was something else to agitate about. From literary sex (this time not represented in photographs), I learned I was missing a "clear burning desire." Clear . . . In that sentence "clear" is not modifying the way the desire is supposed to feel, but that it should have been obvious: obviously there, and obvious what it was. And since in me it was not only not obvious but obviously not even there, how did I know I was *supposed* to be feeling something? From books. Those I read, not those I wrote. In the twenty books I subsequently authored, I tried to understand, and create, what I was supposed to be feeling and how it was supposed to work.

There are sex scenes in books, even some published by friends of mine, that I'd like to call bullshit. People slide so easily in and out of each other. Men even "fuck women's brains out"—the cliché still too easily and readily used. And the women feel something and have orgasms doing it. Yet wasn't Freud's "vaginal orgasm" itself bullshit? Why do fictional heroines still: (a) Lose their virginity so easily and without anxiety, self-doubt, pain, or awkwardness? (b) Feel so much (pleasure) during male thrusting? And (c) Climax every time? Truthfully, I can't read these fictional scenes anymore. They just seem like bullshit. I want every woman who wrote one to sit in a therapy group with me and honestly describe her own sexual experience so that I can gauge her fictional renditions.

Why do women still seem to write the male-centric view of sex? Because men so desperately want penis thrusting to be the ultimate sensation we can experience? This shown in one line in a book by a famous male writer, in a novel where he wrote from a female point of view: "She came as soon as he entered her." What is this, a teenaged boy's fantasy? All it takes is his penis pushing in and she'll be in ecstasy. Either that or the author had a lot of women faking it. That's what I mean by male-centric sex scenes, or penis-centric (or fuck-centric). Women characters who experience so damn much pleasure from the friction of penis-vagina intercourse; it makes me crazy. But this kind of obsessing does no one good when "the moment is right," as Cialis says.

Meanwhile, back in girlhood, after finding the page of penis photos, my next significant (and nonclassroom) sex lessons came in high school from *The Happy Hooker*, a popular pornographic memoir by an infamous madam. From *The Happy Hooker*, I don't remember anything specific except that, to the author, size mattered, which stirred memories of that page of penises. After *Happy*, but before I was brought to a porn theater—by a friend and her boyfriend—to see *Deep Throat*, my literary sex education had continued from Erica Jong's *Fear of Flying* and its sequel *How to Save Your Own Life*. Without going back to reread now, thirty years later, I do believe (the fictional) Isadora Wing's orgasms were always clitoral and seldom "vaginal" achieved during intercourse. She masturbated like crazy to get herself off, she had a lot to say about some men's ineptness, she never mentioned pain, but she did not like going down on another woman; she vilified the smell. I'm sure this greatly assisted my own body loathing, although I was by this time at least twenty years old and had never masturbated.

I've heard masturbation is essential to a woman being able to orgasm with a partner—"teaching yourself how to feel" without the pressure of needing to please a partner at the same time. There's a recent article extolling the same message, except in the 2014 version, it doesn't even include the idea that masturbation is supposed to teach girls how to orgasm; it just says they *need* to orgasm. Like it's a given that they always will.

> Orgasms are good for you. And masturbation means no partner or drama required. Have a migraine? Masturbate. Feeling stuck creatively? Masturbate. Feeling blue? Masturbate. Can't sleep? Masturbate. Mired in stress? Low self-esteem? Sex drive in low gear? Chronic pain? Masturbation is good for what ails you.
>
> It's also good for what doesn't ail you. It feels good to slowly tease yourself until you can't take it anymore. It feels good to rub or buzz or pound yourself into a frenzy full-steam ahead. It feels good to get off and it's empowering to be able to do it for yourself. It's your equipment. There is absolutely, positively, no reason not to use it.
>
> Which brings me to my point—masturbation is really important. It's really important for all women and it's equally important for teenage girls.

It's vital for them to know their bodies. It's imperative for them to have a way to relieve stress. But more than anything, it's paramount that they know they don't need anyone else to bring them pleasure. They can "take care of business" all by themselves. No risk of pregnancy or disease or slut shaming or anything.

—Jenny Block, "The Most Important Thing Teen Girls Should Do But Don't: Masturbate," *Jezebel*, April 16, 2014

Difficult to argue with any of this, except it didn't/doesn't apply to me: I didn't do it, and not out of shame. I had no desire driving me to do so. It wasn't something I ever did simply because my body had and has never asked me to try. And masturbating wouldn't have alleviated any "need" to seek pleasure with another person because I didn't have any drive or desire to get it that way either. I never risked pregnancy or disease to get satisfaction because ... What was *satisfaction*? And what was supposed to drive me to get it?

Where was it, that feeling I was supposed to have? That thing called "horny" that boys obviously had, that some girls claimed to know, and I didn't? That old cliché about raging hormones ... What did it feel like? What had caused it to leave or never materialize?

Perhaps the culprit was fear.

That same *fear* did have another consequence in store for me: pain. And anorgasmia—the physical inability or continued failure to orgasm—which wasn't something I worried about a lot at first, being too consumed by the pain that also led to celibate marriages.

Painful sex and anorgasmia: the latter can be experienced without the former, but really, how could one suffer the pain and *not* have unqualified anorgasmia?

To regret one has a vagina or own one with distaste and resentment; to wonder what the "ecstasy" and pleasure—pleasure written about in both fiction and memoir, shown in film (or porn), or alluded to by friends—is all about or even begins to feel like; to describe sex in words like "friction" at its best, or "scraping," "raw," and "searing" at its worst. These were my initiations into a club no one would ask to join: female sexual dysfunction.

Fear had an unfortunate partner assisting to send me, from the get-go, into sexual dysfunction in the form of an equally unhealthy boy who never kissed me, hardly ever talked to me, never sat with me in a movie or coffee shop . . . but on the way home from school in his van pinned my resistant body so that he could touch parts of me I wasn't advertising or offering. I resisted hard enough to not allow the tussle to lead to intercourse but not enough to stop him completely, and not enough to only allow it to happen once. There was another message fear was delivering: *if you don't like this, something's wrong with you, something that will make boys— and then men—not want you.* So it was several times a week, for several weeks. Memory mashes it into one category of sweaty anxiety. Considering the prevalence of sexual assault on girls who think as I did, I got off lucky at the time. But like date-rape victims, I paid with my future.

I remained a fearful virgin until I was twenty-four. The fear I stewed myself in was not only aberrant but probably the largest part of the cause for my lifetime dysfunction. I waited to seek professional help until a failing marriage might have been (but wasn't) saved with (abysmal, it turns out) sex therapy (which is also not going to a doctor). When I finally got a diagnosis, I found it myself—I don't remember where, but it was before the internet was available. Now that diagnosis is easy to find: vaginismus. But the syndrome only describes the symptoms without explaining a cause.

The cause is easy to theorize: surely the mushrooming fear of intimacy that overwhelmed me in my late teens and early twenties set me up for the involuntary muscle spasms of vaginismus. And once the cycle starts, and a conscious mind is anticipating how much sex hurts and is going to hurt again, each subsequent encounter results in the same pain. There are physical therapies for vaginismus,[1] but none for the simmering brain that cooked it.

1. See "Friend, Partner, Boyfriend."

My sexual dysfunction could have been prevented by some things I couldn't control (I couldn't unsee the porn I accidentally found) and by some I could have controlled (run, and run fast, from that first boy who touched me).

But here's the best therapy of all: A man who cares more about how his partner feels than he does about his own pleasure and is willing to listen and learn. A man who cares more about his partner's self-esteem than he cares how well his partner conforms to culture's depiction of a sexy and sex-loving woman. I actually had to go back to my fearful past to find him. He was back there waiting for me. That's a longer story. One I would likely not trade, now, for that illusory complete and normal sex life.

Like a Boyfriend

2010

Language needs a few new relationship words. Particularly *boyfriend*.

The issue of *boy* having a troubled history speaks for itself. Except it's interesting to note that Black jazz musicians in the 1940s began calling each other *man* because of the Jim Crow practice of referring to them as *boys*. This then is the root of the all-encompassing pronoun-slash-exclamation *man* used by most musicians, bleeding into beatniks and then to many other bonded male groups: athletes, actors, (poets?).

So while women don't mind (even, in my case, prefer) to be called *girls*, men don't usually refer to themselves, individually, as *boys*. As in *I'm a boy who likes* _____. Yes, there's the old standard *one of the boys*. Or *boys' night out*. Or even *my boys* (although that could mean the male anatomy that comes in a pair.)

A few years ago an algorithmic analysis of two online dating sites done by Wired.com discovered that women seeking a relationship with a male received 16 percent more contacts if they referred to themselves as a *girl* instead of a *woman*. But men seeking a female relationship were 28 percent more likely to get hits on their post if they referred to females as *women* as opposed to *girls*.

There was no number crunching for men seeking heterosexual relationships who referred to themselves as *boys*, and I suspect gay men do not refer to themselves, nor the partners they are seeking, as *boys*.

There's an intellectual argument made for why women should reject being called *girls*. I don't know why I prefer *girl* to *woman*. It doesn't, I don't think, have to do with age. I don't dress like my college students, but I think I also don't dress like a *woman*.

Those last words *like a woman* reverberated for a few minutes, sending my inner ear to begin singing "Just Like a Woman." Nobel laureate Bob Dylan's 1966 lyrics—look them up or just let the harmonica-backed tune conjure them—wander through what "you" do that's "Just Like a Woman," until "you" crack like a childish girl.

Dylan's critics over the years debated whether he was being misogynistic in "Just Like a Woman." The *New York Times*: "There's no more complete catalogue of sexist slurs," and "[Dylan] defines women's natural traits as greed, hypocrisy, whining and hysteria." *Allmusic*: "There is nothing in the text to suggest that Dylan has a disrespect for, much less an irrational hatred of, women in general." Unsurprisingly, the first quote was from a woman (Marion Mead), the second by a man (Bill Janovitz).

Yet the misogyny in the lyric never occurred to me. I always both wanted to be the person Dylan was singing about and knew I was at best only half of her. The *takes* part I assumed was related to the *makes love* part, assuming both had to do with intercourse, because I first became aware of the song as a skittish virgin, and then as a recently-not-virgin-any-longer but one for whom sex was difficult. Except the discomfort was not exactly an *ache* (too soft a word), but there *was* pain in there, and no one seemed to fit. I did not *make love* like any woman I'd ever read about or seen on a screen, but it did hurt plenty, and the pain was, indeed, an enduring curse. So I recognized the broken little girl.

I might add here that I thought Ned Washington's lyrics for the jazz standard "The Nearness of You" were: *It's not the pain—oooo / that excites me . . .*

So *girl* has never affronted me. I don't have children, I don't have a *little black dress*, I don't have either *heels* or *pumps* or *flats*. I have some makeup I haven't attempted to use for twenty years. I do go to a hairstylist. Usually, at the end, when she asks if I want any *product* in my hair, I decline. These places used to be called *beauty shops*. Where one, I suppose, bought *beauty* the way one bought meat in a meat shop.

Basically, I say I'm a *girl*, or I'm *female*. Although I might ask, "Why are there no women writers listed here?" and, yes, I'll include myself in the absent names. The term *women's literature* is one of the greatest affronts of all. Because there's never been a category of *men's literature*.

But personally, being a *girl* is okay. And as long as I can still sit on the floor cross-legged and stand up directly from that position, I'll take it. So, *girlfriend*; that's okay too, and, after all, for all female friends, no one says, "She's a woman-friend of mine." (Although just *friend* is fine.)

But at what age can a man still be comfortable with *boyfriend*? Unlike *girlfriend*, *boyfriend* never means a man's male buddies. For gay men in their forties and fifties, if they're still unmarried, how do they refer to their partners? Yes, some still use *partner*. I like *partner* too. But I can also have partners in other kinds of ventures and subsets of life.

A man I'm seeing has come into use. When I tried it, my *partner* cringed. "You're *seeing* me? Is that what we're doing?" Sharing a house, a bedroom, a bed, meals, clean-up, TV shows and movies, snow shoveling, dog-poop pickup and lawn mowing, grocery shopping and exercising. Everything. Plus reminiscing. But if I say he's *my man*, then I'm back to contending with being *his woman*. That word again, but with troublesome possessive pronouns added. The aggravating aura for me is not, like for feminists in the 1970s and 1980s, the word *man* appearing in *woman* (so they changed the spelling to *womyn* and *womin*). For me, maybe, it's the implied *womb* in woman. And at this point my knees should be buckling at the edge of an analyst's sofa.

Except I also loathe *lady*. Who doesn't?

Dylan went from "Just Like a Woman" (1966) to "Lay, Lady Lay" (1969). Given my lifelong sexual issues, I did not ever wish to be associated with the subject of the later song. Nor would it have been better *Lie, Lady Lie*, which is grammatically correct (considering Dylan denied that the lyrics were sexual).

Other "women" in songs I wished I could associate myself with: the "She's Always a Woman" in Billy Joel's 1977 flip side to "Just the Way You Are." I preferred to put these two messages together, that I was always that woman (or girl) just the way I was. Plus there was Joel's "Modern Woman" in 1986 whose detached stare heightened tension. My *boyfriend* (*partner*) says yes, I had that effect.

And here my desiring to be the girl in a song might have ended: 1986. When my now *boyfriend* moved one hundred miles away to marry someone else, because *I* was already married to someone else and he said it was killing him to stand around watching me be someone else's wife. (*Wife.* There's a word that needs looking at.)

It took twenty-five years, but now he's standing around watching me be *his* _____.

Brutality of the Hunt (for Serenity)

WINTER 2011

Campus sits south and west of the Loop, at the junction of the Kennedy and Eisenhower Expressways. In the 1960s, University of Illinois at Chicago wedged its way into and consumed Chicago's Little Italy, grew tentacles into the near west and south sides. At one time called Circle Campus: an urban myth that it was dubbed for the knot of concrete "spaghetti bowl" ramps where the two arteries bisect, but actually named for the architect's circle theme. Nevertheless, like the expressways' raised, rounded ramps, UIC was built of concrete in a style called "brutalism." Another myth remains that this style was meant to emulate Soviet public housing, *and* that "circle campus" was built to be riot proof. The style featured double-layer covered walkways akin to narrow parking garages, an open-air amphitheater, and massive concrete wheelchair ramps to second-floor entries reiterating the circle motif. Jessica Steward on My Modern Met explains, "The word *Brutalism* doesn't come from its harsh aesthetic, but from the material it is made of. *Béton brut* is a French term that translates literally to 'raw concrete.'" Regardless of the actual definition of brutalism, UIC was a miniature replica of an Eastern Bloc city, now including crumbling concrete facades. Falling pieces are stopped by scaffolding erected to protect students and faculty who also mill on (and off) grass-lined footpaths under trees that, in the '90s, replaced the severe web of covered walkways. The round quad in front of twenty-four-story University Hall underwent a decade-long project to add grassy knolls, flowered borders, and (perhaps another wink at brutalism) tile-lined fountains that rarely run because they're perpetually broken.

But I walk campus without envy for Northwestern, University of Chicago, DePaul, or Loyola. They have tradition, bigger trees, vine-covered brick buildings probably called Old Main. We have brutalism. It's where part of me—a native Californian—lives, has lived for over two decades.

One uncharacteristically gentle evening in February, as I walked across the circle quad from University Hall toward the parking lot, a rabbit came hurrying down the sidewalk beside the Behavioral Sciences Building, and continued scurrying down one of the angled paths through the circle. I've seen bunnies here before, usually lazily browsing on a lawn, then hopping, unconcerned, to rest under the daylilies. I wasn't too amazed to see a rabbit in a bigger hurry to a farther destination (albeit sticking to a paved sidewalk), but a few beats after it had gone past, a coyote emerged from the same corridor in obvious pursuit, ears erect, body driving forward, following the scent of the rabbit that had, by then, gone past out of sight. I wasn't the only person outside. Students were on campus to study; evening classes were in session. The coyote didn't flinch at the presence of people—I was twenty to thirty feet away when it passed. It could have been somebody's dog, loosened from its leash to chase squirrels. But it wasn't a dog. It wasn't domestic. It was hunting its natural prey in what has become its habitat.

I wanted to begin with this image. I didn't need to know, at the time, what the narrative that began with this brutalist metropolitan coyote would be about. But now I do know: this is about the place(s) the other part(s) of me live.

I've been house hunting—assisted closely by my soon-to-be exhusband—to live in with a man who was the boy who haunted my youth.

The soon-to-be ex-husband is a man I have hurt. A man nine years older who—after he'd built, then sold a wholesale business; after he'd contracted the designing and construction of his own custom-designed Corbusier-style house in San Diego County—guided and shaped me through my forties. Anti-feminist to claim to be shaped, but I mean it in the way we all shape one another when working/living together in a partnership. And I call it working together not because we shared a profession, but because building a life is a form of working together. We did that: built a life from the ruins of two earlier divorces, a life that included a large twenty-first-century Tudor revival with property adjoining some woods and a creek fifty miles from Chicago (a house whose interior design is now California contemporary); a wilderness house in the Upper Peninsula of Michigan; and the lifetimes (and assisted deaths) of several dogs who were our partners at canine performance events and whose care and training fed our type-A personalities. Then I hurt him and destroyed that almost completely idyllic life we'd built by reconnecting with the other man. A man my age who needs me to help him forget his thirties and forties and face his midfifties and beyond. Help him through the aftermath of being used (and sometimes abused) by a spouse and her children to support them and continue supporting them (and their children) in adult lives of mooching, stealing, child abandoning, drug addiction, some jail time, and runaway credit card debt (that fell to him). He'd put together this "substitute life," he called it—a life to keep himself busy in every waking hour just fulfilling responsibilities of work and home—so that he wouldn't have time to think about the reason he'd taken it on: the creeping lava flow of awareness that a life with me was not going to happen.

I've had to summarize both men's situations and not even touch on their characters, because the whole story would require books—plural—once I let myself follow the tangents and tentacles of other experiences and choices. Spousal abuse of a man—although no injury needing medical care, just soda cans crushed on his head, fry pans of oil flung in his direction, and like incidents—is a tempting subject for a novel. And a man who submitted to it in order to not give himself time to yearn for what he'd originally wanted is a tempting character. But this is real, and for now I can't spare the words to go there.

There are my own emotions I'm consumed with at present.

Guilt, regret, loss, the familiar ingredients of the pejoratively termed domestic novel. These are real too. As is the utter consideration, co-operation, care, and even compassion shown by my ex-husband as we move closer and closer to moving me from a place and a space I love, so that I can start—decades belated—to build another life with a man I love.

Who *he* is and the nature of my feelings for him will have to go undeveloped, as he is two thousand miles away putting in his last few years as a public school band director, powerless (and at times anguished about it) to help with the daily dismantling of my current life: the house hunting, the staggering extent of work and money each new prospect would take to let me feel comfortable there; and the melancholy—I've tried to restrain from him, from both Mark and Jim—of returning home to the Tudor, still home for now, to look out my windows at my tree line, the cornfield beyond, the woods and creek beyond that, after having viewed houses (the realtor insists on calling them "homes") whose square backyards are surrounded by five identical yards, frequently with aboveground pools, colorful plastic play sets, huge trampolines, and—in some cases—dilapidated sheds or travel trailers covered in tattered tarps.

To list the features of a place—outside and in—that nurture me, and the kinds that do not, may unnecessarily offend those who live with fulfillment in houses I reject. Taste is not a hierarchy; I cater only to my own. I spend a vast amount of time at home engaged in this work I do. The hours at my keyboard, and the hours spent gathering the needle drop from the white pines and spreading it to mulch infant trees. The hours I am hunched over a manuscript draft, and those I spend pruning spent flowers from bee balm and phlox. The time I spend lying on the floor in a patch of winter sun visualizing the next scene to write, and the time I am lying on my bed reading my students' dissertation manuscripts. Perhaps some—who bring their laptops everywhere, who write on the train or in coffee shops or writer retreats—think me bourgeois to care so much about my place, my space, my home (used here to mean where I habituate, not a structure, as in real estate jargon). I know that all the pink, purple, and Green-Bay-Packer-themed walls can be painted the absolute white and shades of gray I prefer; I know the fake wood trim and doors can be replaced with smooth plain white; I know the seizure-inducing speckled countertops can be replaced with midnight-sky black granite. But there's no replacing ten years of growth on my Austrian pines and white fir, the curved rural road where houses can barely see one another, or the five-foot windows with no need for coverings providing changing shades of natural light throughout the days on end I don't bother to leave the property.

I am not in a position to complain. My soon-to-be ex is going to use his brokerage account to buy me a house, and I will continue to pay the mortgage and property tax on the Tudor while he continues to live here, perhaps for a few years until he can sell it for close to what it used to be worth. At that time I will get a mortgage and pay him back for the new house, minus my share of the old house. The old house . . . *this* house, where I sit, writing this.

In January the agent called on a Sunday afternoon. I had just come inside from the winter-fallow cornfield where I'd taken the dogs to play in the snow. She said, "Can you and Jim come see a house right now? I mean you have to get there before dark."

It was dusk when we arrived. Like most of the other houses I'd seen in my price range, it was on a suburban street with a row of similar houses, all facing forward, backyards abutting yards of houses the next street over. The realtor explained it was an approved short sale, and there was a time limit for buyers who would live in the house to make offers before the sale would be open to investors (i.e., house flippers); the short sale was only known by agents so far. As though part of the mystique, the key in the lock-box didn't work, the garage door would open only two feet, and the electricity was turned off in the bedrooms (the reason we had to see it before dark). The smallest of the three of us, I crawled under the garage door, went through the garage past a sofa that looked as though a bear had been eating it, then into the small living room to open the front door.

The living room was freshly painted but with only a small doorway access to the rest of the house—bedrooms and kitchen—and had only one undersized window looking out onto the street. The bedrooms were likewise modest, with small windows and white wooden louvered blinds. In general the house looked like one with devoted owners trying to sell it, with a few conspicuous exceptions (like the half-eaten sofa in the garage), not one on the brink of being lost to foreclosure. People losing their houses will sometimes wreak damage, and I can understand the impulse, although my fury might be aimed at the bank, not my lair. Still, there were places where trim had been torn loose, window blinds snapped in half, a wall broken open and plumbing removed, a door hanging askew from the kitchen cabinets, a sink bloodstained with an unknown chemical. In all, it was a paradox: the color of the exterior caulking matched the siding, the three bedrooms (one almost closet-sized) and living room had new carpet and paint in acceptable (for me) shades, but the original generic kitchen and bathroom showed the effects of thirty to forty years of use, besides the random points of destruction.

"They're approved at 113," the agent said. "That's firm."

"You'd have a lot left in the budget to redo the kitchen and bathroom," Jim said. "Everything else is small but in good shape."

I said, "I don't know."

"It's going to go fast," the agent said.

"You could make this kitchen however you want," Jim said.

I said, "I don't know."

Moving steadily through bedrooms (growing darker), the living room, the kitchen, looking out each small window to the square yard with its one tall spruce, down to the basement, back up, my eyes looking out from above my hands, which were unconsciously pressed over my nose, mouth, and cheeks.

"It could be worth two hundred in this neighborhood," the agent said.

"The taxes are low," Jim said.

I said, "I don't know."

"Is it big enough for you and Mark together?" Jim asked. "That's the main thing. Where could he teach music lessons?"

"The basement has a bathroom and space for a music room," the agent said.

I said, "I don't know."

"It's already fenced, and there's a patio," Jim said.

"You could just break out this wall between the kitchen and living room to make it more open," the agent said.

I said, "I don't know."

While we were in the basement a third time, the agent said, "Someone's at the door. Stay down here." She had seen the car drive up and had already turned the lights off upstairs. "Not everybody is willing to crawl under the garage door. This is going to attract a lot of agents."

I was near the space under the stairway, open and big enough for a walk-in closet, containing a boxed toilet, obviously for the hole in the basement bathroom. The cardboard box showed watermarks as though it had suffered a shallow flood—perhaps the reason for (or result of) the wall to the bathroom being broken into and a segment of plumbing removed.

I'd once lived, in some serenity, in a house no bigger than this basement.

"What are you thinking?" Jim asked.

"I don't know."

The agent returned. "I think they left. We have to decide tonight. I brought the paperwork."

And so I started crying. I turned away to relieve the agent's embarrassment. I stifled it as quickly as I could. Wiped my eyes and kept them closed. I was acutely aware of being hungry and dizzy. I said, "Okay." Then signed the paperwork.

Later that night I told Mark the news that I had made an offer. To spare him worry, I summarized the good: lower taxes, high privacy fence, short-sale price allowing me budgetary latitude to design my own upgrades, closer to the tollway, not far from my favorite Mexican restaurant, finished basement with half-finished slate-floor bathroom. "If I were thirty, it'd be perfect," I finished.

Mark could read the nuances behind my every utterance. "Cris, were you pressured into this?"

I tried to reassure him, in order to bolster myself.

The following morning, I took my coffee into my study, as usual. I heard Jim's bedroom door open and his footsteps in the hall.

Then, instead of thumping down the uncarpeted stairs, I heard the creak of the loose board just outside my study. He came in quietly, his face dark with distress. He said, "How are you doing?"

"I'm okay." It seemed true. I felt wrung out, subdued, but . . . okay. The unease on his face was a strange calmative.

"I didn't sleep well," he said. "I don't know if we did the right thing yesterday."

"It's just having it thrust on me like that, having to decide so quickly."

"You know," he said, "we can still get out of it."

The next step in the short-sale process was for the seller to disclose how much of the prorated taxes and closing costs would remain unpaid. These are costs normally absorbed by the seller but understood, in a short sale, to be shifted to the buyer. When disclosed, if those costs are unacceptable to the buyer, the offer can be withdrawn.

Days before the closing costs were disclosed, Jim suggested we go walk around the outside of the house again, look into the windows, think about some new landscaping, then test the route to the tollway when I left from there to go to campus. Like minesweepers, we moved slowly around the outside walls, gazes moving from the ground, looking for junk trees squeezing out from beside the basement walls, up the siding to the windows—inspecting caulking, testing with a thumb for rot—then further up the wall to the soffits, looking for cracks, gaps, broken or leaking gutters. In the backyard we were checking the water spigot when, abruptly, the midmorning hush was assaulted by barking dogs. Not one, not two, and not from different locations up and down the street, as though someone might be walking down the sidewalk. They came from the other side of the privacy fence, several thunderous, deep canine voices and one strident, repetitious bay, accompanied by thumps and scratching of paws on the fence boards.

"Holy crap." I'm not even sure which one of us said it. We moved around to the side of the house closest to that neighbor's yard, where his front-facing chain-link gate revealed the tangle of dogs, still barking, jostling for position to better view us. Three huskies and a beagle.

Normally, in the winter, dogs wouldn't be outside if no one was at home. At least that's my "normal." Sure enough, an irritated male voice shouted at them, repeated the shout, and as Jim and I moved farther away toward the street side of the house, the dogs, one by one, left off barking and went into their house.

"Can you imagine those dogs out there, every time I walk into the yard, every time I let the dogs out—"

"Well, he called them in, didn't he?"

I went to my car, parked behind Jim's on the driveway, while he stayed on the snow-crusted front lawn for a moment, then turned and approached my car, my door still open as I was shedding my coat and settling in. "Since the neighbor's home, maybe I should go talk to him."

"What, to ask how often his dogs are in the yard?"

"No, just to ask about the neighborhood, stuff you might ask neighbors when you're considering a house."

"Okay, call and let me know what he says." I turned my ignition. I still had to buckle the belt, fiddle with the stereo, and plug in my cell phone. By the time I'd just begun to back out, Jim was returning. I stopped and rolled down the window.

"Well," he said, "that was weird."

"You already talked to him?"

"No. I rang the bell, and nothing, so then I knocked, thinking he might not have heard the bell. The dogs are going nuts so how could he not know someone's at the door? Then he came and looked out a window beside the door, mouthing something, shaking his head like really aggressive and waving one hand like *Get away, get away.*"

"Wow. What does it mean?"

"I sure as hell don't know, but you don't want to get stuck next to a weird neighbor. The door had a sticker that said no soliciting by order of the police department. Is that even real?"

"We're parked in the driveway of a house for sale next door. How could we be solicitors?"

"Maybe he's paranoid of anyone knocking on his door, ever. He's at home on a weekday."

"People are out of work," I offered.

"Look at his roof, it's all curled and peeling away. Look at that rusted-out van in the driveway, the bushes overgrowing his house. These are things we didn't see, coming over like that at night."

Flash back to 1986, the house I bought in San Diego with my first husband. Escrow closed, we moved in, I began working in my yard. The neighbor's dog put his front feet on the low cinder block wall, and a war of barking erupted between it and the three smaller dogs I had. Another time, the same neighbor—toothless, holding a beer and smoking while spattering his bare-dirt yard with a hose—tossed his cigarette butt into my yard. I picked it up asked him to please not throw his butts into my yard. He turned and sprayed me with the hose. Weeks later, after I'd erected a board fence against the cinder blocks to double the height, the neighbor, a bit more drunk than usual, broke down the fence and tossed the jagged pieces of cedar, together with empty beer bottles and dog shit, into my yard. Some weeks later, I was awoken in the night by a loud, telltale pop. Discovered the next day that the neighbor had shot his dog.

"I don't know about this," Jim said, as though my memory had been his.

"Yeah, I don't know either."

My drive to campus took an hour. That day, the first half hour was during Mark's prep time between his junior high and the rounds he made teaching elementary bands.

"No, Cris," he said after my report. "Don't do it, it might be dangerous, and you'd be there alone."

"I don't know if it's that. There are more *nasty* people in the world than dangerous."

"Trust your instincts, though. Just don't do it if it feels wrong. What does Jim say?"

"He's real dubious right now."

"Okay, he's not going to let you move next door to trouble."

During the second half of my commute, Jim called. "What did Mark say?"

"He said I can't risk moving in beside a creepy neighbor."

"I know. We have to get out of this."

So we did. The house hunt moved on to the next set of snags I would encounter: The fifty-five-year-old estate-sale ranch where the overwhelmed executor didn't want to deal with ungrounded electrical outlets, unsafe fuse boxes, or an end-of-life roof. The house with no central air I was willing to upgrade, but then I discovered the seller had already purchased "a resort in Minnesota" and couldn't negotiate the price. The gorgeous former three-bedroom that had its smallest bedroom converted into a huge luxury bath, so its value would always be lower than its current asking price. To where I'm going to move: the generic, architecturally nameless two-story (hybrid of the American foursquare crossed with gable-front and center-passage styles) with developer cost-cutting practices like molding and doors made from a resin-and-wood byproduct resembling the fake plastic of second-generation Lincoln logs. But it has storage space enough for my manuscript and photo archives, a dining room that can become a music studio, and a room with a fireplace whose windows view a yard that borders a "common area" and a pond, so, with blinders on, I can still imagine the water's tree line might be habitat for deer, raccoon, and turkey.

On the day Jim and I were to go to the real estate lawyer conducting our transaction, he came into the house from airing the dogs and reported, "There's a deer out in the trees." I went to get my binoculars from my desk and said, "This might be the last time I can look into my yard at a deer."

A few hours later, we were driving from the lawyer to the county government buildings to file a quitclaim on the Tudor at the recorder's office. For homeowner exemption on property taxes, the taxpayer must live in a property with his/her name on the deed, so the new house would be in my name, but I had to remove my name from ownership of the Tudor. Out my window, I watched the progression of houses lining the Fox River and then started to cry. Quietly, I thought. Jim tapped my leg with two fingers.

"Everything's going to be okay," he said.

"Yeah," I whispered.

"You'll make the new house just how you want it. I'll be helping. I'm still there, we still share the dogs, our dog shows. There's the house in the U.P. Then Mark will move out here."

"Yeah." After a calming pause, I added, "He'll be leaving every-thing and everyone he's ever known. Except me."

"You'll show him all the stuff around here. He's a social guy, he'll make friends. And I hope . . . we can be friends too. He likes sports, he and I could be friends. Right?"

"Yeah."

"You know," Jim said a few moments later, "you shouldn't tell Mark things like it'll be the last time you see a deer in your yard."

"Yeah. True."

At night, the deer in my old neighborhood slip between the backyards and walk down the street. And at the little house in the Upper Peninsula—another place, very different from here, where part of me thrives—there'll always be deer in the yard; deer that startle, bolt, and flee much quicker, with less stimulus than many deer here in Illinois. But no matter where they are, deer and rabbits will run from coyote; everywhere they live, coyote will hunt and kill what they need to eat, whether it's a rabbit, house cat, or a nest of Canada geese eggs—geese that used to fly south but now live year-round on ponds and common areas surrounded with houses, like the one that will soon become my new habitat.

House
(What Things Are Called)

I haven't written a fishing narrative, nor sat on a lakeshore writing. The former: I still have not, including this one. It's not about fishing. The latter: I likewise still haven't. Although I set up my camp chair last night at the lake, my notebook remained on the passenger seat of the Jeep. Was going to go back for the paper and pen, but a bluegill took the bait I'd put in the water just before unfolding the chair. Then I never did get the notebook, or even sit, the remaining ninety minutes I stayed at the lake.

"Angler." It means a person who is fishing, or who fishes, with a hook and line. Or a person who gets or tries to get something through scheming. Someone maneuvering for position, designing a tactic, a strategy, a line of approach, of attack. Maybe all of that defines fishing as well. I'm using "angler" here because "fisherman" is biologically amiss and "fisherperson" wretched. But let's see if the other characterization works too.

An impatient angler, I frequently move on. To the next tantalizing contour of shoreline, the next weed bed or stickup, the next creek mouth or fallen tree, the future around the next bend of river. If I don't get that bang-bang hit on the bait or lure, I don't stay.

I've relocated my residence a few times, although hardly excessively. Five different addresses in ten years in San Diego after leaving my parents' house, followed by three different states after leaving San Diego. Then, seemingly ensconced in Illinois, I've drifted from a near-west Chicago suburb to an unincorporated, agriculturally zoned exurb, and now back to a *subdivision* (called a "tract" in my childhood Southern California). I wasn't, in any case, evicted from one or assigned another.

Where I write today: a cabin named Dogwood, on Silver Mountain Road in Michigan's Upper Peninsula, surrounded by the Ottawa National Forest. Although not really a *cabin*. No logs, no chimney, doesn't even have a fireplace. The insurance company wouldn't cover it if it did, being three miles down a dirt road, then half a mile down a forest service route unplowed in winter. No cell reception, no internet, but it offers running well water, propane furnace, landline phone. Locally it might be termed a "camp," since camps (or "deer camps"), like Dogwood, frequently have proper names. The Hi-Lo Chalet, BuckSnort, Big Rack Lodge, Porcupine Acres. *Camps*, however, are not typically year-round houses with electricity and satellite TV. And, to my Californian lexicon, "camp" is not a noun but a verb, something you *do* with a tent in a cleared space with a rock-ringed firepit. To become a noun it changes to "campsite," although admittedly, "going back to camp" means "return to the campsite."

This noncamp noncabin is also nonwaterfront. The nearest lake four miles down a one-lane dirt road with turnouts.

Prickett. An uninspiring name for a wilderness lake. And not really a lake, although truly in as much wilderness as possible for something man made. The word "reservoir" conjures, for me, bodies of trapped, desperately needed water surrounded by steep, rocky, arid hills with scars to mark the former high water levels; an incongruous sea evaporating under a scorching sun and bleached sky in Southern California. I like the words used for man-made lakes in the upper Midwest: "flowage" and, better yet, "backwater." Prickett Backwaters. Still without the poetry of other local lake names: Sudden Lake, SixMile Lake, Vermilac (Worm Lake). By now we all know that Hemingway's Big Two-Hearted River was actually the west branch of the Upper Peninsula's Fox River. He either purposely changed the name to disguise his favorite trout stream, or selected a different actual Upper Peninsula river for the sheer music of its name.

But Prickett fits. In a less poetic, more rhyming way.

When created in 1931—not to store already plentiful water but produce a tiny amount of electricity—the dense forest on the Sturgeon River was to have been harvested before the river basin was dammed. The power company maintained a strict schedule, the logging company not so much. Half the timber was still standing when the dam was closed and the channel flooded. It is now a backwater with a somewhat thinner seventy-five-plus-year-old forest of naked treetops rising from the water's surface, a much denser forest of serrated stumps and tipped-over root-claws lurking submerged, and a vast supply of floating trunks bumping up against some part of the six or seven miles of shoreline.

It is a "prickett" of fish habitat. Normally the water's edge—99 percent inaccessible on foot—is lined with that logjam, easily up to twelve feet wide, bumping against the steep sides of the gorge the river once flowed through. Logs also accumulate on the edges of shallow reedbeds. Maybe not unfeasible to cast out over them, but nearly impossible to land any fish who take the bait out there. Usually when it's too windy, thunderstorms threaten, or—like this week—I have no help to launch a boat, the only shore access for fishing has been the floating pier, installed where the lone dirt-road access dead-ends at a ten-car parking area and boat ramp.

This year, however, the lake has been lowered about six feet. The power company does this, not weather patterns. Now log-littered strips of mud surround some bays and weed beds. Room enough for a camp chair, a minnow pail, a tackle box. To try to be patient; to intend to abstain from wandering and casting a spinnerbait. To instead sit and scratch notes for an essay contemplating the house in Illinois I've almost finished moving into but don't yet live in, while waiting for my bobber's distinctive bam-bam gone-under-the-surface—when the bluegill or smallmouth or even northern pike are *on the bite*.

While I wasn't writing, wasn't even seated in my camp chair, something splashed in a small, shallow cove right up against shore, the surface covered with tiny floating leaves like miniature lily pads in a diorama replica lake. I thought it was probably a frog, then saw something wiggling on the mud right beside the thin line of water's edge. It looked like a minnow. As it tried to squiggle itself back to the water, I put my palm over it, scooped it up in two hands. It was a muskie spawn. Or muskellunge. It *lunged* out of the water going after its baby prey. Three inches. I put it into the minnow pail. I still have the little fish here in the basement, in the larger minnow bucket with an aerator running.

There are aerators in the "ponds" in my new house's subdivision. Rounded-off rectangles surrounded by uniform-size riprap, the water colored a strange, synthetic greenish aqua: they are retention pools. When prairie became farmland, the rainfall and water table didn't need as much new control—but farmland drainage was upgraded with underground tiles and runoff roadside ditches. (I can't even fathom installing terra-cotta tiles under a cornfield, let alone doing so eighty to one hundred years ago.) What I do sort of understand is that when farmland (or prairie) is paved, something has to be done with the predictable rainfall that would have soaked down to five-foot-deep prairie-grass roots and replenished the underground water table. So paved areas need drainage systems to collect that water, and retention pools are commonly employed near strip malls and shopping districts and municipal buildings with large parking lots. The local hospital rents a pair of swans every year (from what, a swan-rental company?). They nest, raise a gaggle of ugly ducklings, then the whole family is whisked away before winter.

My new house is "waterfront" (or "pond facing"), but my view is not the subdivision's retention ponds but a real pond: this one bordered naturally with trees, a few snags (dead trees), reeds and cattails, marsh grasses, and bushes that limit shore access in some places. The color of the water is changeable with the weather and atmosphere, from a genial reflection of summer sky, to dawn-tranquil mirror finish, to steely overcast indifference, to angry gunmetal with wind-blown whitecaps. In the house's yard, right beside the glass slider, in the middle of a clump of ornamental grass, a mallard (which I didn't have to rent) laid her eggs, hatched them, and then led her string of ducklings across the lawn, across the "common-area" grass, to the pond. Out on the muddy bank, in the clouds of flora of a low-oxygen lake, a typical footprint of another introduced species: a half-submerged water bottle, a lid-less worm container, a faded aluminum beverage can.

At Prickett a few evenings ago, mine was the lone vehicle in either the parking area or the line of deep-woods primitive campsites. My footfall in last autumn's leaves the only heartbeat of incursion. But as I took the other rod with the spinner to seek bass near offshore structure, I saw the debris proving others of my kind had seen the same promise. Five beverage cans for five different drinks, from soda to hard cranberry lemonade. They outnumbered the single worm container, the empty snelled hook packaging, the snarl of discarded line. What is the mindset, I wonder, to drain the last mouthful of carbonated sugar or fruity alcohol from the can, then just toss it, as though it's one of the forked branches used for prop-ping a pole now no longer needed so returned to its status of just being a stick.

Just toss it.

A fabricated perfect cylinder of chemically synthesized liquid-then-cooled-and-hardened-metal, purchased somewhere where there were fluorescent lights and automated inventory control—consume it, then just drop or toss. And go on engaged in your wilderness pursuit of *fishing*. How does it compute, how does it ex-ist in the same brain?

Yet I put the baby muskie in a plastic bucket. I only imagined freeing it into one of the ersatz-blue riprap ponds representing the second word, "lakes," in my subdivision's two-word title. I will re-sist the urge to set up a natural-lake aquarium and try to watch him consume prey and grow at an unworldly rate. I can't *make* him a home. He would likely die.

I have carried on a private war with the real estate industry's (and those they've indoctrinated's) jargoned use of *home*.

> Homes from the low 200s.
> Estate Homes of Fox Grove Prairie
> New Home Construction Increases

Somehow a phrase as innocuous as "look at the big homes on this lake" is as white-bread cheesy as the garish "Indian Trading Posts" in Arizona on I-40. Those aren't *homes*, they're *houses*. We each only have one home (at a time), the one we've made that way with anything from our taste for color, light, and décor to our favorite junk strewn in a familiar, comfortable way. "Home" should have a possessive pronoun in front of it. *My* home. *Your* home. *Their* home. *Our* home.

Even "home inspection service" is a service that inspects a *house*. What irregularities might a "home inspection" uncover? That you put dirty socks under the bed? That you store your cooking pots and towels in the same cupboard? That you've hoarded so many different brands of cleaning supplies they've actually putrefied? A *house* has a plumbing system, a foundation, electrical circuitry, a roof, venting that needs inspecting, a code to live up to. A *home's* code? A *home's* safety violations? That your drawers are so disorganized you always go buy new Scotch tape every time you need to tape something because you can't find any?

Maybe the term "home tour" can stand. You're peeping at different people's homes, the *way* they live in their . . . *house.*

I bought a new home.

No, I bought a *house,* and it's only new to me. Right now, do I have a home? This "cabin" called Dogwood can suffice, since I've put my summer stuff in its closets, cupboards, and basement shelves. I've put the food I'll eat in its pantry. I've put pictures I've chosen (and/or taken) on its walls. I've filled display shelves and cabinets with driftwood I've collected, striped and swirled rocks that have caught my eye, and the skulls from roadkill I've cleaned and bleached. I can nap to the familiar cry of ravens from the trees outside open windows, the close-up buzz of wasps outside the screen, the drone of the minnow bucket aerator in the basement.

The little muskie likely won't eat any of the minnows swimming with him in the bucket. "They won't eat in captivity," said of every frog, lizard, snake, or black widow spider I ever tried to keep in a terrarium or jar. But I've already eaten (in captivity) at my new house, pausing in daylong forays of installing pantry shelves, painting closets, or removing carpet tacks to chew a sandwich, standing in the unfurnished "family room" (where I am to be the "family"?), looking out at the lake, the *pond* beyond my fence whose proximity consigns more rules to my house, by virtue of my "pond view" status, than others in the neighborhood. Rules presided over by the HOA.

The *Home Owners Association.* Made up of residents, but instead of a coffee klatch of nosy gossips, it has bylaws, elections, officers, a budget, meetings, and . . . power. "HOA" is a new term for "neighbors." That's what I have now. They—we?—determine whether we'll tolerate elements easily found, and considered unremarkable (or, by me, unendurable), in other places I've lived, in cities and college towns, and the U.P.: an old sofa on a front porch, music that shakes everyone's foundations, a house wrapped in insulation paper then never finished with siding, yard sales every weekend never quite put away, a Chevy painted to resemble the Batmobile in the front yard, or a flower *bed* with a headboard and footrail installed at either end (get it?) accompanied by a toilet overflowing with petunias set out by the mailbox.

Besides the pall of living with published (and enforced) rules, the HOA means people. Neighbors. Well-meaning, friendly, sometimes even intelligent fellow inhabitants . . . living at closer range than I've ever been comfortable. Every time I go out my new front door or emerge from the garage, there are usually people there in their own yards and driveways, needing to be waved at, expecting a smile and chitchat. Is this so awful, so invasive? I've arrived at some of the smaller wilderness lakes up here—the aforementioned Sudden Lake, the less poetic Pike Lake—and have left without launching the canoe because there was *one* other car in the clearing beside the boat ramp, *one* other small jon boat on the water. In these woods, over water, even from more than a hundred yards, voices carry at the same über-rate that the baby muskie will grow. From my new, peacefully gray-and-white office in the new house, I will hear whenever two neighbors exchange pleasantries down on the sidewalk.

The specter of the HOA and its broader definition has distracted my narrative, for a moment. I see I've skipped over (with only the brief parenthetical alert) a key piece: the house's *family room*. And those who will populate it. Not the neighbors I dread having. It will, in fact, become *our* family room, when the *family* becomes Mark and me, together, finally, after thirty years of ... well, two separate lives. For me: a life not knowing what I might be missing but deeply suspecting I was. For him: the whole span of years spent knowing exactly what he'd wanted and hadn't gotten, while also recognizing that what he'd taken on to distract himself from not having what he wanted had itself been a protracted calamity.

Just last night Mark found out that the step-grandson he'd raised until the boy was eight—child of a semiprostitute deadbeat stepdaughter whom he'd financially supported as a child, and again and again as a purported adult, even after she stole from him and painted gang writing on his walls and the police were called for "domestic conflicts" (screaming brawls) she'd instigated with her mother—he learned that the child she'd produced then abandoned and for whom Mark had stepped in to provide shelter, nourishment, medical care, clothing, schooling, Christmas and Halloween decorations all over the yard and roof, kid movies and plastic lawn sports, soccer leagues and Cub Scouts ... in other words a *home* with two adults who loved him ... Well, last night Mark discovered that the kid, now fourteen, had been expelled for drug possession, had scared off his grandmother's new male companion, had taken the state funds she'd gotten for his support and used them, typically, for his own devices, had threatened a counselor's life on his Facebook page, and would, as soon as his probation was up, go live with the disaster that was his biological mother to finish transforming into the kind of lowlife she was always attracted to.

"There's nothing left of who I've ever been," Mark said over Dogwood's landline phone, his voice wavering. "All the houses I grew up in have been torn down, all the people I knew drifted away or dead ... my job—the school district trying to crush the teachers—everything I got close to or tried to care about . . . Everything that was ever a part of me is going or gone. Except you. You've been the same, and best, part of me for thirty years, even when I didn't know where you were and could only imagine what you were doing and what a life with you would have been."

The thirty years, the *would have been*, is probably why I can't imagine the new house in Illinois as *home* . . . yet. Not because I haven't had other homes, or *made* homes out of implausible houses in far more unsavory locations. But because for him, since we'll live in this new residence together, the house he hasn't yet seen is the only home he's ever wanted. Despite the colors I've chosen for the walls—the ideal quiet shades of gray, clean white, dramatic charcoal—despite the closets I designed and constructed to contain my photo files and manuscript archives . . . it can't be mine until it is ours. I left room in the closets for his jazz LPs, his saxophones and amps, space in the family room for his grandfather's desk, shelves in the cabinets for his collection of *Nature* episodes taped to VHS. He's the reason I bought this house in the first place. He's the one, not the house, who knows me, accepts and nurtures me. Certainly nothing about the house, except perhaps the allusion created by the "lake," provides me with . . . What is the best word? Security, solace, serenity . . . ?

Belonging.

An awkward verb turned into some form of intangible noun.

I put the muskie spawn back into the lake last night. After I fished him from the minnow bucket with my left hand, I readied my camera, then opened my fist. He lay on my palm for the picture. As I pressed the button, his body flexed, he lunged—just a little twitch at his size. Someday he'll be able to turn my canoe around, as a hooked but un-landed monster once did in the middle of Prickett. For now, he flipped himself into the water just a foot below. I saw him there for a few moments, tiny fins fanning, blending with every color of green and brown in the idyllic habitat, plenty of sunken log structure, flowing submerged vegetation, reeds that start underwater then emerge to present flower heads to buzzing bees and flies, and a bounty of minnows, beetle larvae, frogs, and tadpoles to feed his growth frenzy. Then he was gone, and I could no longer identify him in the pools near shore. He could live in these backwaters for thirty years.

I checked the camera to see my last shot of him. There was only a photo of my empty palm, open above the water.

How Substandard Closet Design Inflamed My Chronic Dread

2012

People lose things when they move.

Losing things is my habitual worry and keeping organized my worrisome habit.

Anxiety over losing things is soothed by the very method that helps not lose things: order, precision, yet itself another aggravation. Important things like car registrations and deeds to the house, life insurance, the fifteen-digit code that identifies software, keys to the back gate, manual for the refrigerator or cell phone, hardware for picture framing or fixing a hose, devices to cover electrical cords running along the floorboards, filters for the humidifier, sticky-backed Velcro for mounting the tollway transponder, attachments for each of the three different shop vacs, a wallet I used in the '80s when I carried a purse, photos of my great-grandparents. I can put my hands on almost anything I need when the need arrives because I know where it is, because I stored it in a systematic way.

But I'm not a hoarder, not much of a magpie. Giving bundles to thrift stores is also a stress reliever, an anxiety quieter. In the past, even writing a scene that purges stuff achieved some alleviation.

> Then she loaded her boxes of winter accessories—scarves, gloves, sweaters, wool socks and boots—into her car and drove them to the Salvation Army. The next day she emptied [her unpacked]

suitcase into bags and made the trip again. . . . When she climbed
a ladder to put the suitcase back into the closet, she took down
framed posters she'd been saving to put on the walls; box games
of Monopoly, Uno and Tile Rummy; and a briefcase she'd carried
in college. She took them all to the Salvation Army. Then she went
through the linen closet and removed fancy lace-edged pillow
cases, a stadium blanket, place mats, a table cloth, curtains, guest
towels. As she woke each morning she thought about that day's
trip to the donation center and what she would take. . . . On Sundays, when the collection center wasn't open, time crawled, she
was restless and frustrated, tried to sleep late but couldn't, glanc-
ing often at the black garbage bag waiting by the front door to be
taken out first thing Monday.

—Cris Mazza, *Dog People* (1998)

Wrote it once. Can't *keep* writing it; it won't work again.

Now, mostly, it isn't clothes in the bags awaiting the next trip
to the donation center; I *buy* most of my clothes there. My jeans
march steadily down three shelves in my closet, from *best* (although secondhand) to *dog training jeans* to *garden jeans*. It takes
several years before a pair can't even validate its place on the *garden jeans* shelf, and by then the fabric that remains might be used
to patch some of the others. Still, some clothes do go into the donation bag, if I hope the style will never come back, if they attract
and embed too much dog hair, if they're too girly (from a time I
thought I should try harder), if they don't pass a physical or emotional comfort audition (worn to campus for a day to see if I don't
notice wearing them).

Clothes and shoes don't get lost; they only take up too much
of the vital space for arranging other things that might be. Organization. Maybe über-organization. And then reorganizing. The
modus to simultaneously facilitate not losing things and to sift out
what gets sent to the donation center. This also allows both cars
to live inside the garage, allows half my basement to be left bare
for dog training, allows two people to cook in a kitchen that only
has two counters and two drawers. Order. Authority over chaos.
The fundamental anxiety reliever. Shelves, shelf organizers, drawers, drawer organizers, designated and outfitted closets for specific

needs from supplies to archives, all-the-same-size boxes with la-
bels. These are some kind of serenity.

But people lose things when they move. Thrown away or given
away without remembering. Stashed in a "misc." box with no other
label, and there might be fifteen such boxes, some not unpacked
for years (although not in *my* basement). Something loaned and
not returned at the previous residence. Something stored in a place
no one remembered to pack, an attic or under the stairs. The thing
might then forcibly pass the "if you don't use it in a year, get rid of
it" test. But what if it is a photograph or a letter? Do I really want to
read any of the letters I wrote to an ex-husband while I was in graduate school in Brooklyn and he was living in our rented shack in
San Diego? No, I never will, and I really have considered a bonfire.
But the box is labeled, tied with string, and stored where I know it
is but won't see it unless I have to go look for it, which I won't have
to. Why is this important? I can't say. I just know where it is.

Most of my mother's slides as well as her mother's photo albums
are put away and labeled, in archive boxes although without hu-
midity- or acid-controlled environments. At least they're not in
the basement, which gets damp (where a dehumidifier used to
run nonstop until it pushed the needle on my electric bill). Most
importantly, I know where they are. A large scanning and digital storing project is planned,[1] so they await, along with a box of
slide-organization tools—light bar, slide sleeves, slide bins, etc. The
unstarted status of the project creates no affecting angst; it's knowing where they are that's soothing.

Admittedly, order is easiest with mementos and/or artifacts that
I won't be using or even accessing. A Civil War–era blue shawl
worn by my maternal great-grandmother at her wedding in South-
port, Maine. A tablecloth and napkins my mother made in the
1940s as a gift for her mother. A patchwork quilt I made with my
mother in junior high as a Girl Scout project. Each vacuum sealed
and stored in a separate matching box, top shelf of main floor
closet. Dog-show plaques, dog-title certificates, dog-show records,
VHS and eight-millimeter videos of previous dogs I've shown

---

1. Project completed in 2019.

awaiting another large project of digitizing,[2] a swatch of hair from each dog stored in a zip-lock baggie, a few puppy teeth, one nasty foxtail that had to be surgically removed from a dog's groin—bundled and labeled in same-size boxes. Paper items upstairs, plaques in the basement on shelves dominated by boxes of books I've authored, which, despite being paper, cannot be stored in the closets upstairs. They may well rot down there.

Those things whose use is required, whether only occasionally, weekly, or daily, shouldn't live in peril of being lost, but always have higher risk unless put away after each use in the same spot where they came from, and can therefore always be found when needed. Scissors, hole punches, staplers and staples, X-Acto knives, packing tape, twine, twist ties, electrical ties, rubber bands, garden seeds, the metronome, saxophone reeds, saxophone repair materials, any building or painting tool, assorted hardware (organized by type and size), batteries, flashlights, lightbulbs, music CDs (arranged by artist and genre) and movie DVDs (not enough of them to systematize), still also a few VHS movies that I "need" to watch every few years and haven't yet replaced with DVDs. An exhaustive enough sentence to make my point.

I was sure I didn't lose anything in my last move. I was accorded plenty of time; no rush to pack and move during the escrow process. So, while the new house was being painted, retrimmed, and carpeted, and its bathroom upgraded, I prepared the storage areas and closets myself. Paint, organizers, and a plan: Two closets were reassigned from the usual job of holding clothing, turned instead into structured areas for stuff from office supplies to personal files, photographs to software CDs, archived records of now-dead show dogs to promotional copies of my books. The closets that still housed clothes and coats also needed sculpting to hold additional shelves for a collection of baseball memorabilia, blankets, suitcases, the few games I've kept, and I'll have to end this list with the disorganized word "etcetera." Then: What items could be stored on the row of shelves in the (possibly damp) basement, and which required the first or second floor. Which items might need better

2. Project completed in 2020.

access (from certain musical instruments to vacuum cleaners), which could be more difficult to retrieve (other musical instruments to outmoded film cameras). Lastly: Which shelves had to be double braced because they would hold books, photographs, or archived manuscripts? Which could be wire (flat objects and boxes) and which should be solid (photo albums and books)? Could shelves wrap around all three walls of a closet, or which sidewalls had to be left blank to allow for drawers or poles?

I planned the closets in pencil on graph paper. I took the design notebook with me to doctor, haircut, and vet appointments and pored over the plans in waiting rooms. I had lists of measurements of everything, from how tall and wide the saxophone and trombone cases were when standing on end, how much vertical room a row of shirts would need (so I could install a dual row of shelves with clothes bar and maximize space), plus what size board and wire shelves I already had—uninstalled from my previous house, hardware saved in baggies and taped to each. This is why boys used to take drafting while girls had home economics in the '60s. I had neither in the '70s.

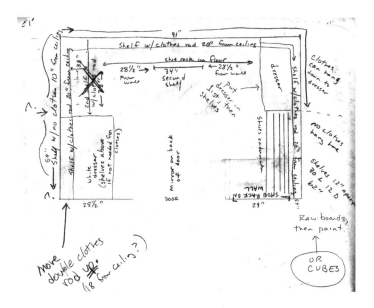

My diagrams almost worked. Strong enough, wide enough, space between shelves, space under shelves. Well . . . The archive and office boxes had to be tipped completely ninety degrees and sideways to be lifted up onto the highest shelves because the front edge of the shelf was too close to the front wall of the closet, leaving not enough room for a normal forty-five-degree overhead straight-on placement. The triangular braces making the shelves megasturdy, which had to be mounted into wall studs, were spaced just badly enough that my matching photo storage boxes couldn't all fit beside each other on the shelf below. And the lower row of the dual clothes-hanging shelves in the walk-in bedroom closet—even with short jackets assigned to hang there—hid the shoe rack mounted near the floor. Plus that same lower clothes-hanging shelf proved to have a second and even more flawed design.

Meanwhile, I discovered I had lost something.

I've had a foot massager for over forty years. My father gave it to me for Christmas my first year of college. After four years of marching band in high school, mostly as a parade band, marching heel first on pavement (as opposed to toe first on grass when I got to college marching band), I always had aching feet. I didn't wear flats or heels, my shoes were always tennis shoes or some kind of crepe-soled oxford (Wallabees a favorite, but I must've had knockoffs). When Earth® shoes came out, I thought they were my answer. I was mostly seduced by the androgynous clodhopper styling, but the promise of returning my feet to their indigenous way of walking lured me as well. After classes, which for three days a week meant after marching band rehearsal, I rushed off to my part-time job as a nurse aide at a state ward for severely disabled children. On my feet there for another four hours. The nurses and other aides started buying their requisite white shoes in Earth® shoe styles. But when I came home with a pair, my father took a rare notice of an aspect of my wardrobe (why should he bother to notice, let alone disapprove, when I was almost always in jeans). He insisted, demanded, that I return the Earth® shoes. Yes, he had a reason, but I don't remember. Bad for my back? My ankles? Unnatural to walk with the ball of the foot higher than the heel? Obviously I argued that my feet hurt at work, but I took the shoes back. And that Christmas my dad, whom we called the Great Gadget Giver, gifted me a Dr. Scholl's foot massager.

My feet have been better the past decade or two, since I don't wear sneakers almost ever. Still attracted to clodhoppers, although crepe soles aren't as common, and too many use faux leather and don't last. Real Wallabees are over $100. But I've remarkably kept myself supplied in barely used Sketchers oxfords from thrift stores. Still, I always kept the massager plugged in under my desk so I could use it when I ached from long days at dog shows on concrete-floored fairground buildings, or from cooking sock footed on a tile-floored kitchen.

Then, after this last time I moved, I couldn't find the foot massager. I didn't seek it out until I'd been in the house for six months, was thoroughly unpacked, my closets humming along in the systemized organization borne from my plans. Every few weeks I searched again in all the reasonable places, from the master bedroom upper closet shelf that held blankets, a suitcase, two office boxes of baseball memorabilia, a plastic bin with four purses I only occasionally use. To the basement in three plastic containers labeled respectively "wheeled tote bags," "film cameras and lenses," and a mixed bin of "jack knives, back-up cell phones, landline phones, and label-maker." To the cabinet in the family room where there was a space for the massaging wand I'd acquired more recently beside three stacked plastic video drawers holding the Beta movies I'd taped in the '80s (the Betamax itself in a vacuum-sealed bag in the basement for future use with a third TV mounted in front of the exercise equipment). To the supply closet in my study, to the photo and music storage closet in the other bedroom, and back to the master bedroom, where I could look up through the upper wire shelf and would see the Dr. Scholls if it happened to be tucked between stacks of blankets.

Had it somehow gotten into a thrift-store donation bag? How could that happen by accident? Had I left it at the old house so it was discarded when my ex-husband moved out after me? But he would have called and, laughing, said, "What's this ancient thing, do you want it?" Dejected by lack of use, had it walked off on its own? How do people lose things when they move? How was I now one of them? How could I have something for so many decades and then suddenly it's gone? It was just an old-fashioned vibrating motor with two places to put my feet; it wasn't my identity; wasn't my heritage, my lineage, my history; it wasn't my intellectual and artistic archives nor the photo record of places I'd been and people I'd been there with. But it was a gift I never would have expected in a million years, and yet so appropriate, and so comforting for so many years, and had been given to me by my parents (who must have been tired of hearing me complaining about my aching feet). Had I finally moved around too much, and too far away, that I lost part of my connection to something larger? Isn't that what we really mean by the symbolic end of childhood?

In 2014, when my mom went into hospice for congestive heart failure and my dad lost thirty pounds and four inches, I (finally) engaged in another obsessive search for what could be lost: my paternal genealogy.

A decade and a half ago, in another period when retreating from reality seemed not just prudent but crucial, I had pulled out a thick typed-and-stapled genealogy research project completed by my mother's cousin, tracing my mother's maternal lineage back to the sixteenth century Earl(s) of Mar. (Another group of distant relatives had started the project to try to lay claim to some of the Earl of Mar's estate. It seems there was a bastard son who fled to the United States in the early 1700s; plenty to facilitate my escape from post 9/11 reality.) As my parenthetical excursions demonstrate, I became so enthralled in imagining the lives at each generation (enhanced by the mysteries of those who died young, men who used up multiple wives and had over a dozen children, two sisters marrying two brothers, etc.), I based my novel *Waterbaby* on my maternal genealogy: the searching, and the utter panacea in the escape of imagining. Escape that, for the character in the novel as well as me in my life, could not ever be complete nor be maintained.

My ancestry and cultural heritage through my father had always been the dominant "tradition," and his was the family we most visited in my childhood, so I'd promised I would someday trace his genealogy. I finally started in November 2014. Stymied at first, I couldn't go back further than two paternal generations. Family lore had told me that my Mazza grandfather had come from Italy when he was fifteen, which would be around 1908, but I couldn't find a record of this Mazza family on any shipload of immigrants coming into New York from 1900 through 1920. The date range was narrowed by federal and New York censuses that *had* recorded the morphing Mazza family from 1920 through 1940 and suggested their immigration date had been 1910. But none of the censuses gave the name of my father's grand*mother*. (My father was no help. He never knew her.) I was stuck, already, three generations back, couldn't find the immigration documents nor the identity of my paternal great-grandmother.

The ancestral disarray thrumming in my mind, I paused on a break to get something from or put something in the bedroom closet, and was distracted from whatever I meant to do by the now two-year-old but suddenly even more conspicuously poor closet-organizational design: I'd put the shortest jackets on that lower clothes rod, and they were still blocking view of the shoe rack below. Sure there were shoes on the rack, but what good was it if I couldn't see them? And for that matter, that lower clothes rack itself *was also a shelf* that was hidden by the shirts hanging on the upper clothes rack. So I'd planned and installed a shelf in my closet that obviously could not hold anything—because not only would the shelved item cause the shirts to bunch up and wrinkle, but nothing on the shelf would be visible. As if to prove that this useless shelf was hiding there, I put my hands into the row of blouses and parted them like curtains.

And there was the forty-year-old foot massager.

As I grabbed it in my arms, the shirts swayed closed over the now empty impractical shelf.

Did restoring this forty-year-old Christmas gift from my father allow me the breakthrough in my genealogy search? I'd like to think so. In the next few weeks, with the massager in its proper place under my desk (plugged in so that I could flip the switch with one toe and rest my arches on the buzzing upside-down cups whenever necessary), I located the misplaced immigrants, including the missing great-grandmother, Fortunata.

In a different search on a new database—one that accessed Ellis Island records—I was able to ascertain that whoever logged the family into the manifest for the passenger ship *Oceania* either misheard the Mazza surname or, in heedless sloppiness, penned the letters poorly. Decades later when the name was entered into the searchable digital files for Ellis Island, the name was read and typed as Marza. Uncovering this error, and therefore finally finding the family on a manifest, was only possible because on the same voyage, the *Oceania*'s records included a list of passengers who were "held" pending a medical authorization. The Mazza family is listed there, spelled accurately, with the correct first names for the males that I already knew to look for, and all the names matched the first names of those Marzas handwritten on the manifest. Both lists provided the first name Fortunata for the individual designated "wife" to Raffaele Mazza. This woman with her own beautiful name had given all three of her daughters the name Maria: Maria Grazia, Maria Elizabetta, and Maria Raffaela. By the time the U.S. census takers were writing the family in their ledgers, the young women had dropped their Marias and were going by steadily more Americanized middle names, Grace, Eliza, and Anne. Until they themselves disappeared off the last publicly available census in 1940. Probably they had married and moved and lost their original surname.

I'd have never found Fortunata if the family had not been held for medical clearance and someone had actually *typed* that list instead of using sea-weary handwriting.

What I found in the closet—in a labyrinth of my own design, in a hiding place I'd been the one to painstakingly create—seems more than a vintage machine to ease my oft-aching feet. The solace of discovering that it was not lost was then strangely equal to the odd comfort of finding those Mazzas, detained on their ship for muddled bureaucratic reasons, hidden by a careless misspelling, not a flawed design.

But what did I find? A woman with seven children, three of them named Maria. A woman who died six years after settling in an immigrant neighborhood in Brooklyn, whose grandchild didn't know her name and couldn't even remember his father or grandfather ever talking about her, even though his father named a daughter for her. A woman carrying her husband's name so there is no way to look for her lineage. Until, that is, with help from a second cousin once removed, we learned that she'd married a man who shared her own Mazza surname. The nature of that premarriage family relationship is still lost, waiting to be found.

My discovery: an enigmatic nineteenth-century individual—defined from "wife" to "great-grandmother"—whose given name is far more beautiful and evocative than the archaic, wretchedly colored foot massager.

Feral

2012

A hole was needed. It was for a knot of daylily tubers removed from a garden at the former house. The ground before me was dry but not hard, loamy from decaying vegetation. Still, it was necessary at first to vault both feet off the ground and land, simultaneously, on the spade's treads in order to penetrate. The blade went through layers of moldering grass clippings, leaves, and valuable Illinois black soil. The hole was just about deep enough when the last shovelful unloaded four or five elongated eggs. One had been broken. Held in my palm, the leathery casing pulled aside, a soft nascent turtle shell was recognizable.

I do not own two houses, but I pay two property taxes—living in the "plastic house" with no mortgage while making payments on a mortgage still in my name on the six-thousand-square-foot Tudor whose deed now no longer includes me. A convoluted separation agreement not completed through an attorney or sanctioned by any court. I have full access to the Tudor and 1.3-acre property where I no longer live. That's full access to weed, prune, mulch, divide roots, till soil, and fertilize as needed. That bigger property will be put up for sale in a year or two, and its gardens have become overgrown, too burgeoning (hence daunting) for potential buyers. I've been removing plants to pots, reviving and revitalizing them, then transporting to the new, more modest property where I now live.

The plastic house—named for its vinyl siding—has empty garden beds, a blank lawn stretching from margin to margin begging for variation. But outside the fence, easily an acre of common area extends to a pond. The common area is also purported lawn. No one treats it for weeds, not the bad (invasive) ones—thistles and dandelions—nor the good (native) ones—mostly Queen Anne's lace. The nonlawn flora seems to have adapted to life in a lawn: growing and sometimes even blooming between scheduled landscape servicing, which has likely seen decreased frequency in this droughty summer. A three-foot-wide band around the pond is also not mowed. It supports indigenous midwestern wetland and prairie plants, especially goldenrod and various bulrushes and sedges.

There are two more features, or topographies, between the pond and my house. They have to be called "community gardens," because they are in the common area. But they have mostly been created by one person, a man I know only as Joe. One is a shade garden and incorporates a copse of established trees. Joe told me he used to plant ten bare-root trees every Arbor Day, but many did not survive much past a year. Besides the few maples and an apple in this group, he planted a line of willows along the banks of the pond. (I did not remark that elsewhere, in forest preserves, gangs of volunteers move about with shovels eradicating willows, an example of an invasive tree species.) Living unfettered in the shade of Joe's thicket are confident prairie plants—daisies, purple coneflowers, Queen Anne's lace, lupine—mixed with likewise unconstrained hostas, daylilies, iris, and other suburban garden flowers donated when the bed was first planted, easily twenty years ago, an estimate based on the sizes of the trees and the establishment of sod between them.

The other common-area patch, the sun garden, is new. The past winter and spring, while I was occupied inside the house—overseeing work by a carpenter, painter, carpet layers, and a plumber, as well as participating in that labor myself, spackling, removing old carpet and tacks, painting closets, and installing shelving—I watched through the windows as a lone man came daily to what appeared to be a fifteen-yard-diameter pile of brush illegally dumped in the common area. He arrived with a wheelbarrow and brown yard-waste bags, and stood methodically picking up one branch after another, one at a time, from the various heaps of discarded clippings, snipping them into smaller pieces to fit into the brown bags. The idea of scofflaws who ditched yard waste on the common area between my property and the pond had already rankled me. It was something the HOA rules would abhor as much as I abhorred *having* those rules. I realize the contradiction here, but if I was going to live in a place where an HOA kept watch over certain kinds of decisions and behavior, it might as well protect me too. I'd watched the man, with some skeptical scrutiny, until it became clear he was not discarding his yard waste but meticulously removing the overgrown brush mountain. It took him all of the two months I spent repainting, reflooring, and refreshing the inside of the new house.

Joe's sun garden was barely a bare patch of ground before it became the relocation home for all the bee balm, black-eyed Susans, sundrops, ornamental grasses, burning bush, and lilies divided from the big property whose gardener I still serve as, even though I've removed my residence from the Tudor. Any audacious flowers that would spread, that were by nature lustful and vigorous and would overwhelm my new smaller yard, that were capable of thriving without additional watering or feeding—those were uprooted and relocated to grow "wild" in the common-area sun garden. Except that this move was being asked of them in a summer of record heat and drought, so all summer, tacitly taking turns, Joe and I attended the garden with buckets. We dipped pailfuls from the pond and poured cloudy greenish water onto the recuperating transplants.

At one time transplanted from California to the Midwest—now to this zip code, this subdivision—this landscape is where I live. Because the basement stores my past—in archive boxes, in photo albums, in a ninety-year-old steamer trunk (originally used to move my twenty-four-year-old mother from Boston to California)—a cliché would claim I've put down roots. An extension of the tired metaphor might replace what "root" represents; exchange the *physical baggage* with *experience*. New tendrils of rhizome have been feeding me information about my new region. I've had the black-ice car crash, the well-water rust ring in the toilet, the mold in a basement cupboard, the dogs who can't put their feet down on the snow in subzero mornings, the ticks, the face swollen from poison ivy, the lightning strike popping light switches off walls and cremating every electronic gadget in the house. Essentially, I have adjusted to new terrain. So now, moving here, to *this* plastic house—moving my plants here, moving my dog here—we'll all adjust even quicker, right? It's only twelve miles away. Nature will take over. That's supposed to mean growing, blooming, and going to seed will all resume, as normal.

The turtle eggs were returned to the earth, reburied, but moved closer to the pond—the treacherous trek to the water will be shorter for the soft, hours-old offspring. A piece of sod replaced over the fresh hole to disguise and protect it from suburban fishermen, teenagers out of the house for a stealthy smoke, and kids with butterfly nets. There's no disguising it from coyote, nor from my dog's nose. Tommy may be finicky about eating carrots and apples, and a bit prissy about burrs in his tail, but he prefers brush or deep woods to a mowed lawn for shitting, relishes gorging on goose and deer dung and carrion (or if completely inedible he wears it on his ears), so a juicy turtle egg could prove irresistible. Part of him goes wild in indigenous topography. Even in a replica.

Feral fe·ral ('fɪərəl, 'fɛr-)—*adj*
Origin:
1615–25; < Latin *fērālis* of the dead, funerary, fatal
Existing in a wild or untamed state, either naturally or having returned to such a state from domestication.
    1. (of animals and plants) existing in a natural state; not domesticated or cultivated; wild.
    2. having reverted to the wild state, as from domestication.
    3. of or characteristic of wild animals; savage, ferocious; brutal.
    4. *derogatory, slang* (of a person) tending to be interested in environmental issues and having a rugged, unkempt appearance
Also:
    1. causing death; fatal.
    2. funereal; gloomy.

Narratives with dictionary definitions: how pedestrian, the true *domestication*—the training, the *taming*—of the essay. I wanted this one to go feral. But I'm having to cultivate, to water, to house-train, or, like a vine, shepherd its offshoots onto a trellis. And what can I do about that last tag of the definition? Does leaving domestication cause death? Or even melancholy? I'm coming to that.

A magazine appeared unsolicited in my mailbox, as though *here* was where it should naturally arrive: *American Lifestyle: Celebrating Life in America.* It claims a big subject, and covers it in fewer than fifty pages, including the advertisements, every other month. Sample featured articles: "The Festive Vegan," "The Art of Temari" (an ancient Japanese craft of intricately embroidered balls), "Doggie Daycare" (this one in NYC), plus the featured recipe "Arugula Scrambled Tofu."

Is *this* really the American way of life? Or maybe the "lifestyle" intended for the address (now *my* address) printed on the heavy, slick covers of this free magazine. One I should be aspiring to or comparing mine against? *Arugula?* Romaine, still sandy from a field in California, was available at the local grocery for seventy-nine cents. Embroidering intricate balls of fine thread? Last night with common cotton thread I hemmed jeans bought for three dollars at the Goodwill. So far this is nothing more than frugality, and debatable whether it's excessive or necessary. Gloating about a less pretentiously bourgeois "lifestyle" (can the word be typed without quotes?) would likely make me just as affected.

Tofu and festive vegans notwithstanding, it's actually the doggy day care that hits a soft target. A prototype that usually earns my disdain: people who insist on keeping a dog when they work sixty-plus hours a week and/or perhaps live in a high-rise apartment, people who pay someone else to feed and play with their dog. But, living here, am I to join them? Even if it's not due to my urban or pressured "lifestyle," but because the move itself, the rearrangement, has cultivated human-style anxiety in an animal, which actually translates to borderline feral behavior in a tame, trained dog.

Tommy can't be left at home alone. He tore up a window blind while trying to keep my car in view as it backed down the driveway. Confined for safety, he bent the steel rod that fastened his wire dog run (housing his blankets, beds, and water bowl) to the concrete basement wall. Given the entire basement, he ripped a coatrack from the door at the top of the basement stairs, tugging on an umbrella hanging there until the steel hook straightened and eventually snapped the plastic anchors that fixed the rack to the door. He weighs only fifty-five pounds but can't stand easily on just one stair. To rip down the coatrack—as well as put tooth marks in the doorknob—was he braced awkwardly on the top two wooden steps, perhaps with his front feet against the door? Did the sudden release when the rack came free send him backward down the stairs? He can't tell me. His joy when I returned had forgotten any trauma. But he needs to be protected from the extremes his angst can cause. To what lengths will a trapped animal go? Leaving a chewed-off leg in the trap: Does Tommy feel that level of fear, just to be left alone in his own bed, in his own house?

Tommy has been taught to perform complex exercises at judged trials for which he has earned many titles, including the highest: obedience trial champion. PETA would claim he is enslaved. But he is the epitome of domesticated canine: he has an instinctive mindset causing him to *need* to be a working member of a pack or partnership. I don't hunt, don't keep sheep, so his "work" has been invented for him. He is not enslaved to his part in this partnership, but perhaps he is a prisoner to his devotion.

Inside the house, he settles (or flings) himself to rest on any floor space I've recently or am about to occupy. He doesn't flinch if I have to step over him going from the sink to the refrigerator to the stove (each trip approximately two short strides, including the step that goes over Tommy's body). But if I go upstairs, even if just to fetch a book or pair of socks, he is compelled to rouse himself, follow (and sometimes pass me on the stairs), then recline again before I've located the book or pulled on the socks; but—*Dammit*, he must think—he has to get up *again* and follow me back down. He is locked into his indicators: Keyboard being tapped, he curls on the floor behind the wheeled desk chair (and how frequently his ribs have been jabbed when I roll back suddenly). TV goes on, he lounges beside the recliner. Food on the table, he lies to one side. Fork stops clinking or my body leans back in the chair, he rises, perhaps sits up on his haunches begging—a trick I taught him in puppyhood—until he's given the plate to lick. Bath faucet starts running, he trudges into the bathroom, thumps his body onto the tile, sighs, and sleeps—even before I've stepped into the tub—until I am finished. Body language might read resigned, long suffering, wearily dutiful. But for a dog it's the comfort of domesticity, the security of being a member, of routine, of knowing what to do and where to be in every situation. Being alone when I am not at home should be part of that routine, but for him, so far in his life, it has not been the norm. This new routine in a new domicile rouses something feral: fear.

I let him come with me when I went to the community garden to plant the last batch of immigrants from the other house. As usual, out at the pond, a different portion of his canine mind went to work sniffing and marking, and soon he was a hundred yards away from me, completely undaunted by how separated we had become. Apparently, space and distance are not disconnection. His fear is specifically named: *abandonment*.

Geese sit on the water and honk at Tommy, and he sometimes pauses in his foraging to pose and watch them. But he won't break the surface and pursue them unless I tell him that's what I want him to do.

The pond. Its natural perimeter. Continuing life cycles of fauna are contained either completely underwater or in the margins between subaquatic and terra firma. None of them need my help. The bluegill and bass spawn. They eat one another's spawn, as well as the tadpoles, mosquito larvae, and minnows. Sufficient spawn survive to reach adulthood. Frogs sit in the muck and gutturalize. Turtles come ashore to spend hours laboring over a teardrop-shaped hole where their dozen to two dozen eggs will be deposited, then methodically covered to gestate anywhere from five months to a year. Unless someone planting a daylily comes along with a spade.

But the wildness here seems . . . tempered. A frog sat atop the algae at the water's edge in the location where I repeatedly dipped the bucket, going back and forth from the garden to the pond, bringing some of his water to the uprooted and resettled flowers. Each trip for another bucketful, the frog remained. I settled the bucket into the water at most two feet from where the frog crouched. Unperturbed by a one-hundred-plus-pound biped repeatedly sinking a large object into the water beside him—the only sound, admittedly, a smooth slurp, a few falling droplets—the frog did not push himself beneath the muck's surface until a finger reached to touch him.

Another time, as I was similarly engaged in the routine of fetching water from the pond for the garden, a bluegill remained near the spot where I was immersing the bucket. Each time, the bluegill made a simulation of the fleeting dart that ordinarily causes fish to vanish from sight as a fisherman approaches water's edge. But this one never completely disappeared. Once, just before the bucket touched the water, instead of darting a few feet away, the fish approached the surface and plucked a spider floating there. For all the bluegill knew, the spider could've been a lure with hidden fishhook. Is *trust* feral or domestic? There might be a shadowy space between feral instinct and complete autonomy, between ability to survive and true wildness.

Mark has not yet relocated to our new house near the pond. All the tending of sensitive new shoots, protecting from weeds and bugs and drought, adding mulch for warmth and nutrition—all *his* adjustment lessons and trials are still to come. Two years ago, before all this even seemed possible, he tried to explain himself to me using a convoluted simile of a guy with a weekday job that kept people who depended on him sheltered and fed, but the job not only didn't stimulate any vitality, it required his time beyond nine to five—evenings and weekends—so he hadn't found a way to seek out new, fulfilling occupations, even hobbies, that might provide him the motive to do more than eat and sleep. "Like"—stuck for an example at the end of his long allegory—"maybe buy an SUV and go to the mountains."

"But am I a new job or a new SUV?" I asked, at the time wretchedly, feeling relinquished.

He still sees a metaphor for himself, his life, in everything. When I told Mark about the turtle eggs, he said that was him, his true self, encased in a shell, waiting for me to disinter him so he could emerge into the real world.

"But turtle eggs will hatch whether I came along or not. The ones here that hopefully *will* still hatch had to be reburied. The one I broke will *never* live."

"Oh, okay, so I'll now finally be able to hatch myself, but only because you've come back to me and changed where my shell is buried."

"But am I the dangerous pond you'll crawl into as soon as you hatch, or the cold, sharp shovel that roused you from the safety of warm dirt too soon?"

Recently, after Tommy had followed me to yet another location in the house and dropped himself to the floor with a loud and seemingly aggravated sigh, I said, "You're a slave to your love, aren't you?" I said it aloud to Tommy, but Mark was with me on the phone, on the Bluetooth in my ear.

Mark said, "Yes."

Now he's taken up the joke, saying he completely understands Tommy's separation anxiety. Mark's servile allegiance is to an emotion he is positive he's felt and sustained since we first encountered each other at sixteen years old. Carried it in his arms, then on his back through our college friendship; tucked within his chest during my first marriage when he played the role of drop-in friend. Finally put deeper into his gut when he attempted to find something else he could call his own, where *it*—the emotion—continued to impede his everyday realm but also became an alternate, private life he tried to live in his head, lasting over twenty-five years, through his decades of symbolically servile financial support of the "substitute life" he sought to overpower or distract from his longings. Yes, he has had beyond-the-time-clock employment as a middle-school band teacher—a career that many in the profession do not find trivial or unfulfilling, and neither did he, on many levels, as he's said, "It was the thing I poured myself into." Plus he had a second job, normally performed by skilled technicians but for which he self-trained, repairing band instruments at the county's only music store. And yes, he had the parasitic family of slackers and reprobates he'd voluntarily picked up and agreed to carry, and then endured degrees of additional humiliation in the forms of flashing police cruisers marking his house as the site of domestic catfights, soda cans crushed on his head, and concealed credit card bills amassed in his name. And yes, despite the wrenching guilt (and escalated verbal and physical punishments), he gave away half of everything he had managed to secure and save—a humble house, two cars, a pension, annuity, and health insurance—so he could finally openly feel and express *it*: this thing, like Tommy's devotion, that made him believe his real life could only happen with me.

When other fenced dogs bark in boredom, Tommy doesn't respond. But if their tone carries alarm or aggression, he does. Stops what he's doing—sleeping or sniffing or rolling on a toy—and stands at attention, eyes trained, ears alert, even nostrils working, flexing, to bring in potential essential information.

My turn: at first it was only voices raised, the strident timbre that one instinctively can tell is not exuberance or joy, not pain or calamity, but anger. Stopped my work in my fenced yard bordering the common area—that undulant, weed-strewn lawn with a few landscaped patches of bushes, plus the sun and shade community gardens—and interrupted my conversation with Mark, as usual on the Bluetooth in my ear. I looked for the source of the voices.

There was a girl, a young woman, in the shade on the common

lawn near a mulched island of shrubs. She was seated, halfway su-pine, her shoulders propped up by straight arms, palms flat on the grass behind her butt, legs in front, feet on the ground, knees bent. The same profile outline as those metallic silhouettes of girls on the mud flaps of semitrucks, the message unambiguous: a volup-tuous woman tendered, ready for and inviting a man between her knees. And sure enough, a young man was standing there, a body's length from her feet, such that if he'd stepped toward her, kneeled, then fallen forward, they would've been coupling out on the com-mon area. Her position so (apparently) voluntarily vulnerable, I thought perhaps I'd been mistaken, that they were just yakking loudly.

But they were battling.

The drama was too far away for Mark to hear it over the phone. So I narrated for him as it happened (with subjective editorial).

It sounded like she just said, "Did you have to play the cowbell?" and now she just kind of screamed, "I told you not to get that can-dle." Wow. I can't hear his answers. His voice is just a buzz. Wait a second, I've only been listening, not watching—they've moved. He's pacing down near the water. I don't know where she is but I can still hear her. Oh—she's coming back from somewhere, coming back to-ward him. Every time I look they've changed positions. The boy is sitting on the pond shore; the girl is marching away again; wait for it . . . now striding back. The boy stood up; I think he just shouted, "So you had to hide my coat?" A coat? In August? Taking his turn to pretend to leave—they're leaving in opposite directions, but of course they've both turned around, coming back. Damn, their breakup is a ballet, the sandhill cranes' mating dance. Coming to its climax: the guy just yelled, "It's just a squirt gun"—is that really what he said?— and he's back to sitting there, as though he's fishing with Huck Finn, and she's going to go through with it this time, leaving; she's around the bend of the pond, going toward those Monopoly-hotel houses on the other side. Maybe she's still having the last word, but he's just sit-ting there.

Mark said, "*No,* don't let her leave, go after her, don't regret it for 30 years!" We laughed—with grief, with shame, with sorrow, with remorse, with elation, with relief.

How, I asked Mark, does anyone ever form a relationship with someone whom they *haven't* known since they were sixteen? The context for this inane yet self-incriminating question has not been memory preserved. Perhaps after one of our gut-funny (only to us) rediscoveries of decades-old shared observations and attitudes. But every time I (do frequently) reconsider the question, examples contrary to my assertion pop up in response: in fact, almost every couple in a stable, profound, enviable committed relationship I've ever encountered *didn't* know each other at sixteen. Most obviously my parents, who met postcollege but have been together over sixty years, so by now how could that not seem as though they've known each other their entire lives? And if I had seen my way, longer ago than three or four years, to understand how Mark belonged in my life, he and I wouldn't have the rousing yet poignant three-way blend of freshness, renewal, and deeply engrained companionship.

Maybe how you grow a meaningful relationship with someone you don't meet until your thirties or forties might be by taking who you are now and going forward with only that, instead of dragging a latent adolescent self along with you. Let the younger self set the older self free. But this kind of being set free has little resemblance to the crux *return*-to-the-wild meaning of "feral." Unless it's returning to the wild state of having no emotional past: regrets, disappointments, hurts, or mistakes, the kinds of memories that disturb natural maturation or behavior. *Baggage.* A metaphor that comes from suitcases—a *domestic* item.

So which would be the true *domesticated animal* (even if not *trained*): a person who is solely his or her adult self . . . or the physically adult person with an ongoing consolidation of childhood, adolescence, and "mature" middle age? Look how the latter seems parallel to the common simplification of *domestic dog*—a canine wolf relative that retains puppy characteristics its entire life (i.e., whining, barking, playing).

So Mark and I are *not* feral . . . yet. We're trying to return.

Camp
(An Unruly Word)

2012

A holiday weekend: Napping as a guest in a friend's place, woken by a loud knock. A new neighbor asking me to move my car. We're shoulder to shoulder, window to window, TVs winking behind gingham or flowered curtains. Several cars bring young adults to a grassy area. They set up a net and begin playing volleyball accompanied by pulsating music pumped from one of the car's stereos. The young men roar. A father also shouts at a kid. Dogs bark (mine included). A baby is screaming. Tarps, some faded and tattered, have been hung for makeshift privacy. Elsewhere, laundry flapping on a line. On nearby playground equipment, kids continue shrieking, and several on bikes go back and forth on gravel paths. A man walks past to the dumpster with his trash. A siren singing, fires here and there in iron pits, plastic flamingos outside doorways. A taxi pulls in slowly, looking for whoever called. A pizza delivery truck likewise looking for a particular locale. Someone's whistle alerts him. Will there be an ice cream truck? If not, it's a missed business opportunity.

This neighborhood, this shantytown, people hollering greetings and playing Frisbee, cooking outside and tooting off to the store for candy . . . This is *camping*.

"Camp" has numerous military definitions related to its mixed origins (Latin = "field," Old English = "battle" or "battlefield").

Modern nonmilitary definitions refer to staying somewhere temporarily, whether as a houseguest when there aren't guest rooms, or a guest staying too long; also when a hallway, office, foyer, stairwell, or other location might be occupied in protest. *To become comfortable and ensconced, but temporarily.* Any of these meanings could fit the campground described (and endured) above. But another dictionary meaning of "camp" also comes in ironically handy for that place: *something that provides sophisticated, knowing amusement, by virtue of its being artlessly mannered or stylized, self-consciously artificial and extravagant, or teasingly ingenuous and sentimental.*

The Americanism "camp-out" connected temporary living arrangement with the outdoors, and used to insinuate an attempted facsimile of frontier/pioneer accommodations. No electricity (OK, propane, also batteries), no running water (except creeks or springs, sometimes hand pumps), no showering, no mirrors, no hair driers, no coffee makers, no shaving. For my childhood family, it went further: try to procure at least some of the food you'll need (by fishing), and no entertainment except what we could produce ourselves, mostly card games and singing around a campfire, maybe with a guitar (none of our other musical instruments could come along).

At one time, that kind of *camping* was the only vacation my father took, with the two weeks left to him after teaching a community-college overload for nine months, then summer school and manning the livestock exhibitor gate at the county fair. Never hammock-swaying leisure, the end-of-summer respite was *camping*, hiking, and fishing in the subalpine eastern Sierra. Five kids in a station wagon that pulled a homemade trailer filled with gear: two military surplus tents (neither with mosquito netting) and seven sleeping bags; propane camp stove and lantern; worms, fishing tackle, and poles; blackened pots and pans, skillets, and pancake griddle for the fire ring, which Dad would have to build with rocks when we arrived. More military surplus for the canvas duffle bags we each stuffed with our jeans, T-shirts, sweatshirts, boots, socks, and underwear. Boxes of the kinds of food that needed no refrigeration: canned beans and vegetables, Bisquick and cornmeal and powdered milk, graham crackers and Cheese-Its, raisins, prunes, and cereal that came in little personal boxes that we only got to have during these two weeks of camp, which made the powdered milk seem manna from holiday heaven.

The wildness, the ruggedness, the isolation, the fearlessness of woodsmoke, ashes, mud, dirty fingernails and hair ... That was *camping*. Where we camped in the '60s, a few other sites might have tent trailers. Over-the-cab truck campers were rare but would be gaining popularity. Yet other than when we passed them on the path to and from the outhouses, or on the portion of the John Muir Trail that paralleled the campsites fifty yards up the non-creek-side grade, other camping vacationers were peripheral.

Most of the sensual details are certain: smell of sage and pine tar, rustle of chipmunk, caw of jay, high feral wind in red fir and Jeffrey pine, and thunder of a glacier creek bordering every campsite, resounding like surf without an ebbing rhythm. Yet under the surface of that din, the burble and tinkle of inlet coves and eddies, the lips of pools, droplets from suspended, sodden branches. We started fishing before dawn, finished after dark, breaking only in the heat of midday to whittle sticks, to search for garnets or grasshoppers or lost fishing tackle, to collect firewood or driftwood or lucky stones.

I admit to nostalgia for camping's rustic austerity, and will concede maybe the absence of other people is simply my antisocial (and idyllic) memory. A baby boomer's grief that the world that was ours, given to us whole by our postwar parents, has been lost.

With tradition comes ritual, and there were expected—anticipated—activities at camp every year. As soon as we were old enough (maybe seven), we began to accompany one parent (usually our dad) on day hikes from the campsites up to the first two or three of a string of lakes on Big Pine Creek, which originated at the Palisade Glacier, the southern-most glacier in the United States. When the youngest of us was of age, both parents could take the trek together with all five spawn in tow (actually one parent at the front of the line, the other at the rear, with our Shetland sheepdog traversing triple or quadruple the distance, as he constantly ranged from the back to the front of his herd). This standard hike to fish the first three lakes was approximately eight miles round trip, starting at nine thousand feet and ending above ten thousand. Such a rite of passage. I still remember my first glimpse of First Lake, nestled far below the trail, appearing as a patch of color between the trees. Astonishing aqua turquoise that didn't seem to fit the subalpine shades of brown and green, I thought it was the roof of a cabin. The unusual color discloses the glacier origin of the creek feeding the lake, as rock particles ground by the glacier (perhaps millions of years ago) are suspended in the water, diffracting light to that "excitation purity" aqua area of the color spectrum.

The other occasion that remains in my memory, separate from blended impressions of five or six years of excursions to the first three lakes, is the capstone camping rite: a day hike of almost eighteen miles to the base of the glacier. It was the golden chalice of hiking: the mythic source of water in the Big Pine Valley and surrounding wilderness, creeping almost vertically on the face of the palisades behind Temple Craig. It could not be seen from the trail until beyond and above the first three lakes that held its opaque aquamarine water. Not possible as an every-year expectation, we'd tried it a year previous and had to turn back because the Shetland sheepdog's feet became too bloody to continue. So my mother stayed behind with my younger brothers and the dog (tied to keep him from following) when my two older sisters and I accompanied our father on this expedition. We may have seen another hiker or two on the trail to the lakes, but possibly did not encounter another human when the trail split from the seven-lake loop for the last oxygen-thin mile to the glacier.

From first light to dusk, climbing to over twelve thousand feet in altitude, with midday views of the three familiar lakes far below when there were still a few miles of climbing to go, through the subalpine zone and into the alpine, above the tree line, where meadows were fields of spongy mosses and the creek was milky. Then the trail became marked on the glacier's boulder field with just three rocks piled atop one another . . . until there it was. A thing almost as ancient as the mountains themselves but weathering time more poorly. A discolored arc of rock-strewn ice, the

whitest tentacles reaching into the crags of the palisade, the whisper of its movement showing in the sweep and streaks of gray extending down to its boulder-studded base against a cloudy proglacial lake, dammed by its own moraine. In a way, the finale of the day's hike was a moment of exhausted disenchantment.

Too fittingly, then, changes started soon after that milestone year. One summer that could have been as late as 1970, our father informed us that we were going home from camp early. The people at surrounding campsites seemed closer, their voices louder, with greater numbers of vehicles pushed into individual sites. More and more pickup trucks with camper shells had come crunching up the dirt road, sometimes towing Airstreams or teardrop camper-trailers. This year there was a large group that carried on nighttime parties with loud music. It's doubtful that a radio could've picked up a music-playing station up there, but starting in 1966, Ford had begun offering eight-track cassette stereo systems on some of its cars, and the format had steadily gained in popularity. That year the Sierra solitude had finally been overrun and overcome, so our parents packed up and fled.

In 1971, we skipped Sierra camping to spend six weeks in our own new pickup camper, dragging a pop-up tent trailer, criss-crossing the United States. We "camped" every night, but we did not consider this *camping*. After that, our eastern Sierra tradition ended. Our parents elected to drive two days through the entire state of California to camp and fish in Oregon. I don't know if they had obtained information that large groups of young adults had continued to live in "our" campsites for entire summers. I recall my father's lament that the area was being ruined "by hippies." I was of an age when I didn't feel much pang over the loss of both place and ritual. My sisters and I began to opt to stay home, get summer jobs, take summer classes, and pretend to be independent while our younger brothers and parents were pursuing annual camping trips in Oregon.

Starting possibly in the late 1970s, however, the Sierra campsites we'd always used at over 8,000 feet had new rules: Campers could drive up to the area and unload gear, then cars and trucks had to be taken back down the road about a mile to designated parking areas near another cluster of "lower campsites" (at 7,800 feet). Even if the vehicles were allowed to deposit a camper-trailer before withdrawing to the parking areas, this would still have reduced the number of trucks and cars, made the area more difficult to access, and prevented the crowded, loud parties, which might have returned the pleasure of camping to us, had we not been young adults separating from the family home. Soon afterward—another year or three—a bridge on the road to the "upper campsites" was washed away in a spring flood, so camping in the upper campsites was only possible with gear carried in on backpacks. Even when the bridge was rebuilt (which may have taken years, not to accomplish but just to have the funds), the forest service chose to continue to restrict all vehicles from the upper areas at *all* times. Eventually, the Inyo National Forest removed the sturdy, monogram-studded, repainted-a-hundred-times picnic tables, and then the outhouses. The former campsites began, as much as they were able, to melt back into the upper montane forest ecology.

There's legislative history that adds to the folklore of how and why our campsites were lost. The Palisade Glacier area is within the John Muir Wilderness. National wilderness areas began to emerge on public lands starting in 1964 with the passage of the Wilderness Act. The subsequent 1976 Federal Land Policy and Management

Act (which also phased out homesteading in the United States) gave the Bureau of Land Management the power to designate and manage wilderness areas. One way of managing wilderness is to not allow motorized vehicles. This time span coincides with our camping area growing too popular, too crowded, too noisy, and the ecosystem probably too stressed; then the gradual decline in access and amenities, until near isolation was returned to the former upper camping area.

My wistful self is glad our bygone campsites had become peopled only by ghosts.

Now all camping in the Big Pine Creek area, other than extra primitive backpacking (i.e., no outhouses), is restricted to the "lower campsites" adjacent to a century-old (although rebuilt many times) lodge and cabins, where many sites can accommodate bigger and bigger motor homes. (I'm not sure if they've added electric hookups.) The lodge—which had been "down in civilization" compared to where we camped in the 1960s—used to have a restaurant and still has a store, clean linens, and showers, and offers a stocked "trout pool" filled with swarms of recently released hatchery-raised giants, guaranteed to swallow hooks. Showers can be also had for a fee for non-cabin-dwelling "campers."

In the 1980s, all of us grown and on our own, our parents bought a small motor home and began returning to the eastern Sierra, to the lower Big Pine Creek camping areas. Every year a few of my siblings would accompany them, sometimes with cousins and aunts and uncles. Adult relatives preferred the cabins, so when my parents sold the motor home in the 1990s, they likewise slept in a cabin. With their stressed and damaged spines, hips, and knees, *camping* no longer meant relinquishing beds, sinks, showers, and electricity. The "kids," ages thirty-five to forty-five, still slept in tents. Propane lanterns were more powerful, camping cookware more versatile, tents fancier—even with screen "porches."

But since my family had first abandoned camping there in 1969 or 1970, I've only gone back twice. In 1977, age twenty-one, I backpacked with my sisters, climbing past the former campsites, then following the Big Pine Creek and John Muir Trail to those familiar first three lakes, camping for several nights and eating the fish we caught. Then again in 1988, when I slept alone in my own pup tent in the motor-home village near the lodge and daily climbed up to where the former upper campsite clearings against the river had grown bushy and winter's logjams were no longer cleared by rangers, providing more interesting fishing.

After that, I have not returned, despite numerous extended-family reunions in the 1990s. My nostalgic stubbornness has meant my continued loss. I did not even return during the last siblings-only gathering in 2013, when my intrepid brothers and sisters and spouses, ages fifty-two to seventy, hiked again up past ten thousand feet, where the chain of lakes is still opaque turquoise jewels in the subalpine forest just below the tree line. Then they continued all the way past twelve thousand feet, through the moraine and boulder fields to the wizened, closer to death, but possibly immortal—and this time magnificent—glacier.

Oneiric
(Another Word I've Never Said)

2013

In a one-minute video circulated on social media, a swarthy, outdoorsy man with lots of dark, wavy hair is holding a black wolf puppy, three or four weeks old, being raised in captivity. The man explains briefly that movements in the pup's ears have indicated that the ears are now open and functioning, so it's a good time to begin teaching him his language. The man proceeds to howl. His lips don't even appear to be open.

It was the most lifelike human-made wolf howl I'd ever heard. Tommy, my golden retriever, got up from his nap and came to stand beside me, ears cocked toward the computer. Seldom does he ever show any interest in audio from the computer, unless I'm playing a dog-show video that contains my voice giving him his commands. I was watching both Tommy and the wolf pup. The pup's head motions were jerky at first. Canine young are born with eyes and ears sealed, both unsealing at around nine to eleven days old. The ears open when they are ready to work and the brain is developed enough to receive the signals, but a pup's new eyes won't focus or follow as well when first opened as they will a week, even two weeks, later. Yet it didn't take very many of the man's howls before the pup had turned his head and fixed a stare on the man's mouth. All his jerky puppy motions stopped. At the video's thirty-eighth second, the little pup threw his head back and joined the conversation. A little squeaky cry that would've only been heard inside a den.

Afterward Tommy went back to his favorite place beneath the window, where he can roll to his back and use the wall to hold him supine, and resumed his nap. He often dreams. Interrupting my work with little yips and high-pitched growls. I usually wake him in case it's a nightmare. But if he were about to catch a rabbit, I've ruined it for him.

It wasn't until later that night that Tommy woke me with a howl. Two howls. I knew where he was in the room, and I knew he wasn't standing up. He was in a foam-rubber bed that's actually too small for him. Who howls lying down? And when had Tommy ever howled? He hadn't. He woke after the second howl, got out of the bed, and flopped onto another of his customary sleeping places, rattling the vertical blinds. What dream had the wolf video inspired?

There were notes on my nightstand, had been there about a week, about a dream I'd had. Until Tommy had his howl dream, I didn't know how to write about mine.

In fifteen-plus definitions for "dream" comprising variations in parts of speech, all but one carry at least tacit ties to "nonreality"—from imagination to delusion. But one definition tries (very hard) to ground itself without the tint (or taint) of illusion: *dream* as *goal* or *ambition*. Some would also call this *hope*, which brings back the whiff of fantasy. Martin Luther King's "I have a dream" carries the *hope* tinge yet was not meant to imply it was far-fetched mirage. He was, however, describing a society that did not yet exist, so his use still sits beside the other definitions of "dream" that retain at least a fingerprint of "nonreality." The oft-quoted (on motivational giftware) quip misattributed to Walt Disney "If you can dream it, you can do it" tried, or wanted, to have a literal understanding. The epigram may not have intended to imply that any implausible to impossible notion will instantly (or even someday) be yours just because you *dreamed* (or wished upon a star) of having it. While King's line can be simplified to its (four-word) bare bones and retain its nuance, the (not really) Disney motto simplifies on a slippery slope to something more resembling "If I want it I should have it." Just today I heard it on an insurance radio advertisement: "If you can dream it, you can have it." I can have a dream to be a brain surgeon or solo concert violinist for the next ten years, but unless I make any of the necessary steps, like going to medical school or taking violin lessons—not to mention unless I relentlessly focus every iota of energy and discipline—it absolutely won't happen. But, my current age aside, even if I had executed those grueling requirements, no matter how much I wanted it, geared my life toward it, and, yes, *dreamed* it in my conscious hours, I simply may not have been able to learn enough or become physically skilled enough to fully achieve either goal. Thousands may dream of being a solo violinist—and do all the requisite work to get there—but never arrive. Yes, they will be able to play the violin. They may play in ensembles from the unpaid community orchestra to world-renowned philharmonics. But if their *dream* was to be a touring solo violinist, they did not get to "have it."

An ambition, a goal, an objective—this use of "dream." Why is it the same word that also means *images, thoughts, or emotions passing through the mind during certain phases of sleep*?

Perhaps the incongruence of the word "dream" meaning both a real-life attainable ambition and some form of hallucination can be blamed (as many things are) on Freud insisting (and thrusting a generation of psychotherapists into believing) that nocturnal dream content was wish fulfillment. And this thin analysis of personality via dream interpretation is also likely behind the pariah status dreams acquired among writers of literature.

Possibly as long as there have been creative-writing classes, and even a little before that, using dreams in fiction was generally known—if I may overstate to make a point—as amateurish, cheap, the work of a hack, too easy, and juvenile. Putting aside the plethora of examples to the contrary (a list could start with James Joyce and Charles Dickens, and at the other end include me), professors of this art have generally stuck to Henry James's view: "Tell a dream, lose a reader." Perhaps he purely meant a loss due to boredom, but "we" professors know how dreams can be inexpertly used by undergraduates as an updated version of deus ex machina to provide insight to a character or reader, to push resolution, to crudely create symbolism, or to explain motive.

Even research scientists have a higher regard for dreams in art than creative-writing professors.

> Most dreams are narratives occurring, and often presented without applied organization, grammar, or expectation of critique. In the dream, we can literally observe the "thinking of the body," and with it, the birth of the literary process. Our dreams can be considered an exercise in pure storytelling whose end is nothing more (or less) than the organization of experience into set patterns that help to maintain order for the thinking system.

> Among successfully creative individuals, dream and nightmare recall, as well as dream incorporation into work and waking behavior, is much higher than in the general population, suggesting that one function of dreaming may be in the creative process.

> —James F. Pagel, "What Physicians Need to Know
> about Dreams and Dreaming," *Current Opinion
> in Pulmonary Medicine* (2012), 574–79

So the *function* of dreaming—the *why* it's part of our physiological/psychological makeup—is to facilitate a creative process? Evolution developed the "cognitive mentation that we call dreams" (Pagel) so that we could be "creative"? Then what's behind Tommy's dreams? What will he do with *his* wordless narrative?

Despite Tommy's *parasomnias*—unwanted behaviors occurring during sleep, which usually do indicate but don't prove dreaming—"most sleep medicine physicians consider dreaming to be mentation reported as occurring in sleep by a human participant" (Pagel).

I love the word "mentation." Loving a word does not set me apart from Tommy. He loves words too. "Supper," "cookie," and "toy" are favorites. Also "squirrel" (any small animal) and "window" (hearing it means he should go look out of one because there might be a squirrel out there). He also has verbs in the form of

commands (which sounds more draconian than he takes it, but I admit, *commands* are not *suggestions*). Humans are always trying to find ways we are like our animals. Do dogs do the same? Or is it simply an assumption, to them, that we want what they want, feel what they feel, need what they need, and don't care about what disinterests them? Without putting it in so many words, *of course.*

The type of dreaming dogs decidedly *don't* share with us: that curiously related meaning having to do with desires and hopes, goals and ambitions. Master trainers say dogs can solve problems during training, but do they *think* about those problems when not engaged in the activity? Can they plan ahead? What kind of *cognition*, which some say is necessary for dreaming, do they have? Then what about the visual evidence: twitching legs and vocalizations—growls, yips, and the recent singular episode of the howl? Puppies, from the time they are a day old, sleep with twitching limbs. I've heard that's how they exercise developing muscles. Tommy is eight years old, fully (and very well) muscled. Add the vocalizing to the leg twitching, and these parasomnia-like motions during Tommy's sleep could be a form of somnambulism: "sleep terrors and confusional arousals . . . associated with incoherent vocalizations" (Pagel).

Or, as I've suspected, nightmares. No dreams of glory killing a squirrel. If he had never caught a squirrel, how would he create the narrative in a dream? But isn't the same true of nightmares, including the three most prevalent scenarios in human nightmares (all, for me, experienced *only* in sleep): falling (39.5 percent), being chased (25.7 percent), being paralyzed (25.3 percent) (M. Schredl, *International Journal of Dream Research*, 2021, p. 61). Other research into nightmares insinuates they are a human-only occurrence, as those who endure them frequently are more likely to be fantasy prone, psychologically absorbed, have "dysphoric daydreaming and 'thin' boundaries" (Pagel, *Dream Science: Exploring the Forms of Consciousness*, 2014, p. 110). While some dogs do have "thin boundaries," I don't know many dogs who are fantasy prone or psychologically absorbed, not to mention the agitated daydreaming.

But there's a *person* I know . . .

Mark finished high school with me, finished college with me, finished secondary-teacher preparation with me. Just before I abandoned the teaching credential for more graduate school, he confessed what I'd already known for five years: that he'd never wanted to be with anyone else, was distraught over our daily contact coming to an end. And couldn't I please reconsider the refusal I'd maintained since his ungainly, overly assertive attempts at love in high school? My response did not change the course of our futures, so he had embarked on his high-school teaching career one hundred miles away, in the desert near the border with Mexico. Two years later, he quit to return to our hometown where I still lived—now with a husband—so that he could stay close to where I was. *He* knew that's what he'd done, but I did not. He substitute taught for a while, then worked a graveyard shift at a printshop.

But back up to a space between the third and fourth sentences of the previous paragraph. January 1980. I was six months past rejecting my plan (but never a "dream") to be a high-school English teacher, six months past Mark's plea for us to remain together, and at least a year away from knowing what the hell I might do instead except the fixated typing of journals and stories that had been going on for almost a decade. Mark was half a year into his foreseen (but also not dreamed) career as a high-school band director. Despite my refusal to consider him romantically, I begged him to be my friend, to let me write to him. One instinct advised him to say no, to break contact, to try to figure out something else he could want. His other impulse, the one that had been with him since he was sixteen, told him to embrace any form of intimacy, the only one he was being offered. We wrote letters. Or I did. He was a man with a job and could answer with phone calls. My letters were typed, single-spaced, and page after page of misspelled, superfluous, angsty laments, questions, frustration, exasperation, rage, doubts, and fears . . . about who I was, who should I be, who would I become, what I was doing, where I was going, who would I eventually go there with . . . and all the gory details about a Jehovah's Witness I thought I wanted who'd rejected me on the grounds I was too worldly, a sin for him to be with. I was still a virgin.

Finally one of my letters to Mark declared that what I needed was to go to a bar and get picked up. Mark seemed the essence of calm when he suggested he could take me to his next gig—down by the naval shipyard—with the Top 40 band in which he played saxophone. The plan was set: he would supply the transportation and the venue; I would take it from there and get picked up. The plan had no exit strategy. It also did not have any hope for achievement because I either sat in self-fulfilling misery in the far back of the nightclub or refused to dance when asked (once). When Mark came to where I was sitting and told me not to sit way back there if I expected to meet anyone, I moved to a closer table. I moved to the band's table. I was there when they returned for their last break. Without a typewriter, I began narrating another tome of bewilderment and despair. And Mark, hot with worry that I'd come there to meet someone, and planning how he was going to prevent it, was available for me to flop, predictably, into his arms. We held on to each other. We moaned. We kissed. He professed his love. He was careful to not repeat the zealous ardency of his teenaged self, but he couldn't stop his words. *Please ... come be with me ... I'll take care of you ...* said against my ear in his car. Modified to *Please, let me hold you tonight ... I promise, I'll just hold you ... Please ...* when we were on my doorstep. Just before I closed the door.

For two months I couldn't even say why I'd done it, any of it, but especially the door closing. When my letters resumed, I tried to blame the book I was writing, my need to focus on it, on finishing school. I created openings so that he could blame the alcohol so as to resume his composure or poise. What I didn't realize, or allow, was his version: I'd received his raw feelings, I'd accepted them, I'd responded with my own; then I'd said I wasn't ready that night. But a mere six months later I suddenly *was* ready, and it was with someone else. I married exactly to the day one year after the nightclub night with Mark. Six months later he quit his two-year-old teaching career and came home to live with his parents, work in a printshop, and drop in two or three times a week after his shift to visit. Perchance to dream.

In 1986, Mark was part of the crew helping me and my then husband move. Mark was teamed with my father. On one trip back for another load, my father, making conversation, casually remarked, "So, Mark, what're your plans now?" I'm not sure how much my father meant by it, perhaps no more than "What've you been up to?" but Mark took it as, *Look, you've quit the teaching job you went to college for (so you could be near her), and now you're helping her move into a house with her husband (who, in case you haven't noticed, isn't you). What's your next brilliant move?*

Mark's next move was to find the first woman who didn't notice his preoccupation—one who had enough baggage, chaos, and problems needing (his) help to solve so that there wouldn't be much downtime for reverie—and bring her back out to the desert, where he was rehired for another teaching job. His former dream not even a dream anymore. A *what-if.* An *"if only."* A reverie put away but not destroyed. Not forgotten. Spoken only by his saxophone.

Twenty-five years later, Mark has embarked on a deferred life in partnership with me, and as a member of my extended family. As difficult as it had been to allow himself the prolonged yearning, that was easier than it has been to get here. In order to be sitting in a dusk-darkened, sunset-illuminated living room across a coffee table from a ninety-three-year-old man he'd thought should be his father-in-law when the man was sixty, Mark had to relinquish half the retirement he'd built over a career teaching middle-school music, half the stressed miracle-it-existed-at-all savings account, half his (sometimes crumbling) physical assets, and had been court ordered to pay a sum equal to half his monthly salary to the woman with all those problems who'd also never worked, whose deadbeat children he'd partially raised and supported even into adulthood, and whose relentless spending created a runaway train of the household budget. Not only had she been awarded nearly half of his retirement account, once he started drawing from his remaining portion as income, he still has to pay almost all of each check to her to meet his monthly support requirement. What might have been fair and just to give a former partner who'd maintained the house, meals, and children was more like ransom paid to free himself. He is only fifty-seven, now without a job, has shed almost everything except his saxophone and his want.

In my parents' living room, my dad on a sofa with the newspaper, Mark across from him, a sunset lighting up the window behind Mark's head and reflecting opaque orange from my father's glasses—while my mother and I struggled to communicate in her newly formed stroke-induced grammar, making *pasta y fagioli* that she used to make by rote but now needs a recipe for—my father said, "So, what kind of work do you think you'll be looking for over there?"

"Pretty much anything I can get," Mark said. "Tutoring, Wal-mart, Home Depot, substitute teaching, music lessons . . . anything."

"I guess you won't know until you get there."

"Yeah, that's what I figure. Get there first, then start seeing what's possible."

As my father lifted the newspaper up to read, he said, "You're braver than me."

Mark sat a while, looking at the curtain of newspaper. Then said, "I'm scared."

My father lowered the paper. He turned his head enough that Mark could tell he was looking past him, out the window to the dimming sunset. The glint on his glasses no longer orange but white, like overcast. "That's why you're brave."

I am now three weeks past the dream whose bedside notes began this essay. The notes preserved enough memory that I still retain the images as well as the emotions. My body recalls the physical responses. Some of the flashbacks are here for context:

I'm the driver, Mark the passenger. I'm taking him on a tour. Of sights. I pull off the road or highway or freeway. The spur off-ramp ends, almost immediately, at an outcropping parking space. Fits maybe two cars. The parking space is not paved but is made of solid gray shale. The shale protrudes out off a cliff, but it's obvious enough to not pull that far forward. The parking place is indeed a viewpoint. There's a similar viewpoint off-ramp on Interstate 5 between Orange County and San Diego, but it's a complete on-and-off circle. I'm not sure what the particular view is on the I-5 viewpoint, except the Pacific Ocean. Mark has told me that he almost drove off the road (somewhere near that viewpoint?) when I fell asleep in our car pool on the way home from student teaching and my blouse gaped open, exposing (thanks to a bra with equally fatigued elastic) a crescent of nipple color. He was twenty-three. It was a year before our accidental-on-purpose, ill-fated nondate at a nightclub where his band was playing.

This dream viewpoint likewise seems to be ocean, but the beach doesn't have the classic sand with breakers. More like the tide pools of La Jolla, the waves come effervescing up across and into Swiss-cheese-pocked flattened rocks. This is what I mean to show Mark. I also (in the dream) recognize it as being the Presque Isle River in the Porcupine Mountains in the Upper Peninsula of Michigan, where I now own a fishing cabin. The tannin-colored water coming out of the Porkies, descending toward Lake Superior, has carved hot-tub-sized circles in the sedimentary rock shoreline. The river swirls into and back out of each tub, a furl of froth always staying behind and circling. Mark and I didn't get over to the Porkies on our brief trip to the U.P. last summer. My foot is firmly on the car's brake, and I shift to park and set the emergency brake. A car pulls into the space beside us, then immediately backs out again. I am aware of my foot, my toes slightly bent backward, maintaining cognizant pressure on the brake. I also know I am only wearing my slippers. I can feel the shape of the pedal under the thin sole. I don't tell Mark out loud, but think to him: *Don't worry; my foot won't slip off the brake.* And anyway, I've shifted to park. But he's ready to go. We both feel nervous. The way we used to feel nervous driving home from student teaching on I-5. The way we each knew the other was nervous without saying anything.

My foot increases its pressure on the brake. Very careful to not let the foot, in just a slipper, slip off the brake pedal. Release the emergency brake. Shift into reverse. Foot will have to jump quickly from brake to gas. The dream doesn't include a clutch (which would have been present in the car driving us home from student teaching), but all of my old trepidation regarding starting motion with a standard transmission when stopped at a light at the top of an incline has returned to me. The fear in that case: stalling (of course), or the car rolling backward into the car too close behind before the clutch engages first gear and the car can begin to go forward. And yet I also know there's no clutch here. I won't make a mistake.

Is this even a surprise by now? I press the gas, and the car, without a jolt, moves forward and is airborne over the beach with flat, pock-marked pools.

My thoughts: *I put it in drive by mistake.* And: *I can't change it now.*

Mark's thought: *We're going to die.*

My answer thought: *Maybe we'll only be hurt.*

We look at each other while also still seeing the view of breakers foaming into the sandstone pools.

Now awake.

The dog on the floor in the bedroom didn't stir. Even if I'd made any kind of sound, I doubt he would have. But since in the dream I didn't cry out or scream (or didn't try to scream but was met with vocal paralysis), I doubt there was any sound to wake or alarm him. But of course, he doesn't even stir if I vomit at night, and what could be a more alarming sound?

Wondering if I'd made any dream sound was not, however, what was on my mind after waking. My deliberation was about how it was one of those mistakes that simply can't be undone. Like cutting off a finger while deboning a chicken. Like accidentally hitting a television screen or aquarium with a hammer—something I've imagined happening when I've walked through a room with a hammer, provided a television or aquarium was present. Like turning on the garbage disposal while I've got my hand in there, stuffing the potato peelings down—something I tell myself not to do every time I have to stuff something down there.

No, listing those other kinds of sudden, ghastly mistakes that can't be undone was also not what I was thinking when I woke. Just that I had made one. In the dream. And I was feeling, still, in a sustained extension of the seconds after, what it felt like to make one. What it felt like seconds before the resounding end.

It was obvious that closing my eyes without replaying the car's gentle leap off the overlook—without rethinking the thoughts, both Mark's and mine, without feeling the hot gush of realization—was not going to be possible. So I turned on the light and began reading a novel where every character was in the slow-motion beginning of a *metaphoric* fiery crash with no concept of the impending dire conclusion, which had started when they were born, or at least when their childhood families had fallen apart. Mark and I have no such background. We have other flashbacks, but not that one.

An hour later, light off and replaying the dream scene again—the same flash of soaring fear—I realized I hadn't ever told him I was sorry.

Neighborhood
(Taking It to the Grass)

2014 WINTER AND SPRING

This morning, *Tuesday, April 22, 5:45 a.m.*, he revved his old pickup, pulled out at 6:00, and returned at 6:10. Last night—after my cell rang around 9:00, and it was him, and I didn't answer, and he left no message—he was outside mowing in the dark. Under a streetlight his silhouette paused, as if he'd hit a bump or the mower blades had become jammed in high grass. But turf barely grows in April, and he had already cut his grass the day before, and not for the first time.

Finally his form lurched forward again, unstuck. As I remember, I think I heard his breath likewise catch and heave. But of course the image was silent.

I'd been warned. My new neighbors on one side told me the neighbor on the other side was odd. People have various definitions of "odd." Theirs was: JD hardly ever comes out of the house, then sometimes he comes out and mows his lawn several days in a row. Sometimes talks and yells to himself. I am sure, now, that they left a lot out of this summary. If they'd told me more before the deal was closed on my house, and if I'd backed out of the purchase, and if the former owners had deduced why I'd reneged, the tale-telling neighbor could be sued.

During a muted first year, I'd noted JD didn't come out of his house much. When he did it was to mow his lawn. More frequently than most. He had no flowers or bushes, but the lawn was a uniform, green crew cut, taller than mine. The difference in how high we set our mowers became a contour of the property line. He did talk out loud, but the Bluetooth earpiece he wore disclosed that it was not a manic conversation with phantoms. Yes, someone had suggested a routine pop-psychological mental illness diagnosis. I slotted that as pop-culture pigeonholing. This time, I was wrong.

Once JD told me I had a nice mower. True, a fly-yellow Canadian-made Cub Cadet with a Honda engine and caster wheels. He saw my White Sox flag and said he was a lifetime Cubs fan. He knew I am from California, and after I returned from a visit asked me, "How was it in Cali?" (Lingo that I've always detested.) He'd been in the marines at Camp Pendleton and liked the zoo in San Diego. Could any chitchat be more throwaway trivial?

I never wanted to live in a neighborhood. At least not again. It was cool in my twenties, renting tiny war-era houses in the college and postcollege neighborhoods of San Diego that attracted vegetarian restaurants, bookstores, and cult theaters. It was tolerable in my early thirties to actually own a postwar slab house in a working-class neighborhood, until the teenaged boy across the street rattled my walls and appropriated my heartbeat with a stereo his parents attempted (and failed) to secure with locks. It was a respite in my late thirties in the Midwest, once more a renter in a train-stop suburb surrounding a thriving village, living in the smallest, oldest bungalow on a street where one-hundred-year-old trees dwarfed houses, even though houses that sold were demolished so a newer deluxe mimeo manor could fill the lot. Sure enough, two days after I moved out, the bulldozers came to flatten my tiny bungalow. Then, finally, deliverance in my forties to again own property, but this time over an acre, with a tree line bordering a cornfield that bordered another tree line that bordered a creek. The neighboring house on five acres, so association with the inhabitants there only amounted to an occasional wave.

But I am back in a cul-de-sac, on a quarter acre, in one of a developer's six or seven floor plans, houses called "homes" before they were ever lived in. Besides the price range suitable for a fractured budget, this one was chosen because behind it lies the common area and a pond with natural borders. It's supposed to be a more responsible way of developing—instead of bigger individual yards with expansive lawns, there's common open-space. The houses on the edge of that space have the most benefit, as the pond, the trees, the birds, the reeds, the plot of wildflowers are outside my back gate.

But on either side of me: people. The gentle curve of the cul-de-sac changes, slightly, the direction each house faces, and on a patio or deck that's snug to the house, each neighbor's patio or deck can barely be seen (or not at all).

This is where I fixed a *home* for Mark when, after thirty years apart, we made the required sacrifices to put our lives together. His forfeit: After thirty years of teaching middle-school band, four-fifths of every pension check goes to an ex who already had banked almost half of the whole account. So after he retired he still pays $2,000 a month spousal support out of his remaining portion. My sacrifice: that finally reached goal of a *non*suburban property, with neighbors only at a distance.

Nature = fortification

No people = serenity

Any contact with my new, closer neighbors changed this past winter. In the midst of one of the snowiest winters on record, I was scraping another overnight coating off the front porch. The snow in the yard was now higher than the step-up porch. But still, my position on the concrete slab outside the front door might have given me another four to six inches of height when JD came across my snow-covered lawn to stand in front of me, ten feet away. Had I seen him coming? Memory doesn't provide that framework. He was just there, saying, "I hear you a dog trainer."

I smiled. "Yes."

I'd done some training outside during the past year. Enough that it was obvious we weren't just playing fetch. My dogs' exploits at performance events are a quiet source of fulfillment.

"So, how you call you-self a trainer. Your dogs bark at me when I go into my yard. You could train them not to, if you a trainer. You not much of a trainer. The way they bark at me."

Thoughts are supposed to race at moments like this. Time stands still when tension speeds up. A fiction writer can add sensual details, stage directions, small movements and gestures, distant sounds. My thoughts did not race. My head went somewhat silent. There were no background sounds or images to swell out of proportion. Snow is not as serene as it is cold. Sometimes harsh. Very quiet.

Only now, in this different kind of quiet at a keyboard, there's another clanging alarm: what I'm *not* saying. What I've said by reproducing JD's vernacular without directly disclosing his race. By making the omission seem unconscious when it's actually the opposite. Sometime in the late 1970s, my budding progressive brain locked onto a policy that it was uncool to describe people using their race. I actually learned this (via a book) from a baseball player who was mugged and refused to tell the police the race of the perpetrator. That code still being maintained in this narrative until it is becoming an evasion rather than a statement. I did want to keep this episode from being something that happened because of race. I still don't think race is the chief reason that the situation arose. But the lived experience and the narrated story are never going to be the same thing. And is the narrative—especially now that I've noticed—at least partially also about my evasion?

Eventually, that day on the cold porch, I did say something. I said my dogs were hardly ever in the yard. Only to relieve themselves, then they come back—it's too cold for them to stay out. He said he was talking about last fall. After another moment of scene paralysis, I mentioned that my other neighbor's dog barks at me in my yard.

"I knew trained dogs in the military. I been around trained dogs. You call yourself a *dog* trainer."

I don't recall how the dialogue ended. At some point I went back into the house and he returned to his property. I don't recall which of us turned first.

I had his email address from when I'd first moved in and had introduced myself. I'd put a handwritten note in his mailbox, and he'd responded via email, just something like "let me know if you need anything." It hadn't gone any further. I give this detail because it was all so innocuous and normal. Accordingly, after this February exchange, I wrote a brief email apologizing for being unable to respond in a useful way when we'd spoken on my porch. I explained the dogs are trained to come instantly when called, so if they bark, I would not hesitate to call them in. He answered that he hadn't meant to sound harsh and he'd been under a lot of pressure lately trying to avoid neck surgery. This still sounds unexceptional.

An over-the-fence dialogue a few days later, on one of the few days of winter clemency (in the upper thirties), was likewise nothing more than conventional. I was trying to exercise the dogs in the snowy yard, and JD stepped out into his. The dogs came eagerly for attention from a new friend, and he wanted to tell me he'd seen the news about my faculty union holding a two-day strike. I was trying to tell him that when the dogs barked, *he* could call the dogs over to the fence and pat them—it would make them stop barking and get to know him. He wanted to talk about his public-employee union and the current fight to protect his pension. Even though we were having two different conversations, it still seemed the typical surface exchange of neighbors who only talk when they are (seemingly) inadvertently out at the same time.

Two weeks later, I stood on the back stoop while the dogs relieved themselves in the snow. In a rapid causal chain, when JD appeared on his deck, the dogs bolted toward that side of the yard, barking; I called them; they wheeled in their tracks and just as swiftly sprinted to the door and came inside.

A day later, an email:

> I HAVE BEEN AROUND DOGS ALL MY LIFE. YOU DOGS RUNNING TO THE FENCE & BARKING @ ME IS INTENTIONAL & BIAS !!!!!!!

Any canine behavior = purposely trained
Familiarity = expertise

Wednesday, April 23, a day after I'd drafted this narrative's first paragraph, JD was conjointly rattled and medicated. Both ungainly and wired. Maniacal and wobbly. I couldn't smell alcohol nor pot. He wasn't slow and dopey nor in physical high-speed frenzy. He couldn't finish a sentence, although he started many, one after another, and saliva both spewed and dribbled.

In the backyard, after he'd produced wooden stakes and a sledgehammer to reinforce his fence posts, he leaned backward on the same wobbly fence—while I held the stakes and Mark pounded them in—as though to disguise that he wasn't standing up on his own power. Once he squeezed my arm with a comment about how strong I seemed. He babbled about his ex-wife who'd just bought an $80,000 Audi; how his grandchildren were graduating high school, and could I email him something to give them because they needed to know what to do next; about the successful professionals in his family and how they could send someone $1,000 just like that if it was needed, and how it hurt him that his sister only contacted him when she needed money; about how he could break a man in half with his hands, and if he got angered he wasn't responsible for what might happen; about his mother, who had washed her hair in rainwater from a barrel and worked in a laundry where the owner tried to make her stay in the back cleaning the clothes, but she insisted that she wanted to be up front where the people were; about how he was going to the pound to rescue a dog, a German shepherd; about how he had a nightmare and could have hurt a woman who was with him. Laced between almost every half-sentence foray, something about how he can't sleep, and when he gets racing he has to take something to calm him down, and why he has trouble trusting, and how it was that the people who used to live in my house came to hate him so much that they moved, so now the other neighbors in the cul-de-sac are mad that their friends moved away, so they hate him too.

Since the first breath of spring, since the grass first greened, his mower has run every day, filleting the front grass. His back lawn has yet to be cut.

Friday, April 25. I gave up writing this today when the cul-de-sac filled with police cars, an ambulance, and a fire truck.

The ambulance and fire truck were first. In the gutter between my driveway and his, just about at the property border, a red traffic cone and a spray-painted white line. JD was still in the front yard when the first heavily garbed fireman came across the lawn from the side. As the first police cruiser circled the curb of the cul-de-sac, JD retrieved the red cone, brought it back to his garage, where he met the fireman. Voices resounded, not angry or arguing. Just unnatural in a midmorning weekday, like a dramatic performance staged beneath our windows.

Because a cul-de-sac is curved, his front porch is not visible from the gallery seats at our windows. JD exited the stage, into his house, and did not return for over an hour. That was when the other five police vehicles arrived. The paramedics waited in the ambulance. Firemen met in the driveway, police back and forth in the driveway. No crackle of loud radios from the cars. No more audible dialogue. The drama continued as a silent movie. One without any development or action. A convention of police cars. The quota, it would seem, for our quadrant of the city.

On the phone with neighbors: *It's happened before. He might have guns. He barricades himself in the house. Last time they evacuated the whole cul-de-sac, everyone had ten seconds to get out.*

Usually, in the calm of past tense, writing a personal account approximates, even surrounds and converges on, unexpected illumination, new perceptions and thus new impressions, some sort of upshot. The in-writing complication of seeing more angles, more possibilities, more layers in the surrounding detail—from what I was wearing to what was happening at work in-between episodes to my mother's simultaneous rapid decline two thousand miles away—would actually (with some semblance of chronology) be a move toward controlling this chaos. Toward sealing a memory like a thorn enclosed in scar tissue. Real-time writing does not feel or work that way. It's like solo cooking a fancy meal for eight people while having a political debate with three of them. Something will be overcooked, something will be raw, something will be missing ingredients, and the cook will have no pleasure in finally sitting down to eat two hours later than planned. A simile fit for one who isn't a good cook in the first place.

Even the mixed metaphors speak the chaos, no closer to a solace of resolution. There is only trust that, in writing, I do usually, after some wandering, get close. Or closer.

So I'll go back to six or eight weeks prior, midwinter. I answered the INTENTIONAL & BIAS email.

> Hi JD, Sometimes I am dense, so I wasn't sure if you were joking—you have to hit me over the head, like write "HAHA" so I'll know.
>   I hope by this you're not suggesting that I am sic'ing my dogs on you. My dogs are not attack trained. There are children playing in the cul-de-sac while I write this, and when I let the dogs out for the last time before bed, they will bark at those kids. My dogs are high-spirited because they are show dogs. They have to have a lot of energy to be able to perform under pressure.

JD responded:

MY (AKC) GERMAN SHEPARD WILL REMEDY THAT !!!

I was unsure what was to be cured with the German shepherd. Kids playing outside? My dogs' high spirits? That I don't get jokes? It was the last time I answered an email.

German shepherd = shut up

Another snowfall had us out shoveling again a week later. For most of the winter, JD had run his snow thrower along the sidewalk around the whole cul-de-sac, but on this day he was keeping close to his driveway, letting the machine sit and run while he tinkered with it, then retreating into his garage. Mark and I began our Sisyphus routine reclearing the driveway, the area in front of the mailbox, and this time also the sidewalk.

JD approached along the cleared sidewalk while I was digging out the space for the postal truck to reach the mailbox.

"I been around dogs all my life. You taught those dogs to bark at me."

My mouth remained closed. There seemed not enough air to begin an explanation of how difficult it is to train negative commands (i.e., "don't bark"), let alone the professional skill it would take to teach a dog to only bark at a specific person based on some kind of "marker" (scent of contraband, scent of internal disease), in which case the bark would not be "at" the person but an alarm for the handler. Had anyone taught dogs to bark at (or attack/hold, as military or police dogs are trained) a particular race? If dogs show this behavior, it's often a result of how the owner acts/changes when in the presence of particular "types" of people. (Long hair and beards, or extreme height, for example; or, I suppose, different races, although I don't know how well a dog would comprehend differences in skin color or eye shape, whereas being able to identify a beard and long hair, or a ball cap, or boots is probable.)

While that was zigzagging through my mind, Mark was answering. Probably pointing out that we'd created a barrier in the yard and the dogs could no longer access the side of the yard where JD's house was.

"I know dogs all my life. I was around dogs in the military; they bark at who you want them to bark at."

"They're not military-trained dogs." My voice as flat as my momentum, while lifting yet another load of snow to the mountain on the parkway.

JD was already leaving. "I know what I know. I know what I see. You send those dogs to bark—it's *bias*."

By the time he was back in front of his house and had started fiddling with a porch light, I had returned to our garage. Mark had the wider shovel and would clear the rest of the driveway. But Mark followed JD.

"You're wrong. If you just knew her, if you could possibly know, you'd know how wrong you are."

"Mark, you can stand there and tell me this snow is green, but that not going to change that it's white."

Snow = white
Dogs bark = racism

On an isolated stretch of mild weather in mid-March, the doorbell rang. The dogs barked. I stuffed them behind me and slipped out, closing the door most of the way but staying in front of it, perched on the doorjamb and sandwiched by the glass storm door in front of me, which I held partially open. JD stood on the porch holding out two solar patio lights. "What's this?" I said as I took them. As soon as the lights were in my possession, JD extended a hand to shake, which I did. He did not answer—at least not in full sentences—my stammering attempt to ask why he was bringing me a gift. Of course I recognized it was some sort of apology, so I ignored what it was an apology for and shifted to building goodwill. Flattery. Interest. Attention. Basic human needs (and uphill work for the antisocial among us).

It looked like he was full of misplaced spring clean-up energy (he had hung some ugly plastic sunflower wind chimes in the walnut tree between his driveway and our front yard). He said he had to get the place in shape, he was a good neighbor, and he liked to help the older couple across the street. Falling in with the looping of non sequiturs, I said I'd noticed he cleared their snow, and it looked like he'd lost weight. He said he was going to the rec center every morning. I asked if it was expensive. He said he was trying to avoid surgery on his neck. I asked if it cost a lot to go. He said he did everything over there, even used the pool. In a while I learned (for the first time) that his ex-wife had bought a very expensive German car because he'd been fleeced in the divorce, that he had a speech impediment (which makes him difficult to understand), how many kids he had (two sons), where his eldest son went to college (University of Illinois), where JD went to college (also University of Illinois), what he majored in (criminology), when he'd graduated (1978), that he'd lost his front teeth playing college basketball (which is the speech impediment). He was down off the porch by this time, sort of swinging from side to side, shifting his weight, unable to stand still, grinning widely, gradually moving away from the porch. I let the storm door close behind me. Maybe it was relief that the bizarre accusations had been lifted. I got chatty too, told him I'd also graduated from college in 1978—of course in San Diego, he already knew that—but that Mark as well had graduated in 1978, from the same college as me. In fact Mark and I had also gone to high school together, had known each other since we were sixteen.

Mark came home from his afternoon music lessons before we were finished. JD continued his swaying retreat into the driveway to extend a handshake to Mark. I took the opportunity to return into the house.

Solar lights = spring
Gifts = good neighbors

My gift to JD was to set a paver landscape border around a tree planted by the city on the parkway straddling the line between our properties. JD had purchased the pavers, along with bags of red mulch, on one of his daily trips to the hardware store around the time it opened (between 6:00 a.m. and 7:00 a.m.). But when he mounded the mulch up a foot high on the little tree, then jammed the bricks against the pile in a tight circle, I told him I would create a bigger circle out farther to make sure grass didn't grow up through the mulch. Also because the "beehive" look of mulch piles against trees was not good for them; trunks need to breathe. He smiled and said he hadn't known that, and proceeded to pull a second, bigger mountain of mulch away from his walnut tree, so it appeared that tree was growing out of a red volcano.

During the two hours I spent on my knees in the chilly spring mud removing turf and leveling the bricks, JD puttered in his driveway and garage, the door rolled open. The first year I'd lived here up through this past winter, two of his cars fit into the garage with the old truck always in the street. Now his slicked-up Nissan and new huge black SUV were always either in the street or the driveway, his garage door usually open, and a pile of paraphernalia growing in the garage. I'd seen him move a used organ out of his truck one day. He said he'd bought it off Craigslist. There was also a lawn tractor with a snowplow attachment, four new lawn chairs he'd purchased as soon as the hardware stores featured the trappings for outdoor living in earliest spring, more bags of mulch, and the remaining jumble of junk unknown to me because I had never stood there long enough to take an inventory. How I knew as much as I did: his coming and going was not difficult to not only notice, but to watch. And my watching would become even more acute. Plus the doorbell had rung more than once, the barking dogs stuffed behind me or Mark, and JD would be on the porch to request Mark's help to load or unload something into the old pickup.

While I was on my knees finishing the tree, I learned that JD or his son had lost the garage door opener, and he'd been on the phone with LiftMaster all morning trying to get the universal code, and then found an opener in a jacket pocket.

Days later, this time just after Mark got home from his private lessons, the doorbell rang. The dogs barked. I stuffed them down the basement stairs while Mark went to answer. I heard Mark's amiable neighbor greeting, "Yo, JD, what's up?" I heard Mark say, "What?" And I heard him say, "What are you talking about?"

When I got to the door and joined them on the porch, JD said, "What do I hafta *do* to lock this place down?"

I echoed, "What?"

JD stepped backward. Swaying again. "What do I *hafta* do? Mark just drove in and was messing with *my* garage door from his car."

My head cocked to indicate I was having trouble hearing him (i.e., I couldn't understand him; I only figured out what he was saying from Mark's response). I leaned, touched my ear, then stepped forward again.

"*Don't* come closer, I'm special ops." By that time JD was on the edge of the lawn. "I'm dangerous when riled. Keep *back*."

Meanwhile, Mark had already said, "I'll show you I didn't open your garage." He went into the house, into our garage, opened our door, backed his car into the driveway, closed the door, backed into the cul-de-sac, opened the door, drove up the driveway and into our garage, closed the door.

"You said you just reprogrammed your garage door the other day," I told JD.

"Don't crowd me, I'm dangerous. I was special ops. I react."

And during the sound of our garage door closing again behind Mark's car, JD either said, "I got guns" or "I know what you done."

I added the incident to the log I'd started after the last accusation, several weeks previous. The rest of the afternoon, the evening, the attempt to read before sleep, the half hour to an hour before the Ibuprofen PM had any effect, Mark and I tried to think and talk about benign frivolous things: the week-old baseball season, whether to do an early spring lawn feeding, how the dogs lying on their backs and holding toys over their faces was an example of evolution in action. It was all edgy and eerie.

"There'll be an apology," Mark said before we slept; and the next morning, "Your apology is here."

Four bags of dark-brown mulch were stacked in a bare place in my front garden. As much as I could use them, we decided that Mark would go out and give them back.

"Did he seem mad?" I asked as soon as Mark returned to the house.

"No. He claimed he bought brown by mistake, and instead of taking them back thought you could use them because you like brown better than red. He looked like his back wasn't doing so well, so I put them into his truck for him."

No mention, by either of them, of yesterday's scene.

But the gifts continued. JD began to cook outdoors, and he brought portions of grilled chicken and bratwurst over to us. He tried to hand me a shopping sack with a brand new pair of men's pants, too small for either him or Mark—"I don't know why I bought these"—and he seemed surprised they wouldn't fit me either. The same shopping sack was used again on Easter to hold a box of chocolates, handed to me over the backyard fence. Mark's Easter gift a case of beer.

In the name of social living, which I was supposed to be learning to do—that is, living as a neighbor in a neighborhood where front lawns had no physical demarcation on property borders—I asked JD if his lawn service would give us both a discount if Mark and I used it too, on the same days. He said he would call and find out, then asked for my phone number.

I hesitated. "No, I don't want them calling me."

"Okay, write your number down and I'll call you with the answer."

What could I do? Tell him no, I didn't want him, my neighbor, to have my number either? Give him a fake? Admit that I'd already put a filter on my email to throw any of his messages into a folder titled "neighbor issues"? I gave him my number. That day we exchanged three calls regarding the lawn service (which did not give either of us a discount, but continued to court me for two months anyway).

Then one evening soon afterward, my cell rang, displaying his name. After a hesitation, I answered. I'm not sure I ever knew what the chief purpose of the call might have originally been. He talked and talked. About the new state pension overhaul and how he'd worked for the state as a youth probation officer for thirty years, only to have them yank everything out from underneath him. Similar to how his ex-wife had raked him over. About why the police had been by his house earlier that week ("sometimes they come to pick my brain about cases they're working on"). About how he had to go get something from a friend who lives in a ritzy neighborhood but couldn't drive his old truck, and maybe not even the metallic-red Nissan, or it would look like he was going over there from the 'hood to clean out some cat's house. About a law firm named Duey, Cheetum, and Howe. About how he'd thought someone might have broken into his house and taken an attaché that contained, among other things, a microcassette recorder where he stored ideas he might forget, but that now he thought it was an "inside job," done by someone who'd been visiting him. And then: "So if I met a woman at 7-Eleven and then go to where she's staying in a motel, what do *they* know? It might be my sister; see what I'm saying? They don't know if it's not my sister, right?" It was either before or after that when he informed me: "I don't date Black women; not that I don't appreciate them, see, but I been burned, they out for what they can get, see? I leave 'em alone. I have an Asian girlfriend, a RN, but she went to her country to help out her people there." Somehow he brought up the price I'd paid for my house—"It's public knowledge, you know that, right?"—and how if he'd known they would be selling so cheap, he might've bought it himself and rented it out. Then about the people who used to live in my house: "*She* didn't travel for work; she hardly worked. She had to lay out in the yard any time the sun was out, had to catch her some rays." Invisible threads between the non sequiturs were starting to show.

I stopped answering when the cell showed his name. There were also texts I didn't answer:

4/10/2014 5:25 p.m. What days u work in Chicago?
4/10/2014 6:13 p.m. I be in the city.
4/14/2014 4:21 p.m. Hey C, how are u ??
4/14/2014 8:51 p.m. How was your day ?

My calendar tells me I was in New York April 15 through 17. I'd asked Mark to let JD know—as soon as the next circuitous dialogue inevitably occurred—that we didn't have texting in our cell plan and had to pay for each text. This had recently become not true. We were changing: One of the things Mark said he'd always loved about me was my staunch candor. And Mark, the one who could (and would) strike up conversations everywhere, with anyone, in grocery stores and on airplanes (offended by the social dictum that says, "Don't bother the person next to you on an airplane"), suddenly didn't want to go outside if JD was patrolling his yard and driveway.

If this account has the same unruly sense of time and logic as those dialogues with JD, it's because my memory careens from static moment to frozen image when I try to construct plotted narrative. And there are elements I can't shoehorn into the fragmented timeline, like how my ex Jim—who'd helped me search for, then refurbish this house, and loaned me most of the entire purchase price—nearly wept his angst over the mounting incidents and tried to figure out a way Mark and I could buy and live in the twice-as-large house on a private acre and a half I'd moved out of and quitclaimed to him. Meanwhile, it's been several weeks since I started writing, and JD has sliced the tops off the blades of his front lawn every night, starting around 8:30, the last glimmering of twilight.

So I'm back again, not to the beginning but to the week I started writing this account. April 23, the day JD was weaving, unsteady, and babbling apologetic excuses while Mark and I pounded the posts JD had bought to stabilize the fence bordering our backyards. That afternoon of fence-mending (an obvious idiom that I swear wasn't invented for this purpose) was just after the frenetic nighttime grass cutting of my opening paragraph. It was the middle of the week that ended with emergency vehicles flooding the cul-de-sac. There is still the rest of that week, both the before and after, to try to navigate here.

Lawn mower = identity
Mowing = displaced ferocity
Freshly mowed lawn = order, harmony, peace

Thursday, April 17, the day I returned from New York, we stopped on the way home from the airport to purchase our rain barrel.

Friday, April 18, I brought Mark to campus with me for an afternoon lecture. Afterward, in my office, my cell rang. I held my phone at arm's length to show Mark it was JD's name on the lighted display while the phone rang and then stopped. We waited for a voicemail chime, but none came. The plan we arrived at was that Mark would call back on his phone, and say that I was busy at school and had asked Mark to call JD back. Seemingly unruffled by this, JD told Mark that he'd purchased a small snow thrower at a yard sale and Mark could have it if he wanted.

When we returned home and spotted JD lurking in his open garage amid the junk that had continued to amass, Mark muttered, "I'll get it over with," and headed over there while I went into the house to greet the dogs. "Don't let them go outside and bark," Mark added.

"OK," I said, "and don't bring home the snow thrower."

So he told JD that he appreciated the thought, but shoveling was good exercise, and we didn't have room in our garage for a snow thrower anyway because we had two lawn mowers. I don't know whether JD asked for an explanation or Mark offered more: we each like our own mower better, my yellow Cub Cadet and the standard red one Mark moved from California, so we kept both. JD's response was to mockingly chide Mark for being sexist (which he called "chauvinist," but I'm not sure what Mark could have said about my lawn-mower partisanship to earn it). He said that he'd seen me pushing the Cub Cadet around last summer, and it was too big for me. At some point JD asked to borrow the red mower because his was broken. Mark said the mower needed an oil change, and JD volunteered to do the spring tune-up. By the following morning, Saturday, April 19, the borrowed red mower crooned tranquilly from JD's garage, and then out on JD's already mowed lawn. He was still the first in the neighborhood to have started a mower that spring.

Saturday, April 19 we needed to install the rain barrel and till the vegetable garden, both located on the side of our yard adjacent to JD's, so we checked through the front-door glass to see whether any of his vehicles were gone, or whether his garage door was open. Not the first time we expressed to each other that we shouldn't start living like hostages. Mark would have to leave at 11:30 for afternoon music lessons, so we got our tools and went into the yard. Besides, there was an extra car in JD's driveway, so perhaps a guest would keep him too busy to come give us food or clothes or yard ornaments.

But in fact JD wasted little time in introducing his guest. It was an Asian woman named something like Theresa or Amiya (I believe he used both). When he called her over to the fence, she was circling his house with a watering can, pouring water on volunteer junk trees that had sprouted in his fallow garden beds over the past several years. She shook our hands and said hello, not much more than that, then there was an opportunity when she went to water another big weed for me to ask if this was the nurse he'd told me about. "She a nurse, yeah, that's right, but a different one."

As always, looking for something more than chitchat to occupy myself, I wiggled the fence post a little, looking down to where it disappeared into the ground and must be rotting. "I'm getting to that," JD said.

Later in midafternoon, Mark still gone to his music lessons, I bathed and washed my hair. I had a dog show the next morning and would be getting up at five. We would eat an early supper, watch part of the ball game, then go to bed. I was still soaking in the tub when my phone rang. Leaving pooled footprints of water on the tile, I went to get the phone. Mark often called to tell me when the last lesson was that day, or if he was stopping on the way home for something to grill. But it was JD. I put the still-ringing phone back down. Instead of returning to finish my bath, I dropped to hands and knees and crawled from the bedroom to my study and crouched below the window, where I could see JD's driveway. The guest's silver sedan was still parked there. The dogs stood on either side of me, rattling the vertical blinds, chins on the windowsill, to share what I was watching. When I crept back to the bedroom, I called them in with me and closed the door to prevent them from charging downstairs barking, should the doorbell ring. Back to kneeling, bent forward, huddled in warm water in the tub, waiting for the voicemail chime, but it never sounded.

I was still there when I heard Mark came home. The bath water growing tepid, my bent body curled into a tighter ball.

It seemed to take longer than usual for Mark to unload his instruments, carry them into the house, then begin the trips to bring them upstairs. I was finally wrapped in a towel and preparing to dry my hair when Mark released the dogs from the bedroom and came in to ask why we were closed off in there. Did the doorbell ring?

"He called, just a little while ago. But his friend is still there."

Once again, we planned how Mark would call back, tell JD he'd come home, and I was sleeping, and he saw a missed call on my phone. If that made it look as though Mark was checking my phone log, Mark would call back on *his* phone, make it a signal that Mark's phone is the one he should call. Or even tell JD outright my phone is for my writing and school business and Mark's is our "home phone." Our strategy as disheveled as it sounds. Probably good that little of it was used, just the part where Mark used his phone to call back. "Hey, JD, we noticed a missed call from you. What's up?" JD's reply was it must have been a "pocket call."

Is this it? The race part I'm avoiding—where a white woman is afraid to tell a Black man to stop calling her because it'll look like a white woman telling a Black man he can't call her, a demand laced with flagrant assumptions on why he's calling? And is that even what's happening? Twice in the months after this, JD has asked me why Mark answered my phone, but that's not what Mark did.

———

Monday, April 21, before breakfast and again afterward, I scanned the conditions outside. Every time we behaved as though under siege, we commented that we shouldn't, then went on living as though barricaded.

But sometimes our garage had to be open, like that day when Mark went to prepare my Cub Cadet for its first use of spring. The door rumbled open like an invitation, and before Mark could even check the oil, JD was on the driveway, just like a neighbor sharing the relief of an early spring day when the lawn mowers reemerge. I could hear their voices from upstairs in my study.

It was the kind of day that brought other adult males out of the two houses on our other side. Raking sticks and leaves scattered during the winter, checking mailbox posts for heave or snowplow damage, a sweatshirt-only day in a week of revisiting the winter coats. After JD had gone back to his own garage, Mark joined the other two men for a moment on the sidewalk. He'd recently shared with me reveries of enjoying beers in the backyard with Tony and Joe—the former, like Mark, recently retired, the latter a much younger father of small children whose daughter took weekly flute lessons with Mark. The klatch didn't last long. Sweatshirts weren't really enough, unless you were raking more vigorously.

When I came downstairs for lunch, Mark told me that Joe had asked him if we were going to use a lawn service for feeding and weed control, and when Mark had said that it cost more than we were willing to pay, Joe had said, "Good, I'm not either." Since now we wouldn't be the first to mow (and thereby look lawn neurotic), I suggested maybe Mark could shave off the rowdy sprigs and tufts of our no-professional-lawn-service patch of grass in front of the house. Our red mower had already growled across JD's seamless grass more than once.

So before Mark walked two doors down for the flute lesson, he went the opposite direction to JD's garage, as usual standing open, with JD tinkering or shifting things around inside. He asked if JD was finished with the red mower. "If not, go ahead and use it all you need to, but if you're finished, I'd like to use it because Cris wants me to mow and I don't like her mower." His memory believes his inquiry about his red mower was met, at worst, with neutrality.

At some point during the half-hour flute lesson, the dogs bolted to the door and barked. Braced for the doorbell, I froze. Nothing. My hand went to my phone in my pocket, waiting for the vibration. Nothing. After enough moments had lapsed, I went to check out the door's window, and saw the red mower had been pushed onto our front lawn and left there.

Coming home from Joe's house, Mark called out a thanks to JD but received no response. Nor, he admits, did he wait for one.

One of those scattered-showers passed over. Enough to forestall the ritual first mowing. Enough to propel Mark to the rain barrel to check his first harvest and discover a five-minute shower will half fill the fifty-five-gallon barrel, so he set about attaching a hose to the overflow nozzle.

By now it might have been unsurprising that when Mark went out to that side of the yard, at some point JD was there in his backyard as well. His is one of the few houses in the neighborhood with a door from his garage to the backyard, an easy flow from driveway to garage to backyard and back, with access to his kitchen from another door inside the garage. Mark called, "Hey, JD," but before he could process JD's starched body language and lack of response, Mark was reporting the news that the rain barrel was already half full.

"Don't talk to me." JD began to walk away, but parallel to the fence. A dismissive wave of his hand, his back still only half-turned, and he continued, "You the same—that coward who used to live here, *he* was racist."

Unable to simply retreat into the house, Mark asked what JD was talking about.

"*You* know. You tell *me*. Go look it up if you don't know; go find out who the grand wizard of the neighborhood is."

"What are you talking about, JD?"

"You call me *Mister* Davis. I told that guy before you, I'd kick his ass if he called me JD again, it's *Mister* Davis to you. That guy, *he* thought I wanted his woman. That skinny Olive Oyl. I can get any woman I want, and I want someone with meat on her bones. You just go ahead and look it up, go find who's the grand wizard of *this* neighborhood."

This is the day before I began writing, still Monday, April 21. JD purchased his new mower late that afternoon. That evening my cell rang and displayed his name. Not fifteen minutes later he resumed the nighttime ritual of detonating the spinning blades.

Wednesday, April 23 was the afternoon we mended his fence. It was a Band-Aid applied to a concussion. Plus Mark and I had to stop the not-yet-finished tilling of our vegetable plot when JD came to his side of the fence to restart the oscillating dialogue that had been going on all week.

That morning, as Mark and I returned from an errand, we did not think to immediately close the garage door after pulling in. Or maybe we did, but when Mark reached for the transmitter, he saw JD already standing in the driveway behind the car. As we unloaded our groceries, JD wandered into the garage with his face tilted up, admiring the shelves and organizers we had installed, burbling about how he's also tidy and women who visit him notice, but skeptically. Then he spied two unopened cans of wd-40 and said, "I need somma that."

"Take one," Mark said. "I'll never use that much in a hundred years."

I was going in and out of the house with bags, and only have a last image from that encounter: JD back on the driveway, still talking, holding the wd-40, his mouth foaming a little at the corners from the excessive babbling. His speech lubricated but no easier to follow, so my memory holds the image, not any gist of what he was saying.

Some time after that, in the backyard, when JD first came out, Mark left what he was doing and met JD at the fence. I did not, at that point, abandon my task. I couldn't hear them well enough to follow anything. It was later that Mark reported to me that JD had wanted to apologize, by way of explanation, for the things he'd said two days before. The explanation was circuitous, (like time in this narrative), twisty, a switchback trail that sometimes ended up below the point where it started instead of zigzagging up toward a new message. But JD did have a theme, once again having to do with the people who used to live in our house: how they were at first friendly, and the woman even brought JD portions of meals when she made too much, but then she started coming over to see what JD was doing, and maybe the man himself sent her over to find out things, or else the woman was trying to shame her man into getting off his butt and working like JD did (he gave both possibilities, but did not use an "either/or"); then the man started to think JD was "after his woman," but "he shoulda never been allowing her to be coming over with food to give; what would you think if your woman did that?" With the upshot being that when those people rather suddenly decided to sell the house and move, the two other neighbors on the other side were upset that their friends moved away, and they blamed JD, so when JD saw Mark talking to the other guys on the sidewalk, and right afterward Mark asked JD if he could have his mower back, JD knew ("When you add two and two you get four, right? Am I *right?*") that it could only mean the other two neighbors had told Mark not to trust JD with his mower and advised him to get it back.

It's possible JD was wiggling the rotten fence post during this monologue. After they parted, with the apology aired, JD returned a few minutes later with a package of cedar garden stakes. He was unable to even unwrap the cellophane binding the stakes together, let alone pound them in with the full-sized sledgehammer he'd also produced. Mark, still or once again over at the fence, called me over. "JD says you told him to get these to shore up the fence. How do you mean?"

I'd actually suggested he get rebar stakes that could be pounded in alongside the fence posts. But it was clear JD was in no condition to receive a new explanation any more than he could have wielded a sledgehammer. His speech was slurry, his mouth still foaming, his gestures wonky, his gait and carriage lurching and weaving. I got my own tools, including cordless drill and screws. Mark and I pounded the sakes on three sides of the most rotten fence post, then fastened them with screws to the post. JD watched us, blathering a string of non sequiturs. The fence was somewhat, but not entirely, more sturdy when we finished.

On *Thursday, April 24*, JD wasn't physically as precarious. When Mark went to get the mail we'd forgotten the previous evening, JD was already lurking between his driveway and open garage. When Mark asked how he was feeling, JD returned that he's always better when he gets his rest. That was probably 7:00 a.m.

At 8:00 the doorbell rang. "You never got back to me," JD said, "about who's the grand wizard of the neighborhood. Did you look that up? Who leads the neighborhood Klan?"

"I'm not going to talk about this shit," Mark said. "When you have something worthwhile to talk about, come back and we'll talk."

At some point on Wednesday I'd heard the news about a mass killing in California, then on the morning of Thursday there were more details on how a distressed young man had fulfilled his plan for retribution against all girls who would not relent to his need to have sex with them. He killed six people, then himself, and wounded thirteen.

That evening I spotted another man with JD on his deck. Probably I was checking to see if I could go outside. Or because I had heard voices outside. Or both. JD was speaking animatedly, pacing and making broad gestures.

Friday, April 25, like a daily appointment, the doorbell rang. Mark was in the middle of his bowl of granola and cantaloupe, still chewing. I'm sure he said "*fuck*" at the sound of the bell. Maybe we both did. Tasks we'd been conditioned to perform on cue: he went to the door while I sent the dogs into the basement. Then I stood well behind Mark, where I could hear without becoming a participant.

"I'm dressed *down*," JD declared.

"You look nice," Mark said. JD was wearing khakis or maybe canvas painter pants. Even though much earlier that same morning, he'd been wearing a suit, he still looked dressed to go somewhere. Mark asked if he was dressed up for something.

"No, I dressed *down*."

"Yes, it looks nice," Mark repeated.

"You saw my man here last night—he's special ops too. What's it going to take, how many men do I have to bring in, to lock this place *down*?" Once again, JD began shifting his weight side to side.

"What are you talking about?"

"Go get those two cowards from over there on the other side, those two cowards Tony and Joe, get them out here, let's settle this right here like men."

I was first to retreat to my soggy granola, my tepid coffee. Mark finally joined me and we sat staring. Not at each other.

> down = sometimes up, sometimes not up
> cowards = not men

Not much later was when the ambulance arrived, then the fire truck, then the police cruisers, three or four of them plus an SUV. Across the street, a Nicor Gas truck, a worker returning to it and driving away as the cul-de-sac filled with emergency vehicles, blocking our driveways. The story we heard later: JD had reported a gas leak, but the responding agent had sensed a different kind of problem. Whatever occurred between them, the Nicor man chose to dial 911 instead of just leaving.

We watched from the windows, occasionally on the phone with another neighbor, until JD came out of his house, walked beside a policeman and paramedic to the ambulance, climbed in, the doors were secured behind him, and one by one the vehicles began to depart.

It was a strangely calm, strangely calmly tense, strangely tensely tranquil day.

This has got to end. I know I've got to find an ending, even though there isn't one, JD is still next door, Mark and I are still spontaneously coordinating our time outside to when one of JD's vehicles is gone. Then we rush, do sloppy work with too much frustration and too little joy. Is the same true of this essay?

JD was only gone until early evening. My ex Jim was over to visit the dogs and have dinner. The doorbell rang. On cue: the dogs barked, I pushed them into the basement, Mark went to the door.

"He tried to talk to me when I got here, but I just said 'Hi' and got into your garage," Jim muttered before following Mark to the door. I stayed behind, as usual, staring this time at congealing pizza.

"Hey, you saw what went down this morning, now you people ducking me, let's get this out, let's just take it to the grass, come on out, let's settle this."

"There's nothing to settle," Mark said.

Jim added, "We're just trying to live our lives, trying to enjoy our dinner, let's just let each other relax at home, no one wants trouble."

"I know what you think, you think I don't know? I *see*."

"There's nothing to see, we're eating dinner . . ."

". . . Just like that last guy living here, all up in my face about how I mow my lawn and sending his woman over to ask me what I'm doing and why."

It went several more exchanges, and could have continued to circle, until Mark said, "If people are avoiding you, it's because they're afraid of you. Because you do things like this. The police talked to us, this morning, know what they said? That if you ever act like this, like what you're doing right now, we should call them, call 911. They'll come back."

JD's swaying retreated back, to the step below the porch. He was no longer as close but also no longer taller. "I don't sleep and I have bad nerves. I hear 'em going off over my head. I'm supposed to take something, for my nerves, you know?"

"Then take your meds, JD," Mark said. "I'm sorry you have to do that, but we shouldn't have to pay the consequences when you don't take care of yourself."

This is so anticlimactic, so unexciting, me sitting there listening, face toward the tabletop, pushing my finger into hardening pizza cheese, two men, the former and the present, shielding my doorway. Our doorway.

Even before today, *Saturday, May 31*, when I have resumed my work to complete this narrative, the news had already emerged that several weeks before the California gunman's rampage, the young man's mother had sensed something amiss—and she didn't have to use a mother's intuition to understand his flagrant, internet-available rants—so had called his psychiatrist, who then requested a police welfare check. Approximately half a dozen officers arrived simultaneously at his apartment. But the law enforcement contingent determined that the young man did not meet the criteria for an involuntary hold and psych evaluation. Then I discovered this today: A spokesperson for the police department told a reporter that the police had no information or reason to believe the young man possessed any weapons. But according to the *New York Daily News*, the young man's "ownership of the semiautomatic weapons was available in law enforcement databases, which apparently were not checked despite his increasingly erratic behavior."

That day the police and ambulance had come to our neighborhood, and after only one police cruiser remained, we had joined neighbors gathering on the sidewalk around a police sergeant. He told us they were aware of JD and his unbalanced, even volatile behavior; they kept an occasional eye on him, sometimes stopped by unannounced, but they didn't think JD had weapons. The neighbors said they thought he did, but perhaps they'd been taken away; they told the sergeant about the time the cul-de-sac had been evacuated, so they weren't there to see who or what was brought out of the house. We didn't ask specifics about how they'd ended JD's reverse siege this time. JD had walked on his own to the ambulance, so the psych eval was voluntary; they couldn't hold him.

A few days ago, I was out beyond my back fence, at the edge of the pond where a community garden is allowed to grow and bloom wilder and more feral than the plots in my yard, and I am the community of one who cultivates there, keeping the thistles at bay and the prairie flowers in balance with the perennials I've introduced. I can go out there whenever I need to be outside but want to be alone, especially if the conditions are such that a closer proximity inside my yard isn't advisable, for these now-obvious reasons. But, this time in the community garden, I did not let my view of the houses become obstructed, and I was not working with my usual focus-on-the-ground obliviousness. So I saw him coming.

"Here." JD extended three plant pots, three near-dead begonias swimming in muddy water because the containers didn't drain yet had been watered faithfully. "From my Mom's grave."

"Thanks." I took them. "They'll be happy out here."

I expected a verbal barrage would follow. I'd be out there trying to follow (and end) a fragmented non sequitur monologue that might well contain something funny, something true, something informative, but would also always be about how the world has treated him—and wasn't I part of that world?

But he didn't. He turned and returned home. Soon I heard the lawn mower dependably reverberate to life, then calm to a throb and dwindle to a purr as he mowed down the parkway and around the corner, joining the other subdued, docile ambient sounds of the community.

Northwoods Nap
(Classically Conditioned)

2014

Four in the afternoon is the hottest time of day, even in a place
where one can escape the worst of the Midwest's summer heat and
humidity. In winter, four in the afternoon is dark. In June, it won't
be truly dark—dark enough to see the billions of stars and streak-
ing comets freckling the sky—until after ten. I cannot start evening
fishing until seven, and even that is prompted from impatience,
not twilight. I'll be in bright sunshine for an hour. The four o'clock
nap helps to defer me. Suspends me between whatever chores I've
given myself to accomplish after the morning fish and before the
evening fish.

Chores may include working on a new essay, revising one, or
getting emails ready to send when I next visit the motel parking
lot twelve miles away where I use the Wi-Fi. Other tasks: Scrub
the concrete basement floor with lemon- or pine-scented solution
where the last of the winter melt's dampness still shadows the base
of the walls and the foundation's cracks. Go out to set the minnow
trap or go back and harvest the minnows. I might paint a doorframe
or hang laundry. Sandpaper a driftwood project—a fish likeness
I plan to mount with a lure in its mouth—or restring a spinning
reel for the real fish I pursue. Tend the woodland garden where the
bee balm, sundrops, turtleheads, and mint I've planted have been
joined by wild daises, buttercups, and goldenrod. Mow the "lawn"
that's mostly not grass, which I would leave to be a minimeadow of

more daisies and hawkweed, but it's mosquito and tick habitat, so a ring is kept clear around the cabin with the edge of the forest well defined. It's there that I exercise my forest-fanatic dogs.

Why *wouldn't* they want to root around in the woods? So a Frisbee on the mowed area keeps them happy and engaged and away from potential skunks or porcupines digging for termites in old logs, or fleeing deer leading the dogs too quickly into the forest, disappearing into Northwoods wilderness.

Still, if the dogs do go too far in, they're not lost except to my eyes. No worries, unless my call isn't met—after, at most, two beats of silence—with the crashing of their feet on layers of leaves and sticks as they sprint back to me. They have been habituated to respond to the word "here" by returning to me at a run. Potentially a lifesaving practice.

Initially, training them did involve teaching them to associate receiving a cookie when they came (back) to me. ("Cookie" = any treat, from dog biscuits to cheese to hot dogs to leftover steak.) But a response to the call, the drop everything and *go*—especially when a dog has his nose full of the vast, wild world—won't be achieved with any dog without making an impression, early on, in controlled-environment training, using something that is capable of making that impression without my hands on the dog. Defense (not apology) for the stimulation (not shock) collar starts with understanding the definitions of classical and operant conditioning (or training) and how they work together.

Classical conditioning (which is not usually called "training") is an association formed between two stimuli, most commonly illustrated by Pavlov's dog, conditioned to salivate when he heard the ring of a bell because he had heard the bell every time he was fed. The conditioned association can happen through a planned experiment like Pavlov's or by accident. I don't like the taste or smell of dried banana chips because I once threw up after eating them. These kinds of associations are also often faulty logic: B followed A; therefore A caused B. (The ringing bell did not actually *cause* salivation.)

But classical conditioning *is* used in animal training: most often (or most successfully) with aquatic mammals. When they hear their "bell" (actually a click), their classically conditioned association that it means food causes them to feel the same pleasure as having *gotten* the food. Afterward they do get the food, but since they hear the click and feel this pleasure *while* doing the desired behavior, it's the behavior itself that starts to trigger the pleasure. So they happily repeat it when asked to.

It sounds so pure, so kindly cooperative. But what if an animal, a dog, is gaining pleasure from his nose, his taste buds, his chase reflex, so that any conditioned pleasure received from responding to a human call is lost in the blizzard of other naturally occurring endorphins?

Enter *operant conditioning* (which *is* called "training"), with its grossly misunderstood positive versus negative and reinforcement versus punishment. Basically, in a training context, "positive" means *adding* or *presenting*. "Negative" only means *removing* or *taking away*. And "reinforcement" applies to increasing a behavior, while "punishment" refers to decreasing a behavior.

Setting aside how immediately the *positive (presenting)* or *negative (removing)* has to happen, here are the possible combinations and how they're supposed to work:

1. Something good can start or be presented so that behavior increases (*positive reinforcement*). Dog sits when commanded and gets a cookie.
2. Something bad can start or be presented so that behavior decreases (*positive punishment*). Dog barks and receives a spray of lemon juice, so resists barking.
3. Something good can end or be taken away so that behavior decreases (*negative punishment*). Puppy bites while playing, so owner yells OUCH and stops playing; puppy learns not to bite.
4. Something bad can end so that desired behavior increases (*negative reinforcement*). Head harness (instead of neck collar) turns a dog's head sideways if the dog pulls out away from trainer, so when dog walks without pulling, harness stops turning dog's head. Dog learns to walk on lead without pulling.

Too frequently, most people—even some who train dogs— think the first two are the only training methods. Many misname the second one as "negative reinforcement," with *both* terms used incorrectly.

Once operant conditioning with positive reinforcement teaches a dog to come to a trainer on a particular command—pairing the word "here" with running to his person to get a cookie—the dog needs to learn that responding is not a choice. Ever see a dog let loose in a park, with his owner calling and screaming, but the dog never even turns to look? Collar-conditioning training with low-level stimulation (negative reinforcement) ends that. Similar to spaying and neutering or shots, the lesson is insurance to possibly save a life.

Once—not in the Northwoods at the cabin, but home in Illinois—Tommy and I were out in liquid predawn, past the property's tree line on the edge of a soon-to-be-harvested tawny cornfield with a creek bordering its far side. Not for the romance of the setting, which was stop-time tranquility, but because I needed Tommy to poop before leaving for a dog show, and he is an artist and politician with his shit: must be placed correctly and where his newest constituents might notice. Both the tranquility and poop finesse ended when three deer hidden in the cornstalks bolted for the creek and Tommy followed, all of them bounding like porpoises breaking the surface of the water, until, in seconds, all four animals were out of my sight and the cornfield was once again silent.

Until I gave the call: *Here!*

First it was my heartbeat drumming. Then his footsteps crunching, and I saw him a few times, momentarily appearing among the tops of the corn, until he was back beside me. Glowing from the classically conditioned pleasure of returning for his praise but also from the joy of the chase.

Not just that chase but The Chase, the canine business, a feral part of him that may be domesticated but still detonates, his brain flooding with dopamine the closer he gets to the quarry. This is why the farther a dog gets into the chase, the more difficult it becomes to "call him off." Which is why the recall has to be not a whim or an option but a serious *transaction*.

A more crucial save-your-life recall situation had occurred at the cabin several years earlier with previous dogs, Tommy not yet born. I had two Shetland sheepdogs, twenty-four and twenty-eight pounds, noisy and full of stupid confidence—or all three of us were. Despite the cabin compound having no fence, I stayed inside and let them out every morning, shutting the door after them to hinder mosquitoes. The shelties' desire to be fed was so strong that they would pee and return in sixty seconds. Usually, I watched through the door's window, although they could easily go out of that range of vision. One morning, I couldn't see them but heard their outburst of territorial barking. I jerked the door open and saw a wolf loping across the driveway and then into the woods, head turned over his shoulder, appalled at the strident strangers in pursuit. It lasted no more than three seconds, and in that same span I gave the call. My memory image after that (with a palpable echo of the hot gush of not dopamine but adrenaline) is their cocky faces as they trotted back to me. And how I held them, muttering blasphemous curses, while they writhed to be free so they could eat.

Foundationally, it was the initial classical conditioning that formed an association between a stimulus (the word "here") and immediately returning at a run. And isn't this how we're all always being trained by life? To seek, to avoid, to achieve, and to stop discomfort. That doesn't mean that some, or even many, accidental classical-conditioning life lessons don't go awry. I won't eat dried bananas.

So it is also the associations of stimuli that make a Northwoods nap in late afternoon soothing beyond mere sleep. The sheets retain a tint of DEET from my neck, arms, and shoulders—for me one of the smells of summer. The forest protects the cabin from direct sunlight, and a curtainless window is open above the bed. Breezes flutter or rattle leaves in maple and birch. The conifer needles hum; branches may creak. Birds twitter, call, mutter, sing, occasionally screech, or knock a rhythm against a dead tree. When all else is still, sometimes a loon keens from the nearest lake, three miles away. Or the gurgle of a sandhill crane, far overhead. During rain, the music is a faraway waterfall with the nearby patter of individual drops hitting the closest branches, then spattering below to the matted layer of last year's leaves hosting this year's ferns among moss-coated, rotting logs. Before and after the afternoon's passing showers, sometimes in between, with the forest still breathing in the background, a bee or a wasp, even a common fly, drones up close, a zigzag buzz, then quiet again.

One night, or premorning, in sleep likewise beneath the open window, I woke to a chilling canine scream. The pitch, the abruptness, instantly suggested coyote instead of wolf. Not native, coyote moved into the far northern forests after the old growth was decimated, around the turn of the nineteenth century during a logging frenzy without foresight. The woods were transformed to a badlands of stumps, perfectly comfortable to the opportunistic, desert-dwelling coyote. Now, a century later, the forest restored (albeit very little can be called old growth), the coyote are at home in deep woods as well.

But even more likely, it was the sound of a fox, perhaps the cry called a vixen's scream, although both genders are known to use it. The shriek lasted no more than five seconds. Whichever it was—even possibly a cougar?—the sleeping dogs beside my bed never stirred.

There are other sounds the dogs don't notice, but I do. Gunshots. I try to imagine target practice, not poaching or thrill killing (coyote, considered vermin, are legal year-round) or frustration. (A man I knew took a shot at some spawning steelhead he couldn't get to take his bait. Thankfully, he missed.)

There's a sound I used to think was the slow rev of a generator, one that fired automatically when needed (if there is such a thing), but only at a remote deer camp with no electricity, farther into the woods than my cabin. I now know it's a male grouse drumming, a noise he makes with his wings on a hollow log. Starting slow then accelerating. More felt than heard. So adroitly cadenced, I must have been beguiled—actually, more like provoked—into assuming it was human made. Until I discovered its natural source, a shy bird calling a mate, I had perceived the reverberation with dismay. It sounded too much like the thumping heartbeat of a stereo. The kind I couldn't escape in the late '80s, in my postwar slab house on the pre-gentrification east side of San Diego, assaulting me from across the street. A swaggering sixteen-year-old in orange parachute pants and untied sneakers marking his territory.

My apprehension when hearing the grouse: classical conditioning. Now that I know, I will begin to desensitize.

Not easy for us, but even less so for a dog. Rational explanations—learning the truth, understanding his own basic psychological responses—aren't available to the canine brain. Even if abstract comprehension were possible, there's sometimes not anything rational *to* explain. One of the most common fallacies about dogs, voiced by almost every well-meaning person who's adopted a pet from a shelter, is that a dog who cowers, who displays submissive fear, has been abused. First, pet adopters like to believe they are rescuing an animal from a tortured life—just springing him from a concrete-floor cage with certain death in a week or month isn't enough for them. But dogs can be genetically submissive, and the body language of cowering is instinctive. If you're waving your arms or stomping your feet, it will appear as a dominant gesture, so they naturally display submission. Even reaching over a dog's head when offering to pat him can stimulate a submissive response in a dog who was never struck by a human hand. Some dogs are born requiring socialization to human gestures, human noise, a complicated environment. A captured fox will probably cower too, so was it abused while living in the wild? But you can't just explain to it that there's nothing to fear.

In the absence of rational enlightenment as therapy, more crude methods, like flooding, often backfire. A dog is afraid of fireworks? Lock her in a chain-link kennel and put on a half-hour show twenty yards away—now she'll be terrified of chain-link kennels and the backyard as well.

I might never stop the stress response when a stereo-booming car passes through my perception field, even on the farthest edges.

Last June, we were down for our late afternoon nap, hot and weary from chores and errands, which included a trip to a creek-side meadow, not yet in full growth, so the dogs could chase retriever bumpers in excess of fifty to seventy-five yards. (The forest-surrounded cabin compound only offers distances of twenty to twenty-five yards.) The bedroom simulated dusk while the sun, at four, was still only forty-five degrees from straight-up midday, and at this point probably hotter. The dogs settled on the floor with sighs. I read for a few minutes, then turned off the bed lamp and rolled over. The forest was whispering, tittering, rustling, droning. Lulled but not yet asleep, I felt a warm, gentle pressure on my ribcage. It was Tommy putting his chin on me. He only does this when he seeks direct interaction. A request. But for what? He does not sleep on beds, he knows that; and even in motels when he is invited to share the mattress, he leaves after only a few minutes.

"Lie down." My voice flat, neither cajoling nor annoyed, not playful nor angry. He did as told. Again the drifting began. But again, the warm touch of his chin on my back. I couldn't believe he needed to go out when we'd just come in, but I got up and took them both to the door, let them burst into the sunshine of the clearing. "Go hurry up," I told them, their instruction to take care of business (a response created with classical conditioning), so the young female did so, and Tommy covered hers. Back into the bedroom, they both thudded to the floor, then released the customary breath before resting. I stretched out on my stomach. A few quiet moments later, his chin again lighted on my shoulder.

"What is it, boy?" I rolled over, put my hand on his ear. Immediately he hooked one paw over my wrist, his traditional gesture, either demonstrating shared affection or shared dominance. "Lie down, Tommy. Time to rest." He tried. But the routine was repeated. And I started to think I discerned a pattern. Each time, just before he'd touched me with his chin, there'd been one of the transient buzzings of a wasp or bee at the window screen.

Once again, I roused myself from the bed, slid the window shut, then turned on a fan for white noise. An experiment.

Which worked immediately. Tommy reclined (with his usual thud) beside the bed, and soon his breath slowed, and he slept. We all did.

Had he been stung that day? He hadn't swollen anywhere, wasn't scratching or licking. But some dogs don't react to a sting except when it first happens, and who says it was even a stinger? The deerfly, circling noisily, just bites, and it hurts. I once wiped one away from a dog's face and it left a smear of blood between her eyes. Whatever Tommy had experienced, his classically conditioned response of stress when hearing this sound was the only way I would know.

The next afternoon, just as sunstruck and drained, I led the dogs into the bedroom so we could revive ourselves for the evening hours of fishing. It would still be warm enough at 5:30 for them to come with me to a pond where they would swim before I put my line in. Their first leap into the water would not be tentative, despite not knowing anything about the slope of the bank, the location of subaquatic logs or rocks, or even what monsters might live in the water—none dangerous to them, but how would they know? They'd act the same in Florida where alligators are the sunken logs.

The window had been open all night while we'd slept, so I left it that way. Moments after we all settled, a bee buzzed at the window screen, and Tommy's chin was on my back. I turned to face him, and in almost staged behavior, his eyes rolled upward to his left, toward the window. A gesture so clear I could put it in quotes as dialogue.

I closed the window, turned on the fan. Classically, he'd conditioned me to hear him.

A Finished Brain

2015

> Poetry is not a turning loose of emotion, but an escape from emotion; it is not the expression of personality, but an escape from personality. But, of course, only those who have personality and emotions know what it means to want to escape from these things.
>
> —T. S. Eliot, "Tradition and Individual Talent,"
> *The Egoist*, 1919

Part 1. Compartmentalization

A rude light in my eyes, a camera on my periphery, I was answering questions, intimate questions. I was not uncomfortable. I was not holding back.

Anything a person says, any personal story, is edited. This has always been my mantra about first-person narrative. All people have an agenda, even if they haven't articulated one, even to themselves. There's a way of telling so that the story matches what the memory means to the speaker. A way of representing so that the listener will visualize the experience as the teller does. What is left out, what is detailed compared to what is glossed over, what is shaped by metaphor and how the chosen metaphor manipulates: these are only a few examples of editing. In written literature what's most intriguing about the first-person narrator is what we, the readers, can perceive or appraise *about* him or her in the *how* and *why* the story is being told, not just in what happens.

This time with the light, with the camera, with spoken language coming out of me faster and with less control than when my fingers tap words—which can, after all, be deleted and replaced before anyone receives them—what's apparently been edited is not so much the particulars, not the specifics, but the emotion. The director told me I needed to show more emotion. To provide emotion. Otherwise, he explained, the viewer won't develop any emotion *for* me as the character, as the subject of the film.

Why I am to be the subject of a film is itself snarled up in some spent emotion. My last book, a memoir called *Something Wrong with Her*, concerned female sexual dysfunction, anorgasmia, body loathing, and a return to a man I'd known (and had rejected) twenty-five years before, including the hot snarl of tormented

writhing it took for us to see our way through to being together again. Because the traumatic reunion happened while writing the memoir, the book became both a look back twenty-five years at the beginnings of my sexualization and a real-time discovery and journey for the author doing the remembering. A filmmaker reading memoirs to locate a subject for a film selected mine, contacted me, and assumed I would be able to easily access the raw sensibility oozing from the book's real-time portions, as well as from the images of my college journal in a girl's agitated handwriting.

The film will be a fictional sequel to that memoir, and I agreed to write the screenplay. Meaning I wrote a story that contained events (and emotion) that haven't (yet) happened. But also meaning the backstory, the characters' lives and conflicts and fears and experiences and obstacles, are all the same as in the memoir. Mine. Or ours, since Mark, the man I'd returned to during the writing of the memoir, is costar.

Certainly, as in a novel, the characters' pasts can be sewn into what they have decided and how they behave in the story of the film. But the details of those pasts, and how these "characters" assume their pasts have affected them, were dramatized in the film via interviews, after which the interviewer's questions, prompts, and pushing for more will be deleted, leaving only the characters' voices—frank and sometimes uncertain, searching for ways to articulate, as well as (hopefully) swinging between raw, bewildered, angry, troubled, even distraught. Emotion. Shown by a character recounting experience.

Except me—or the character-me in the filmed image. I couldn't (or wasn't) escaping also being the author who was relating experiences and past anxieties that I have already written, sometimes in more than one genre, and rewritten, and proofread, and edited, then read at readings. Written material is supposed to still contain the sensibility of the writer (at the time of writing), but the author has already mastered the material. In other words, the author is no longer that same mess.

The interviews for the film are also supposed to include a new round of confusion and doubt (inciting the film's *fictional* story), but it is, this time around, a fake real-time. I'm supposed to display raw reaction to real past events that I have already mulled and refelt and pondered and relived and looked at through multiple prisms, plus *new* emotions that I am inventing. I am being frank, honest, unguarded. But . . .

Over a bowl of chili while scouting one of the film's locations, the director says, "Maybe you just don't have feelings."

Getting older has compelled me—thus allowed me to learn—to pause longer before retorting. During the pause, my brain didn't even deliver to me, until this writing, a memory of having been told more than once in college that I was excessively, messily, and problematically emotional. At that time there was no "handling" the seeming chaos of incoming controversy. I cried a lot. Vented in a journal and in long letters to peers and supervisors alike. Stormed about, moped, brooded, agitated, and couldn't accomplish any simple task as long as I was throbbing, an oily cycle of more throbbing.

The pause: my eyes on the bar area, three or four loiterers with nothing to do on a February Sunday at midday except sit on a stool with a beer (the waitress had told me one of them was also a professor). Finally I replied, but without any flare of passion, "That's a mean thing to say."

During our filmed interviews, Mark was performing (or accessing) his past emotions more successfully than I. Other than with his saxophone in a jazz quintet, he hasn't had as much previous opportunity to express a bottled lifetime of frustration, melancholy, even rage. I told Mark about the director's complaint while we prepared dinner together. Then just as we sat down to eat, my brother called for my help with the challenge he was facing to put his dog down while his children were away at college, and at a time his wife had just lost her mother, and his own mother—*our* mother—was slowly dying of congestive heart failure in a hospital bed in the bedroom we'd each once called home. We talked about the vital responsibility of doing what's best for the dog, enumerated the growing list of the qualities of dog life that have slowly and then suddenly more rapidly been lost for his pet; we lamented that nature does not take its course without suffering and that we have to act for the mute animal who, as my brother noted, lies there and looks at him.

Only after I hung up the phone and started to tell Mark what the call was about did I have to wipe my eyes and steady my voice ... even though it wasn't happening directly in my life to a dog I live with.

In 1931 a film director needed his child star Jackie Cooper to cry in a scene. As an adult, Cooper revealed that the director arranged for a security guard to take Cooper's dog and pretend to shoot it backstage. The director got the desired tears from Cooper in the scene. Cooper's memoir *Please Don't Shoot My Dog* may have snuffed the technique from further use.

It's been twenty years since I first faced that decision for one of my own dogs. For several weeks afterward, I had to go to bed medicated, with talk radio playing, to keep myself from picturing certain details about the moment of euthanasia. The scar tissue around that experience is a thirty-page personal essay using the thirteen years of that dog's life and death as a structure and means to explore related events in my life. Six years later my third loss of a dog occurred just after my mother's post-heart-bypass stroke rendered us unlikely to be able to communicate as two adults. My then husband became frustrated because I wouldn't respond to (i.e., take care of) his sorrow over the dog. Of course, I couldn't look at his because I was *avoiding* my own. Until I wrote it. Another thirty pager—again using the structure of making the decision to end the dog's life to also look at my mother's stroke and the aftermath.

So writing, either fiction or nonfiction, has obviously been my way to, first, look directly at the source of emotion, and then to control it. Dramatize in language, so the thing felt is contained within. The emotion has become part of something I made. Part of something I created, then revised, then edited, then saw go into production and had to help copyedit, promote, and sell. There I am on the outside, doing a reading or talking to a class of undergraduates, and the thing felt—some things so hard to feel I had to use radio advice shows to distract me—sealed away inside that thing I made. It's still mine, but it can't hurt me.

The kind of fresh raw feelings the author seeks to put away during the writing process *can* erupt later, but they have little to do with the enflamed content of the writing. Yet the results of having written—the published book—put a bullseye of sensitivity on the public author ego.

Several years ago a trendy independent press picked up what I thought would be my breakout novel. The publisher was edgy, innovative, and had been noticed with interest by the book-media establishment. Early in our publicity planning, I'd suggested we propose an event for The Associated Writing Program's conference in New York. "They often like to highlight the lit scene in the host city," I explained. The publisher asked me how one made such a proposal and I sent him the guidelines, to which he responded, "Much too complicated for what looks like minimal outcome, I think I'll skip it."

Dismissing a bureaucratic proposal as a waste of time was entirely in his MO, so I forgot about it, especially since a printing mishap threatened all of my distribution. Discovering that the novel had been printed with two fifty-page signatures in reverse order launched me to the floor of my study for the brand of hot, slimy crying that produces a days-long sinus migraine. But that kind of frenzy over sheer bad luck was easier to put behind me than was the chronic dull bewilderment when it took my agent some prodding to get the publisher to confront the printer for a reprint.

While I was already carrying that steaming pile in my gut, my next meltdown was close to public. While attending the aforementioned conference in New York, I discovered my publisher had, in fact, proposed an event, *A Celebration of X-Publisher Books*; the event had been accepted and scheduled . . . but I was not one of the authors who would be sharing recently published work. My heaving, blubbering display took place behind a friend's literary magazine table in the bookfair. She hadn't been given a prime spot and the foot traffic was light. Later, only a little more composed, I called my agent and managed, through my blubbering-warped words, to explain this new trauma. My agent must have suggested that I go talk to him, go ask him why. I must have done so, because

I ended up reading at the event. Was it my puffy, blotched face that prompted my publisher to invite me to join the lineup (or did I wait for some post-hysterics facial paralysis) . . . or did my agent again have to call and prod him? Maybe I didn't want to know, because I have forgotten how it came about.

I understand weeping is common at this conference. The potential for it is now at the top of my "con" list when deciding whether to attend. These last two dispassionate sentences might be a method of not revisiting what it felt like to discover how entirely insignificant I was to that publisher. An example of *compartmentalization*. (I'm getting there.)

But the act of writing itself—the frequently harrowing hours of composition, revision, and more revision—had never been, and is still not, the source of any inconvenient pathos I sought to avoid. One doesn't produce seventeen books in thirty years without the writing (as opposed to publishing) being the prevailing method to put away emotional turbulence. Writing is a common compartmentalization method in therapy, used even for nonwriters. And for most adults, compartmentalization is something that should be made possible, or instinctive, by simple maturation. Although now I wonder if the method itself can become overly successful. I'm sure my film director thinks so.

As I stop for some research of *compartmentalization*—my crude understanding incited by therapy sessions during the last time I was a roiling wound, the years of the real-time memoir—I actually *am* compartmentalizing: using fact searching to escape the disconcerting accusation that I don't have feelings.

First stop Wikipedia, which views compartmentalization's therapeutic effects as a mixed bag:

> Compartmentalization is an unconscious psychological defense mechanism used to avoid cognitive dissonance, or the mental discomfort and anxiety caused by a person's having conflicting values, cognitions, emotions, beliefs, etc. within themselves. Compartmentalization allows these conflicting ideas to co-exist by inhibiting direct or explicit acknowledgement and interaction between separate compartmentalized states.

Despite admitting it's a psychological defense mechanism, the writers of this Wikipedia entry don't seem to have a positive opinion of compartmentalization:

> Compartmentalization may lead to hidden vulnerabilities in those who use it as a major defense mechanism.

For example, one can be vulnerable to being told she has no emotions.

I thought that when my therapist used the word in 2009, teaching me behavioral methods to handle depression, that it was a common therapeutic concept. But a paper in *Counseling Psychology Quarterly* in 2012 *calls* for the use of compartmentalization in therapy, as though it was, at that time, new.

> It is proposed that compartmentalization and absorption can be applied as psychotherapy strategies. Therapeutic compartmentalization and therapeutic absorption are easy to learn and master, and can be used to treat anxiety, depression, and other adverse emotional states. (307)

Compartmentalization and absorption: my therapist used the first word without the second. What she told me to do: Be as obsessively focused on my angst as I wanted to be for an hour a day, preferably in the morning. Sit and write everything I felt, address it to someone if I needed to, spew and describe and describe again, go over the details, just completely grind on it. What she didn't say, and what I'm guessing now, is that this was the *absorption* part. After the time is up, she said I should not allow myself to do any more of that kind of writing, even if it meant not writing at all. Conceive of other things to do if I have to. Shop. Cook. Garden. Don't go on a walk (too much brooding time). Do something that requires consciousness: Train a dog. Organize the garage. Sort and scan old photographs. That was the *compartmentalization* part.

I was, however, not equipped to do this during the year I was weekly sitting in her office. I could do the *absorption*, but not the *compartmentalization*.

Back to real time, I admit to withholding the title and *first* sentence of the above quote:

Milder forms of dissociation often provide a defensive function di-
minishing the impact of disturbing emotional states.
    —Brad Earl Bowins, "Therapeutic Dissociation:
    Compartmentalization and Absorption," *Counselling
    Psychology Quarterly* 25, no. 3 (2012)

So, compartmentalization is a form of *dissociation*. Dissociation
is not supposed to be a good thing. But in a mild form, it's also
fairly common, including the feeling that one is watching oneself
in a movie, a sensation that followed me for several weeks after
the film wrapped. Other more common mild forms include daydreaming, being "lost in a book," or binge-watching TV shows, etc.
Severe dissociative disorders include amnesia and the condition
formerly known as multiple personality disorder.

Searching *dissociation* resulted in far more articles relating to
psychology and behavioral therapy than did searching *compartmentalization* (which also yielded essays on closet organization,
which just happens to be one of my compartmentalization methods). But I found another researcher made the connection
between dissociation and (therapeutic) compartmentalization
in a piece ironically (for my purposes) titled "Dissociation Isn't a
Life Skill."

I wonder if digression is another form of dissociation.

A piece on grieving (which has since been removed from the
website where I found it) seemed to hit closer to the mark to explain myself:

> Compartmentalized grievers are very different from other
> styles. . . . It is rare to see compartmentalized grievers display any
> real emotion toward loss. They will have difficulty relating to
> others who are experiencing the same loss. It is easy for compart-
> mentalized grievers to go about their daily work and personal lives
> as if nothing has changed. Some people may consider these griev-
> ers to be emotionless, "empty" on the inside.
>
>   —Sandra Brown, *Psychology Today*, November 22, 2012

This selection almost describes me being filmed talking about
personal experiences that I'd already developed in novels, stories,
or memoirs. Did the director (also the interviewer) view me as

empty on the inside? During one interview I took a sip of water, and it trickled down my throat too close to my trachea, so I had a moment of difficulty speaking; my voice cracked, and a few moments later I asked for the cameras to stop for a moment so that I could blow my nose. The director, whose interview questions had been pushing me into more and more intimate areas, perked up, but I had to inform him I wasn't sputtering in emotive sensitivity; I was *literally* choking. He appeared genuinely disappointed. I must have seemed a dry husk.

So much the opposite of myself at twenty-one, in a university office I habitually filled with the foul and often stormy humidity of my prolonged angst. I wonder what my supervisors would have thought, hearing the director's complaint that I was emotionless, or seeing me able to (re)relate delicate personal stories on camera without any outward appearance of distress.

But this change shouldn't be surprising. My surfing foray (or digression) through layman psychology articles, abstracts, and book reviews has helped me understand why my younger self was so emotionally beleaguered. An unfinished brain, awash with more emotion than rationality, cannot compartmentalize.

> Scientists have discovered that . . . the brain is not fully "installed" until between ages twenty to twenty-five. . . . Scientists have [also] discovered that in the teen brain, the emotional center matures before the frontal lobes. Emotion therefore often holds sway over rational processing. When we realize that the prefrontal cortex allows reflection while the amygdala is designed for reaction, we can begin to understand the often irrational and overly emotional reactions of teens. . . . Researchers at the University of California at Los Angeles compared scans of young adults, 23–30, with those of teens, 12–16, looking for signs of myelin which would imply more mature, efficient connections. As expected, the frontal lobes in teens showed less myelination than in the young adults. This is the last part of the brain to mature: full myelination is probably not reached until around age 30 or perhaps later.
>
> —Pat Wolfe, "The Adolescent Brain—a Work
> in Progress," *Mind Matters, Inc.* (2012)

So by now I would assume my gray matter has prepared, learned, and insulated itself enough to protect me from ever feeling that way again.

Part 2. Depressive Practice

In the months after two intense weeks of filming, I spent no more than three hours working on a new writing project (actually, this essay). The rest of the summer I built block borders for my garden beds, planted baby trees, took pictures of fungus and insects and birds. I fished, I trained and showed my dogs, I tended a vegetable garden of greens and spent a good deal of time harvesting, washing, preparing, cooking those greens for a new way of eating adopted in March. I watched baseball games and mended my tattered garden jeans with patches. I did anything and everything I could do to not think about: menopause stripping away any possibility I'll ever re-create the sex life I never had; my mother spending her tenth, eleventh, and twelfth months in a hospice bed, muscles puddling, lifetime of experiences converging in dreams as her life dwindles; and, likewise dwindling, the remnants of my identity as a writer.

Despite the fact that my activities have largely been solitary (or accompanied only by Mark), no claim could be made that I wasn't participating in living; that I wasn't finding pleasure in the results of my labor, in terrestrial beauty where I fished and took photos, or excitement in dog-show victories and hooking large bass. I know because there was a period not so long ago when I couldn't enjoy any of those things.

Ways to describe that interval in 2009 have become cliché. Word descriptions of the combined physical and emotional impact seem vapid. Once I tried this: "[Like] a pony that's lost a life's companion; won't come out of the dark stall or shake the flies out of its eyes." And this: "*Oh shit, it's morning again.*" My version of suicidal ideation was to imagine car crashes every time I approached a stop sign, and how learning to walk again would consume my conscious hours. Yes, something was happening. Nothing was happening. Too much was happening. Something was ending. Something was frozen. Everything was ending or frozen or already dead. Loss piled up. The compartments got too full. Instinctive automatic compartmentalization failed. The system crashed. When the aforementioned therapist tried to teach me to compartmentalize in 2009, this hadn't been the first occurrence. I had titled 1989–90 *The Dead Year*. Toward the end of that bout, I got myself into a marriage—chased him, pursued him—because I wanted to get as far away from that feeling as I could. It worked for a while, a long while. A span that saw eleven of my seventeen books written and published. While I also fished and planted gardens and trained dogs, designed closets and painted rooms, took photographs; even cured, bleached, and rebuilt skulls of wild (dead) animals I'd found.

Somewhere during those eleven books, in 2004, a writer for a small Ohio newspaper who had already reviewed one of my books requested my forthcoming novel. Against long-standing reviewer protocol, he made email contact with me, told me how interested he was in my work, informed me when his new review would be coming out . . . and then, timidly—although looking back, it could have been *warily*—asked me whether I suffered from bipolar or clinical depression. I don't remember whether he'd also read my first nonfiction book, out a year prior, containing an essay about my paternal aunt hospitalized in a state institution from 1936 to her death (coincidentally in 2004) for paranoid schizophrenia. Despite The Dead Year of 1989 and all its obvious characteristics, I hadn't sought treatment or taken meds, and the only therapy that time had been a group thing more concerned with codependency than compartmentalization.

After I answered him *Not that I'm aware of*, he decided not to review the current book. The reviewer wrote back that he wasn't really as interested in the book as he'd been saying. In fact, didn't even care for that book. I never heard from him again.

The book he *had* reviewed was *Dog People*, which included a fictionalized version of The Dead Year. And the novel that provoked his question in 2004, *Homeland*, contained the most re-clusive of all my introverted, name-changing characters.

How could this incident not inform me of a growing trend? One's writing is only as worthy, artistic, and provocative as one's real maladies. Without a diagnosis and meds, the book he'd so re-lated to and the one he had asked for to review were no longer interesting. Nor was I.

A man in my former writing group pointed out that it seemed if one wasn't on Zoloft, one couldn't claim to be a serious literary writer. That wasn't why I did in 2009 eventually take my turn with an SSRI, and had a moment, six or seven weeks in, when I real-ized I was smiling as I blew bubbles for my dogs to chase, and that I hadn't felt myself do that for a long time. I wrote in a journal, "I have been to an isolated static place. As I start to come back, flashes of unnamed fear . . . that I'll settle, that I'll let feeling OK or 'nor-mal' make me decide to do nothing. Cause me to let everything fade back into vague, distant yearning."

I have left out the trigger, the particular source in 2009, when Mark, receiving threats and ultimatums from his then partner, tried to stop our nascent communication. I've already written a book about it—a real-time memoir I wrote while the episode rolled out. And then wrote and produced the film that was meant to be the fictional sequel to that book, where the "characters" in the film had experienced what my book had preserved and exhibited. Which then elicited the complaint during filming that I "had no emotions." Maybe I just had none *left*.

I tried to explain compartmentalization to the director. He tried to incorporate it into the film with vignettes of me tilling, casting a lure into a pond, play training the dogs, exercising, cooking, star-ing at a computer screen without moving except to get up and look out a window.

Not long after, I began writing this essay. Another real-time es-capade? Hardly. Except for how the "research" (otherwise known as needing validation) clarifies or even bends the road a little for me as I go.

––––––––––

Is it odd that Walter Bonime, MD (1904–2001), author of the efficiently titled psychotherapy classic *Clinical Use of Dreams*, has no entry in Wikipedia? (Case in point, there's one for me, and I didn't put it there.) Bonime's second book was the equally methodically titled *Collaborative Psychoanalysis*, and yet according to Silvia W. Olarte, a former student—who put her 2002 tribute in the *Journal of the American Academy of Psychoanalysis* instead of any existing networking domain—Bonime was "forever an optimist and worked hard at experiencing life as a challenge, an opportunity, and a journey that could always offer something new, creative, exciting, and engaging."

This anecdotal data about Bonime's nature would likely be used as hard evidence to challenge him, and no doubt rudely, if his theories were to jostle among the flotsam of social media now.

> The proposition is offered that depression is not a passively experienced or reactive interpersonal response, but an active means of relating to people.
>
> —Walter Bonime, "Depression as a practice:
> Dynamic and Psychotherapeutic Considerations,"
> *Comprehensive Psychiatry* (1960), 194–98

> Depression, rather than being an affliction, is a practice—a distorted way of relating to other people. It is a way of interpersonal functioning which unavoidably results in misery. (11)

> Despite the uniqueness of each life, the concept of the depressive personality can be generalized in terms of six cardinal elements. Enumerative presentation carries the hazards of rigidity and reductionism. What follows will, I believe, nevertheless, offer the opportunity for an authentic grasp of the basic problems. The elements are: despair, manipulativeness, aversion to influence, unwillingness to enhance others, anxiety, and an affective core of anger. (207)

> These people, always ones who have been deprived of affectual nurture in childhood, develop techniques of eliciting by multiple methods a sort of compensatory care from others. (208)

It is an exceedingly difficult undertaking for a depressive to give up depressive practice. He or she has spent a lifetime trying in complex, idiosyncratic ways to be recompensed for an initial loss. (217)

—Walter Bonime, *Collaborative Psychoanalysis: Anxiety, Depression, Dreams, and Personality Change* (1989)

Yes, it's dated. Or has been superseded in the forty years since publication, although I could not find an article refuting or even *referring* to the notion of depressive practice. All I was looking for was something that said it could be a habit. A familiar fallback mode. It could be a cycle at least partially perpetuated by practice. One that for some reason became comfortable. The way a 200-pound body seeks to return to 200 pounds after its brain made a determined lifestyle change that brought it down to a vigorous 155. When I was twenty, my supervisor said of me to someone else, "She goes from crisis to crisis without learning anything." In the early 1990s this kind of behavior became the more familiar *drama queen*. Since that time, the characteristic has taken on a more positive spin . . . er, I mean a respectable (even sought-after) clinical diagnosis.

None of this suggests it's not due to a disorder, genetic or otherwise, in the secretion of chemicals or incomplete pruning of synapses. Which one could have to a lesser degree that warrants no meds or shrink. Which millions could have in low-grade variations causing them to weep more easily, feel rejected, excluded, or affronted in trivial situations (called, interestingly, "narcissistic injuries" by psychologists). But something is also causing some to want to wear moodiness or brooding or melancholy as a badge of enhanced artistic sensitivity, instead of seeking instead to evade the discomfort—from chronically fatigued eyes to sinus headaches to obsessive inertia to existential helplessness.

For me, compartmentalization became my evasion. Change the subject. I watch myself doing it.

Have I been (more successfully) fighting against depression this summer? Four years too soon, according to my every-ten-years routine. This time a triggerless bout? Or is it actually some kind of horrifying contentment?

When people asked the disposable "How are you?" there was a time I used to think (not say) "Still searching for serenity." Just now *serenity* has been suggested by a thesaurus as a synonym for *contentment.* This—my current psychic state—can't be what I meant. So what's missing?

Start with motivation. More than just daily stay-busy resolve. I mean incentive (or energy) that's fed by future-looking with hopeful, excited anticipation. Something my father also, now, has none of.

A few weeks ago I spoke with my father on the phone. A ninety-five-year-old man who often forgets to eat, living in the house where he raised his children, alone except for a twenty-four-hour caregiver and his bedridden, dying wife. I said, "How are you doing?"

His voice grown foggy this year: "It's hard . . . waiting . . ."

"What are you waiting for?" Oblivious, or deflecting.

"Oh, you know . . . your mother . . ."

How did I answer? Maybe just "I know." The only future he can anticipate is not going to generate enthusiasm.

Yes, my mother's looming death is also in my future, and I've had my compartments to avoid paralyzing feelings about that. And now there's little eager expectation for a future of continued triumphs for Tommy, my over-ten-year-old competition dog. And what kind of future achievement is there for bass fishing and wildlife photography, except catching or capturing anything on the next occasion? What's the ambition or hope for the garden that produces the basis for how I eat, except health, perhaps a longer life? A longer life to do what with? Write?

This motivated-momentum thing, aspiration and anticipation, is most missing in that part of my life where it used to rage: *writing.*

I don't even like that word anymore. What does it mean? Making literature—too pretentious. Artists call what they do *making* art, musicians *make* music. Do writers *make* literature? *Make* fiction? Do you hear me?—I'm digressing.

What else could be recently absent? What's *not* missing is companionship or love. And yet there's some measure of isolation. But isn't it isolation by choice? Day after day, I don't leave the house except for resupplying the pantry and material for yard projects, an occasional dog show. But my only human interaction of substance is with Mark. By tacit reflexive decision. I do rely on the radio to keep me company when he's away teaching music lessons. Not news. It's an election year—too vexing. Sports. An enclosed compartment.

Tommy seems to be having the same dilemma, except he's not a natural introvert. His favorite pursuit is not squirrels or ducks or even tennis balls, but meeting and cultivating new human friends. (In his years as a stud dog, he had one other more beloved endeavor.) Throughout the two weeks of filming, the house was daily full of people. These were engrossed, hungry young filmmakers, but Tommy could always steal a little of their focus to win himself affection and laughter. Also, his lifetime dog friend was having one of her last prolonged visits. Tommy and his daughter Crash had lived together since Tommy was three (and for Crash's entire life). During the almost three years it took for the collapse and transformation of my former life, resulting in Mark moving two thousand miles to live with me, Crash and Tommy remained together three-quarters of that time. Every morning when I went into the basement to exercise, the two dogs rattled down the wooden stairs and played rope tug-of-war, which turned into WrestleMania (teeth allowed, but no full-on bites). Together they inspected the yard for squirrels or the Loch Ness monster that had taken up residence at the bottom of the groundwater drainage intake grate. Together they each took a training bumper and raced across the common area to the pond for daily swims.

Then when filming wrapped, the crew stopped coming, and Crash went to her new home in St. Louis with my ex.

There were days when I forgot to feed Tommy because he didn't seem to know how to remind me, when I didn't wake and rise at six because Tommy wasn't going to get up until I did. Some of his other symptoms are more anxious than withdrawn. He has become (even more) afraid of flies. It used to be a fly or wasp buzzing on the outside of the screen at an open window that caused his chin to rest on the most convenient horizontal part of my body in eye-bulging alarm. Now any fly loose in the house sends him squeezing

under my computer desk (if I'm sitting there) or smashing himself between my knees and the kitchen counter, or crowding with our legs under the kitchen table so he can lay a chin on my thigh. He relaxes again after I search the house and kill the intruder. At training and shows Tommy has begun to let his treats dribble from his mouth instead of chewing and swallowing, the dog rendition of "I'm so stressed I can't eat." Mark and I both leaving the house at the same time means fortifying the area where Tommy will stay, to prevent rugs or mattresses from being ripped, blinds from being shredded, or doorknobs from receiving tooth marks. Tommy can't be crated; he does not view a crate as a protective den but a trap, and he'll ruin his teeth on the wire doors and windows in desperation to escape. So I've started trying to make sure one of us is always home. Since I so seldom want to leave, it isn't a problem for me, but Mark sometimes wants to go to dinner, a movie, a museum, a concert.

The only time I've cried the last six months—despite the marathon parental demise strangely paralleling the evaporation of my writer self—is at the prospect, looming, of having to retire Tommy from competition. The compartment of dog showing is starting to need other compartments to protect me. With the formerly primary protective compartment of writing having lost effectiveness as a shield; with the approaching winter sending my garden, bass, and most subjects of my photography into dormancy; with my reluctance to elevate cooking and eating and planning cooking and eating enough to warrant any *more* of my attention; and with my Facebook feed too full of (well-intentioned) political brawling and abused animal shockers while baseball season has ended with disenchantment and disillusionment . . . A new compartment is sorely needed.

And now the rough-cut edited film is going to return for my viewing and response. I should be enlivened, aflame, eager, yet I've never been impatient for this step in the process to occur. I'm not sure I'm ready to feel disappointment as I watch myself not show the emotions my brain must have been so determined to control.

I do want to feel something. Why am I afraid?

AN○RGASMIA

Faking it in a Sexualized World

A FILM BY FRANK VITALE AND CRIS MAZZA

Intercourse in Absentia

2015–2019

It seemed I had not lived the kind of life that a writer needs. I have not, nor has anyone in my immediate family, recovered from an addiction, nor from a catastrophic injury or disease. I've never lost everything in a natural disaster, never been arrested. I was not abused (sexually or otherwise) by my parents, nor by any extended relative. The most lucid, documentable, unambiguous gender discrimination I've faced was when the local newspaper took away my paper route when they found out I was female. I have not come out to and then been rejected by a hostile family. Sexual harassment . . . well, of course, but I wasn't outright raped (notwithstanding gray-area incidents with complicated complicity). I have not had a special-needs child. I have not had any child at all. And yet I wrote a memoir orbiting another thing that never happened to me. A book concerning the absence of it: orgasm.

Perhaps—although I didn't realize it while writing—the absence of sexuality itself.

In Erica Jong's sequel to *Fear of Flying*, sadly titled *How to Save Your Own Life*, the feisty and candidly sexual protagonist has her first "zipless fuck" with a woman. The oral sex seemingly goes on for hours, until the other woman barely, or maybe, has only a tiny orgasm. A groundbreaking lesbian sex scene in fiction . . . *but*: In this scene we are supposed to feel for and with the oral-sex *giver* for having to "endure" doing it so long. She doesn't like it; her "*nose felt like it had spent its entire life in there*" (121). Yet what of the woman who maybe had a small "shudder," or else pretended to for the sake of her provider? She was the scene's *loser*. She couldn't even orgasm with oral sex, for God's sake. She "made" Jong's character do it "forever." Not designed for compassion, she is only drawn with contempt, and on two fronts: her lack of sexual response, and that appalling, putrid place where, regrettably it seems, the other's attention must be focused.

Reading that book was at an unfortunate stage in both my sexual development and evolution as a writer. As a teen, Jong's character longed for breasts and her first period, while I, in preadolescence, dreaded the onslaught of body changes. Somehow, though, according to Gina Frangello in *Experimental Fiction / Poetry*, I became a bold and audacious provocateur, "infamous for . . . explorations of gender politics and (sometimes deviant) sexuality." And in that identity, I hid my secret: I was living in the wrong time and belonged in the 1950s or 1960s with legions of women who had been branded "frigid."

I've lived my many decades of life with the identity of heterosexual female with a pronounced androgynous style. In crude semichronological summary, starting as early as memory goes back: I liked boys, hated my female body, frequently wanted to be a boy, didn't want to touch a female body, and never touched my own. I pretended to be a boy at Girl Scout camp and felt the power of primitive patriarchal animal attraction to a group of girls. I did not want to start my period or grow breasts. I still liked boys and wanted them to like me. I never used the word "woman" to describe myself. I liked being mistaken for a lesbian. I still did not want to touch another girl (or myself). I hated dresses and high heels and makeup (although I went through periods of trying). And I was terrified of sex.

I've been married twice. Sex was always painful in the first case, frequently painful in the second, and never much more than friction in either one. Both marriages ended after years of celibacy. I've done couples sex therapy and intervagina electric stimulation therapy for vaginismus. Basically I had a triad of sexual dysfunction, each issue probably inflaming or reacting to the others: sex was painful, nothing "called" me to need or desire sex, and I'd never had an orgasm. Quoting myself: "a wall of thick clear glass between me and the sensual, lascivious world that is paraded, painted, filmed, flaunted, blared, boasted about, advertised, analyzed, danced to, dramatized, and even purred about softly in every subliminal white noise." While the estimated proportion of women who have at least some form of sexual dysfunction hovers between 40 and 50 percent (WebMD), percentages of women with anorgasmia—no orgasm at all, considering all forms of sexual stimulation—ranges, in sources, from 26 percent (Najafabady, Salmani, and Abedi, "Prevalence and Related Factors for Anorgasmia among Reproductive Aged Women in Hesarak, Iran") to 10 percent (Hayley MacMillen, "What I Learned from No-Orgasm Sex," Refinery29), or as low as 5 percent (Elisabeth A. Lloyd, *The Case of the Female Orgasm: Bias in the Science of Evolution*).

If I were born blind or deaf, would I consider the lack of sight or sound as *absence*, something I lacked? Or do I only label anorgasmia as "absence" because of societal and cultural *expectations*? These are present in almost every facet of daily life, not restricted to the media. The first being that pejorative word "frigid" signaling that culture deems this absence a damning personal flaw.

Hugh Heffner died in 2017. The eulogies and obituaries gave him credit for starting the sexual revolution. Apparently the free and easy enjoyment of sex only needed someone (a man) to "start" it, and then it would happen. But what of those for whom it didn't? In my pre-sexual-harassment-era college years, a mentor told me a story[1] about a professor who "grabbed a girl after class and physically told her how he felt. He said he should have the right to follow honest impulses."

"Wasn't she scared?"

"Probably. But she liked it, she might have been hoping for it. If a girl hasn't experienced those feelings by that age, there's something wrong. They were married in three months."

I was, at the time of this private conversation, still a virgin. And I *was* scared. And I *didn't* want it. *What* was wrong? And where

1. See "Nothing to Offer" (p. 169) for the complete story he told.

had the wrongness come from? At this time I'd already experienced those assertive hormonal boys, but hadn't *every* girl? It was in those years that I had my first pelvic exam. When the speculum was jammed in and cranked open, I wailed . . . then continued sobbing. The male doctor at student health services barked, "I'm not hurting you." The first man to push something inside me and inform me that it didn't hurt.

Ratcheting up expectations further: media. Magazine cover blurbs that tell me what I'm supposed to want: *Wild Summer Sex . . . Hot Late Night Sex . . . How to Get Exactly What You Want in Bed.* And what the result of this desire should be: *Sweet & Sexy Moves—Orgasm Guaranteed.* If these examples are high on the crass, commercial, and sexist spectrum, how about a radio therapy host who tells her callers that orgasm is the best way to relax and de-stress. The examples of sexual expectations on social media are more numerous and the most effective at showing me my deficiency, because they can't be dictated or influenced by corporate standards . . . *Can* they? Besides the pouty, pursed lips and pronounced-cleavage seductive (and highly filtered) selfies from serious authors, there are examples like a successful/intellectual woman's announcement that she had worn out (yet another) vibrator, and photos from an all-woman literary event titled *Sex and Power*—to which this androgynous "explorer of gender politics" had not been invited—where some expressed that "power" in alluring clothing. Difficult to deny, but also to articulate, the brand of power in appearing without apology as your true sexualized self. If it is indeed *true*, and not created by a patriarchal culture that determines how one does and does not get attention/validation/voice. The sexualized universe of which I am increasingly not a member is truly expanding.

Anorgasmia . . . the Movie

The set called for silence. I slid in slippers toward a stool at the nucleus of screened lighting, ducked under the boom, and lifted my feet over the cables, careful not to jiggle any of the light or reflector tripods or jounce, even slightly, either of the cameras, which both had operators so close behind that they were a fusion of human and instrument. From my place on the stool, the two cinematographers, sound engineer, and director were fixed and silent silhouettes. Now I was in the center of the focused attention of lights, lenses, microphones, and four men. Three of the men were decades younger than me, the fourth a decade older. I was dressed in a gray T-shirt and sweatpants. My hair was washed and brushed, thankfully covering the thin spot on my scalp. I wore not a particle of makeup. It wasn't the independent low-budget project that eliminated costume design or makeup. Makeup was not part of my life, so I wouldn't start here, on the set of a film I was coproducing, had written, and was starring in. A film that was the semifictional sequel to a memoir published the preceding a year. A film about my dysfunctional sex life and body loathing.

The director said, *Quiet*. The head cinematographer said, *Speed*. The director said, *Action*.

I looked out of the darkness, into none of their eyes, and said, "I'm a person who didn't want to be sexualized, who didn't want to have sex, and didn't want any of the things that led up to it. . . . Wanting to be a boy was a way to avoid that. . . . It felt like his penis was studded with razor blades."

How and why would I write and star in a semifictional film about this? And let men have so much control of the medium? The latter issue is one I haven't yet entirely unpacked. The former: it was a way to playact my way to some clarity about my sexual self, if I even had one.

Something Wrong with Her is the memoir that finally faced my sexual situation head-on. *While* writing it, I was also reuniting with Mark, a man I'd known from age sixteen to thirty. To make it further disorienting, he'd been one of the determined boys breathlessly wanting something from my body. Now a man, he felt responsible for my life of sexual dysfunction; he wanted to be the solution. For a year of correspondence, before the reunion was complete, I believed he could be. But, despite receiving from him forms of physical enthusiasm I'd previously not experienced, I still felt no "call" of desire, and still no orgasm. Now as much of a life partner as a man can be, a man for whom my androgyny is as much a part of what he loves in me as is how I laugh and crumple against him when he does a quip or impersonation . . . Mark made the film with me, beside me in scene and out, bearing my frustration and disillusionment . . . and his own bewilderment over what I was "saying." *This* complication is not the same as the one involving the all-male film crew. He, or who he is to me, has to be part of any identity I profess.

Essentially, after I wrote a book that contained more than one story that developed *as* I wrote, I then helped create a film sequel where I learned what the real subject(s) might be *while* the cameras sped. I was making a film ass-backward, researching while filming. Gender diaspora, asexuality, heteroromantic, nonbinary—identities that hadn't been offered or available in my teens and twenties. But film technology was too fast, and I didn't learn enough before we wrapped. Nor could I even stand to watch the various cuts I was sent during editing. Unable to go back and redo certain scenes, to let my "character" explore the identity she couldn't quite grasp, all of it desperately thwarted by her age and muddied by her devotion to a partner, I had to let filmmaking's usual brand of teamwork help the final product, *Anorgasmia*, become somewhat less confused than I (still) was.

Four years out from the wrap of filming, a year out from the film's release, no longer looking for "solutions," can my private evolution continue? Androgyny easy enough to claim, but is anything else an answer that can settle this question that society seems to be asking? A natural outgrowth of being anorgasmic in a highly sexualized world? Are sexual dysfunction and anorgasmia a means to knowing who I'm supposed to be? Or the collateral damage I'd mysteriously become.

Friend, Partner, Boyfriend

2017

It was still 2017 when I put several pages of chaotic notes—memories, or words to represent, hopefully to preserve, memories—into a folder marked "Tommy." The project I intended was to make each separate memory into one exquisite sentence. It is no longer 2017. This mission has leaked beyond the decade of this book's title. I was never "ready." The folder sits beside me now—in 2022.

In 2017 the most I accomplished was to fill and label the box also marked "Tommy." A ritual of compartmentalizing, a performance of archiving—preserving—the beloved without resorting to taxidermy. A swatch of light golden hair, his collars, his title certificates and most important rosettes, a doorknob with his teeth marks. Onto a shelf in the archive closet.

The week preparing Tommy's box may have ended with the arrival of his ashes. The outer white box still never opened, still sitting on a bookshelf behind me in my home office, surrounded by favorite photographs of him and other dogs he swam, played, and slept with. After that I was ready for nothing more. To have successfully compartmentalized, it was not safe to reopen the "compartment." I asked my brother via email to tell our dad for me so that I wouldn't have to form the words with my throat. Dad, living alone without his wife, our mother, for the first time in almost seventy years, was having trouble sleeping. I was too. I sent him boxes of Sleepytime® tea, a gesture to speak what we were sharing.

I was able to preserve, seal closed, what had happened on January 20–23, 2017, by turning to fiction. A compartmentalization method that had for decades been my go-to and has steadily since then lost its preferred place. But, at the time, I had a stalled novel with a dog-trainer character, whose dog had barely survived a rottweiler attack. Tommy's spinal infection slipped into place.

> The facts listed over and over: to front desk, vet tech, ER vet, neurologist, next ER vet, next vet-neuro. Memorized but harder and tougher to say each time. Can't see keyboard through pooling eyes, typos in every word. Digressing so the words won't get typed. If it's not written, maybe it's not real, didn't happen—he's *gone*, best friend, partner, soul mate . . . he collapsed, 48 hours ago, middle of the night heard him plod toward the water dish, maybe dragging feet—a telltale sound probably started days ago—then the ka-thunk. Thought just down to sleep again . . . didn't check til *my* need to pee, then he's in the way, wouldn't move . . . *couldn't* move, swam on the tile floor. Lifted him but legs like noodles, crashed back down, chin hit hard. Somehow, that mysterious super-strength, could pick him up to race to the car. But couldn't do without his serrated wail—will never un-hear it. But he never stopped recognizing me, knowing me, needing me, my slimy face hot and bloated, smelling of panic.

—Cris Mazza, *Yet to Come* (2020)

The fictional sudden-emergency paralysis was actually, in life, not sudden at all. "I'll have that possible disc lesion X-rayed in January," I'd said to the vet, when blood tests told us of an inflammation somewhere. I had registered Tommy's periodic yelps when his collar or neck was touched during motion; and he'd recently started having trouble making his twenty-two-inch jump height at performance trials. The costs of his ITP treatment had been mounting, and I was still paying a huge property tax bill on a house I no longer owned or lived in. I didn't realize that putting off diagnosis of a bulging disc might be life-threatening because his immune system was being medically suppressed. The vet didn't disagree with the postponement.

And, in actuality, there was no superhuman strength. My character was alone and had to get her (smaller) dog into the car by herself. That real night, if I hadn't had Mark to help me, how long would I have stayed with Tommy on the floor after trying to lift him into a stand and he crumpled, hard, screaming, then holding his head in my lap, hearing the sound of his pain? A foreshadow of where we would be in three short, very long days.

> Me kneeling on the floor, bent forward, a fetal pod people step over and around, the noise of the hospital blurs, glaring lights dim with my face against his shoulder, but an occasional whimper means he's being hurt, I'm *hurting* him. . . . When I return in the morning, he recognizes, jerks and heaves his head up, yowls, just a squeak, his chin lands in my lap and doesn't move from there again, heavy warm weight, trusting me, needing me . . . decision had to be made . . . let him go . . . fucking let him go . . . as though that's what he wants . . . He wanted to be *helped*, taken care of, and I couldn't, didn't, *my* fault, I didn't listen, wrapped in my own selfish woes, just let his physical decay and malaise be the evidence of mine.
>
> —Cris Mazza, *Yet to Come* (2020)

The preserved perception of a real-life event rendered in fiction hasn't changed in retrospect. Granted, *Yet to Come* was written during the decade of letting things go. But I see now, I didn't let go of *any* of this. It's so distressing to endure the memories that I have allowed myself to rely on repeating how I first represented it in a novel rather than forcing myself to relive it in narrative again.

Three days. And then he was gone.

The usual guilt following euthanasia involves questions: *Did I wait too long? Did I do it too soon? Did I prolong suffering? Did I rob him of days of pleasure?* Mine, this time, was magnified, complicated, by that decision three months prior and for purely financial reasons to postpone diagnosis and treatment of an injury of unknown origin. In the meantime, the treatment for ITP was making him sicker. He'd stopped eating; his kidneys showed signs of deterioration from the toxic medications. The blood-test indication of inflammation, the pending X-ray and pain treatment or even disc surgery, had all slipped down off my mental screen as other urgencies were added at the top.

The Sentences are still undrafted, a photo untaken, a painting unpainted. A body unroused, unexhilarated.

Many other things stopped in 2017. Feeling was one of them. Not just emotions sealed over with compartmentalization. Physical, tactile sensation. Not all of it. I'm sure there were headaches. And there was a familiar form of raw pain.

Back in 2011 I had (self-)diagnosed vaginismus. Sex is painful. Has always been painful. For me, in addition, it was also without much of what they call "pleasure," the superlative sensations people crave. And if, by "pleasure," they mean "orgasm," then there was none. If pelvic floor therapy could eliminate the pain, perhaps pleasure would fill the void. A urologist called it pelvic floor dysfunction, and I embarked on a plan called pelvic floor therapy.

> Biofeedback, electrical stimulation and Kegel exercises, are . . . therapies for pelvic floor dysfunction. . . . My understanding of the use of the electrical stimulation—which was only as painful as a 15-minute pelvic exam, and included a rhythmic insect-sting somewhere farther inside than the probe was jammed—is that it causes the pelvic floor muscles to tighten and relax on a nonspastic schedule, simulating normal function.
>
> During biofeedback, with the split screen showing the activity of my pelvic floor muscles above the graph of my abdominal muscles, it took just one session for me to isolate which muscle I needed to control. . . . The most interesting feedback on the graph, however, was in the weeks after I'd successfully isolated which muscles to exercise: During the rest period when I was supposed to be relaxing the pelvic floor muscles, sudden spikes would appear in the graph, which the therapist explained were muscle spasms. I couldn't feel the spasms, but would have experienced them as pain if they'd occurred during sex.
>
> —Cris Mazza, *Something Wrong with Her* (2014)

The weeks of therapy had an effect. Sex without pain was *possible*. Visits to Mark in 2011 and 2012 bore moments of proof. A dispassionate way of telling it. Because there wasn't much more than the absence of pain. It was basically still just *friction*. The gratification, for me, remained his want, and seeing him satisfy what he'd thought he'd wanted for twenty-five-plus years. I allowed myself the self-centered slant because I knew there would not be much more than that, physically, for me. That, and some sensation in my secondary erogenous zones. (Again, so clinically stated; part of the pathology, I suppose.)

But then, menopause. For one, then two years it was manageable, but eventually genital dryness, compounded by a refusal to take hormone-replacement drugs, brought back the pain, which reminded my pelvic floor muscles that this activity required spasms.

To come live with me, Mark had given up half of everything he'd spent most of his life working for. I realize that "being with me" had more depth and breadth than finally "making love" (a term I loathe) with the sixteen-year-old girl he'd decided was the one he wanted. But I wasn't going to ignore his years of wondering what a *whole* life with me could mean. We invented ways to simulate actual intercourse; we used our hands and mouths. It wasn't easy to be spontaneous, but it was never in the last conscious moments of the day before sleep (that is a different form of tangled intimacy). Sex, I might add, was never an effective method of compartmentalizing, and 2016 marked a time when avoidance of reality with intimate physical sensation would have been welcome, had intimate physical sensation not been so fraught.

Our efforts were tacitly and, we thought, temporarily put on hold during Tommy's two months of illness and treatment. Our sleep was still a knot of bodies; it was winter, and we've always turned down the furnace and made our own heat. But when his hands and mouth resumed seeking to stimulate me to some level of arousal, there was nothing. After Tommy was gone, so too was any sensation in my secondary erogenous zones.

It felt—*I* felt—gross, lying there while Mark worked at trying to find something I knew, and knew it with finality, was not there to be found.

———

I've not tried to explain, not even to myself, what possible kind of distorted relationship there could be between Tommy, the loss of Tommy, and the final end of sexual sensation. Tommy had been a registered stud dog of some distinction, but, as is borne out by previous essays that feature him, it was not his sex life that created the balloon of joy in my gut that had been there ever since he came to me at ten weeks old.

Maybe The Sentences were never going to be adequate. I'll try two flash scenes.

In a car, both of us staring straight ahead, my ex Jim and I on our way to the cabin named Dogwood in the Upper Peninsula of Michigan. It was early summer 2008. Four dogs in travel crates in the back of the SUV.

I sighed and said, "I'm sad and I'm happy."

"Okay." White noise of tires over pavement, perhaps a rustle of dog bed, a canine echo of my sigh. "What are you sad about?"

"My book."

Released six months prior with prophecies of fanfare, *Waterbaby*, my long-awaited breakout book, had an independent publisher who'd been featured in *Newsweek* as the future of publishing. Perhaps the ghost of the family-lore lighthouse legend I'd used in the novel was not pleased. The publisher was bought by a larger company and made into an imprint; his new duties would have priority, then illness in his family made him not only unable to work his usual magic, but unable to respond when a major printing error was discovered, two fifty-page sections bound in the book in reverse order. Returns were being pulped. The errant printer agreed only to a mere six hundred new copies. Two large reading events either had ordered no copies of *Waterbaby*, or only had the print-error versions. The mood quagmire had caused both a flurry of attempts at emergency self-promotion in the form of a mass mailing, and a lot of time spent lying on the floor with Tommy. The mass mailing had resulted, months later, in an email from Mark, after he'd received the book promotion mailing with one of my business cards, for reasons unexplored, slipped inside.

"And what are you happy about?"

"My dog."

Not too many years later, probably 2012, Tommy and I drove west to visit Mark in California. The more than just cordial division of property with Jim had been completed, my new house was purchased, and Jim was overseeing the contracting work to upgrade the interior to my taste specifications. Meanwhile I was, during visits to Mark, helping to clean out his ex-wife's left-behind hoarding, holding "all free" yard sales on his front parkway, and painting some walls. On the way back to Illinois, Tommy and I stopped in Phoenix to visit a friend of thirty-plus years. *My* friend of thirty-plus years, but Tommy's friend of easily that much in dog years as soon as he met her. We three were sitting on the balcony of her apartment, Tommy beside her but at a ninety-degree angle so that he could look at her face and put his paw onto her leg periodically while she stroked his head.

My friend was telling me about her last long-term relationship twenty years earlier, during a time she and I were not in contact. She was explaining why she'd not only left the man but moved two thousand miles away from him, having to eat up a retirement account and change careers to do so. Even with the fraught situation of trying to restart her life, she did not regret leaving behind the man who had been abusive not in physically harmful ways, but in the most humiliating ways, including once leaving her in the woods, knowing she was an urban girl with unease about the wilderness, and once at a table full of friends for some kind of celebratory dinner, pouring a pitcher of water over her head from behind. As she recounted these and other examples of insult and degradation, tears welling, her voice going raw, Tommy again lifted his paw to her leg. She looked down at him, his eyes smiling with pleasure that her hand was stoking his head and one ear. "Why," she said to him, "couldn't you have been my boyfriend?"

Condom Races

2018–2019

> I can give example after example, seemingly trivial things he said, and me-then slicing them open to examine in my journal, one day agonizing over a hex of hero-worship, the next grateful I met someone so worthy of respect.
>
> —Cris Mazza, *Something Wrong with Her* (2014)

Shouldn't I start with the latest and most jarring incident? Before character introductions; before the narrative pondering of questions raised; before metaphors for the sadness, disillusionment, even fear aroused? And fear of what? Being wrong to begin with? Sensing a narrow escape? Somehow . . . being abandoned?

The initial questions already listed, the primary emotions already announced, why is it so hard to simply dramatize the event? Because it was an email exchange, without setting, facial expressions, background noise . . . details that I know impact a dramatic scene. Maybe my title can do the job of the lead-in hook, and I can continue blathering.

He is fifteen years older, and long ago had become the only person who received a copy of every one of my books—eighteen at the point of this occurrence. A mentor during my inwardly tumultuous twenties, then he was personified, with only the thinnest of camouflage, in four novels and easily a dozen stories.

The latest time span between book publications had been longer than usual (I'm getting tired, and the world is relieved). Plus I'd delayed sending him the latest book for a year and a half after its release. So as I had for the last several books, before addressing and mailing the package, I emailed to find out if his address had changed. Asking about his address had always been an excuse: I needed to know if he was still alive, and it's not polite to ask outright. But this time there was no coy substitute question to also discover if he'd recovered from being sucked into an ideological black hole. I was aware he'd run for his local city council in the 2010 Republican primary, as a Tea Party candidate. In fact, the last time we'd communicated, just a year and a half earlier, he'd told me he needed to go speak with several groups about why Hilary Clinton could not be president. I do think he said "could not" and not "should not," and I'm positive he said "needed." While searching for that email might validate those details, I don't really want, right now, the visceral face-to-face of words he actually typed.

The comment about Clinton probably and partially explained my delay in sending the most recent book. I probably had deliberated permanently suspending the book-sending tradition. So this time, even though I had already searched local obituaries to make sure he was still alive, I still did not inquire about his address wholly without trepidation.

His answer came back promptly: yes, his address was still the same; yes, he and his wife were enjoying decent health, playing golf for exercise. And . . . "worrying what was going to happen to California when in the schools they have relay contests with 5- and 6-year-olds racing to put condoms on models of erect penises to see which team is fastest."

> In his office—not the same one where I'd worked for him, a bigger one—there was a George Bush calendar on the wall right behind his head. I didn't want him to notice me looking at it, didn't want to hear him say anything about it, didn't want to *know* what he would say, although the fact that he had it says enough, and says, above all, that I couldn't have known him the way I thought I had.
>
> —Cris Mazza, *Various Men Who Knew Us as Girls* (2011)

Why are there people in our pasts whom we can't forget, can't shake, even when it's healthier to do so? I mean besides the former spouses or former lovers or a love interest who never reciprocated. And not parents who abused or abandoned or siblings who broke ties. Not close friends who died or converted to a restrictive religion. These are *good* reasons for the termite trails left in our brains.

But why is it sometimes so difficult to forget, break from, or merely leave behind some of those from a mentor class: bosses, teachers, professors; maybe a coach or choreographer, music or drama director, club adviser, Scout leader? And why the yearly or biyearly dreams that we still have daily or frequent contact, or that I've returned, that I'm still a student-employee working for him although I seem to have no duties, no purpose, not even a place to sit?

Did the mentorship ever go bad? Not in the old-fashioned way: the pupil did not eclipse (then neglect) the mentor. We were in different fields, but even a comparison of our career trajectories had a zero factor in any mutating of the mentor relationship.

Also, it didn't go bad in the now #MeToo-established ways. The mentorship never turned sexual, romantic, or even flirtatious. For curious reasons this is considered bizarre or a suspicious claim. Why should it provide a problem? . . . But it does: in defining the relationship. The interpersonal dynamic I pondered in all those stories and novels was inexhaustive and resilient as "material" *because* it was an undefined relationship, or defined in the negative: not friends, not lovers, not colleagues, not peers, not professor-student, not family. As employer-employee it was once removed. Was he my "boss"? Yes . . . and no. Was this a complicating factor? Yes, but not in a simple line-of-command way. And some of what did make the "boss" aspect an issue has only been perceived lately, as he was in his midthirties, and a comparison of his demeanor, insight, and ability to reflect doesn't jibe with thirtysomethings I've met since then from "the other side," nor my own bumbling thirties. But remember, my perception of him was that of a twenty-two-year-old, and *that* image also doesn't jibe with the Tea Party candidate conspiracy believer. It's possible his sagacity, grace under pressure, and calming leadership were a sham, created in part by my unfinished brain's stewing anxiety over my impending but latent, even delayed, adulthood.

But the true complication in our unofficial mentorship relationship came primarily from the "real" boss, the one with official charge and accountability for my position, who was also my mentor's senior faculty program director. We both worked under an egomaniac conniver whose motives always came from his desire for power and prestige. This seems almost comical, but power and prestige exist in every little world and society, even dog training, even Boy Scouts, even Little League, even collegiate bands, even university English departments.

My first sense that something was amiss between the two men now seems an almost comically lucid example: when the senior boss wanted to win a teaching award, wrote a letter of recommendation for himself, and asked his junior colleague, my mentor, to have it typed up and then sign it. My mentor did as asked. When I, the letter's typist, realized the unmistakable sound of the senior boss's strutting rhetoric, I looked up from my keyboard, aghast. My mentor said, "Just type it exactly as is."

I recognize now that my mentor's senior colleague (my "real" boss, and referred to from now on as "the monster") was gaslighting and manipulating my mentor, "requiring" certain behavior and decisions out of sheer jealousy—the threat my mentor posed on a popularity scale, on a future-prestige scale, on a future-glory scale, etc. So their tension started with jealousy, but that was manifested by my observable, laughably enthralled regard for my mentor. "There's too much allegiance to the desk in the corner," the monster said to me on one of the too-frequent times he was there without my mentor present. And then the monster manufactured a situation where he could give me a longer private schooling. He arranged for me to house-sit for his neighbor, and then he asked me to stop by *his* house. He took me into his study to "warn" (i.e., gaslight) me about my mentor: *He's all image and no substance, basically a charismatic, and you shouldn't "chase after personality" because you'll lose yourself.*

I am certain I told my mentor about this as soon as was feasible, but I can't remember the time lag. I know I was looking to him for . . . What? . . . Protection? Relief? Cover? Shared misery at being gaslighted? Some kind of assurance?

Instead, while I was not privy to what the monster may have said to my mentor, my mentor started cautioning me that he might have to ignore me, couldn't be seen talking to me, and couldn't call me the name I was currently trying to use instead of a childhood nickname, because "I can't appear to have knowledge about parts of your life that have nothing to do with your job." What was he told to do, or what did he deduce? What did he fear?

So *betrayal* was how this conflict became defined in *my* POV. But the monster had a lasso on my mentor's future. I did not. Maybe what we really shared as a relationship was that we were both thrashing around (maybe simultaneously cowering), trying to figure out how to react or survive this monster's style, posture, and conduct. For decades I've always referred to this boss as the only human being I've ever hated. Just now, trying (again, again, *again*) to describe him, I realize he was, not so astonishingly, a precursor but comparatively trivial Donald Trump. Someone my mentor would someday vote for.

True, it was my mentor who struggled the most under the ego-motivated, manipulative, sometimes illegal practices of this monster. The worst example was when a state employee who was also a student elected to go home for the summer. The monster ran a scheme whereby the government paycheck was mailed to the nonresident student, and he sent back as a personal check made out to the person (mea culpa) who was actually doing the work. He also falsified addresses in order to get paid summer jobs for non-eligible students in an employment program for inner-city youth. But even as my mentor was pressured into participating in a plan to drive me out of my part-time employment, he still tried (without grand success) to advise me in being able to function without emotion, to help me perceive more of what was going on around me besides my mess, to warn me, to validate my abilities and attempt to redirect my attention to what should be my full focus and real life mission. Have any low-level White House staffers (in their thirties) mentored a troubled twentysomething to get out of that administration and find their real life's work while simultaneously finding themselves being asked to lie, falsify reports, or perform illegal practices? Perhaps my mentor's lasting impact and importance (for me) lies there.

The previous five paragraphs were written by hand in a notebook while I waited for an oil change. On the way home, without cognizant reasoning, instead of my usual practice of listening to MSNBC or CNN news on satellite radio, I chose the 1970s music channel. The playlist gave me "You're So Vain" . . . "The Way We Were" . . . then "To Sir, with Love." Sing along or look up the lyrics of "To Sir's" second verse until Lulu belts out the title again, "To sir, with love."

Instead of bestowing him ownership of the moon or inscribing it across the sky, what I gave him was the first eighteen books I authored. Now I find myself wondering about the right-and-wrong, weak-and-strong concepts I might have absorbed from him. So I'll go back to the only source I have—my college journal, where I saved and pondered the things he said.

- *Are you explaining or defending?*
- *A person's character can be judged by how he responds to not getting his own way.* [He could have used female pronouns but probably didn't; he was referring to the monster.]
- *When the main concern is who gets the credit, little is accomplished.* [Again, the monster.]
- *Only idiots follow instructions without asking questions.* [Who was the idiot? Him? Me?]

Some of these, with thirty-plus years of retrospect, may have been said to me as a means of convincing himself.

- *Look around, be perceptive. You're the center of the universe to yourself but not to the rest of the world. Things are not going to be so level, so pure as you want them to be.* [Did he say "level"? That's what my college journal claims he said. Or did he say "simple" or "equal" or "balanced"?]
- *When you leave home like this, all you have to do is go 100 miles up the freeway and your life doesn't seem real anymore, everything's out of phase, out of proportion, like worrying late at night.*

> • *Have you ever fried an egg? Then you know how you can let it get too hard, turn it over and over-do the other side. The cell breaks down, changes composition, corrodes, changes color, and gets really ugly. That's like thinking too much, especially when you haven't slept, you have no resistance, everything changes color.*

A forecast of the future of his own perception?

The Believing Brain

No need to repeat the facts about and research on how long it takes the human brain to fully mature. Heightened emotion, impulsiveness, varying amounts of narcissism can continue to stew up to one's late twenties. I've already wondered how that unfinished brain's condition may have impacted my perception of my mentor's character, personality, integrity, as well as the onetime conclusion that he ultimately betrayed me.

Now, however, I don't know what fog or agenda in *my* perception wants to find a good excuse for the mentor's turn toward the extreme outer limits of conspiracy theory. But first, a look at research in conspiracy-theory belief shows researchers are not considering physiological brain aberration, but only the evolution of how a "normal" human brain works and why—with *danger* or *survival* being chief factors.

"Belief in conspiracy theories appears to be driven by motives that can be characterized as epistemic (understanding one's environment), existential (being safe and in control of one's environment), and social (maintaining a positive image of the self and the social group). . . . This research suggests that people may be drawn to conspiracy theories when—compared with non-conspiracy explanations—they promise to satisfy [these] important social psychological motives" (Karen M. Douglas, Robbie M. Sutton, Aleksandra Cichocka, "The Psychology of Conspiracy Theories," *Current Directions in Psychological Science*, 2017, p. 538).

A related study by Jan-Willem van Prooijen and Mark van Vugt proposes that "conspiracy beliefs are part of an evolved psychological mechanism specifically aimed at detecting dangerous coalitions" ("Conspiracy Theories: Evolved Functions and Psychological Mechanisms," *Current Directions in Psychological Science*, 2018, p. 1).

In other words, belief in unproven, hyperbolic, beyond far-fetched "facts" happens through *normal* brain function. "From sensory data flowing in through the senses, the brain naturally begins to look for and find patterns, and then infuses those patterns with meaning. Our brains connect the dots of our world into meaningful patterns that explain why things happen, and these patterns become beliefs. Once beliefs are formed the brain begins to look for and find confirmatory evidence in support of those beliefs, which accelerates the process of reinforcing them, and round and round the process goes in a positive-feedback loop of belief confirmation." (Credit goes to whoever wrote the book blurb for *The Believing Brain: From Ghosts and Gods to Politics and Conspiracies—How We Construct Beliefs and Reinforce Them as Truths* by Michael Shermer.)

Further exploration might have also led me to research forms of tribalism rising in opposing political principles, and the tendency, therefore, to see hidden life-threatening (or life*style*-threatening) danger in "the other side." April 28, 2019, a conspiracy theory was born: In a rally speech, the forty-fifth president told the crowd that in blue states that allow late-term abortion, "the mother meets with the doctor. They take care of the baby, they wrap the baby beautifully. And then the doctor and the mother determine whether or not they will execute the baby." (Found on PolitiFact, Talking Points Memo, Scary Mommy, a few other websites.) No national media outlet—newspaper or broadcast network media—carried the outrageous hyperbole (i.e., lie) as "news."

From my (biased) perspective, it does seem that "my side" doesn't hold as many scientifically unsustainable (i.e., crackpot) conspiracy theories. Maybe *The president is a mentally ill psychopath* counts as one, but I'm not sure what the *conspiracy* is (what's the *story*, the cause and effect?). But when juxtaposed to *he was sent by God to fix America*, the quotient of irrational derangement doesn't seem to be of the same dimension.

But all of the above research is only interested in conspiracy theories adopted by large swaths of people. The researchers give examples like anti-vaxxers and flat-earthers, government staging of the 1969 moon walk and terrorist attack of 2001, and the contrail-is-mind-control-poison myth (interesting note: conspiracy theorists may have either mistaken or changed the word "contrail" to "chemtrail"). Searching details from any of these conspiracies displays an abundant list on Google and Snopes. But "condom races for five-year-olds" or "five-year-old children forced to run condom races"—in any rearrangement of specifics—exhibits zero results. No one is talking about, spreading, or believing this story. The closest hits are actual condom races sponsored by AIDS organizations in the 1980s for college students. These couldn't be the "patterns" perceived by an evolutionarily wary brain that is alert for danger.

So, what if it sounds like a conspiracy theory, but you can't find anyone else who believes it? My conjecture is there must be a how-the-brain-works difference between believing current ballooning conspiracy theories—easily available and passed in tweets, posts, blogs, or email—and adopting one that can't even be found anywhere on the wide swath of information available except in a different form thirty or forty years ago. This, to me, tends to put this particular belief in the realm of paranoid delusion.

The Injured (but Believing) Brain

My mother's brain was injured via stroke just days after a triple bypass. At seventy-five, she had time left for speech therapy to improve the resultant aphasia—not a physical difficulty forming words, but a neurological language-processing malady. Pronouns and prepositions were snarled ("from" the same as "to," "here" the same as "there," "he" and "she" inexplicably reversed in every case). Family relationships ("sister," "daughter," "mother") scrambled. Verbs ("go" and "come," "eat" and "drink," "give" and "take") a jumble to be unraveled.

A worse consequence of aphasia was in understanding incoming language, complicated by hearing loss. She began to sit in an isolated bubble at family dinners and parties. She could read large-print books but not watch TV. She had basic know-how for email; she had my father correct her outgoing messages and actual letters (slathered in Wite-Out corrections). Just months after the stroke, when I'd experienced my usual airsickness returning home after visiting her, she typed in an email, "Sory for the terrible sick on the plane." She eventually wrote an essay that started: "Time to decide to write." There was something beautifully unique about her diction and sentence structure. Even in November 2008, when, in the weeks after the presidential election, she nearly sobbed, "This new one is going to take all our money." It was not Obama who took their money, but the twenty-four-hour care she required in her last year of life.

But following her stroke under Bill Clinton's presidency, she slowly got better, until she started to get worse again during George W. Bush. Congestive heart failure was shrinking the amount of oxygen sent to her brain before anyone realized. So before the longer and longer bouts of sleeping, before the fainting, before the monthly then weekly trips to the ER, followed by over a year spent in a hospital bed on home hospice care . . . Long before any of that, she began pestering my father to help her enter the Publishers Clearing House sweepstakes. "A person wins," she would say.

Over a decade earlier, my uncle, in the early stages of Alzheimer's, was discovered to have spent thousands entering the Canadian lottery. A *New York Times* article in 2010 by Gina Kolata on the financial hardship of early-onset dementia gave a profile of a man who was "sending substantial amounts to lottery schemes." (I'm not insinuating the Canadian lottery is a scheme.)

This kind of belief suggests brain injury. Call it heightened belief. Or delusional belief. Now add *paranoid belief*. Commonly, dementia manifests in paranoid delusions, most frequently involving caregivers and family members. My ex-mother-in-law reported that her caregiver ran out the back door with all her laundry, that the hospital was a "clip joint" and her son was "in on it with them," and that a stranger knocked on the door to tell her that her new curtains were beautiful (not all delusions are paranoid).

"Paranoid symptoms [e.g., believing that someone is out to get you, or is taking your stuff, or is in the house at night] falls [*sic*] into a category of mental symptoms . . . technically called 'psychosis,'" according to Leslie Kernisan in "6 Causes of Paranoia in Aging & What to Do," *Better Health While Aging.* "Psychosis is uncommon in younger people, but becomes much more common as people get older. That's because any of these symptoms can emerge when people's brains aren't working properly for some reason."

And those reasons range from the earliest signs of dementia to a late onset of schizophrenia to other *neuropsychiatric* [emphasis mine] disorders, concludes Naresh Nebhinani et al. in "Late-Life Psychosis: An Overview." *Neuropsychiatry* deals with mental disorders and behaviors—including psychosis, anxiety, and disinhibition, a few I cherry-picked off a longer list—that are the result of a nervous system *disease.* And a "disease" like dementia could itself be considered a traumatic brain injury. But what if there was a prior *event* of a corporeal traumatic brain injury?

My last visit (out of only a handful) to my mentor in the years since my first book was published was in the early 2000s. It is also the last time he told me a story to make a point in answer to a "situation" in my life . . . and that moment between us spawned another novel, *Various Men Who Knew Us as Girls.*

For complex emotional reasons (i.e., too long a digression), on that visit I had decided to tell him that twenty-five years earlier, when I was in a student-teaching program with a master teacher he had selected for me, the master teacher spent the first half of the semester in a titillating flirtation; then when my mentor heard of it and made a call to the high school's principal, the flirtation abruptly ended. After summarizing this series of events, I told him that it had been an emotionally bewildering outcome, but also that his part in stopping the master teacher's behavior had possibly changed the course of my life. (What I didn't do was specify the roiling hypothesis that letting the flirtation take its course instead of having it snuffed out might have mitigated or at least moderated my sexual dysfunction.)

My mentor locked onto the "moment that changed the course of life" theme, and suddenly the conversation reverted to mentor and mentee as he told me a story: He had a girlfriend in high school, but it was "just dating, someone nice to do things with." But one night his girlfriend suggested going to an amusement park and going on a dark boat ride. She tried to seduce him during the ride, but he, "a morally concerned boy," didn't think it would be right. It turned out the girl was pregnant and thought if my mentor believed he was responsible, he would do the responsible thing. The trajectory of his life would have been entirely different. "You can't help but bookmark a moment like that."

When rereading the fictionalized dialogue of my mentor telling me this story, one detail, a throwaway, is his voice being "more scratchy" than it used to be. It was an aural detail I had perceived and recalled, so there it was, included in the scene. But the background of the scratchy voice was another story he'd told during that same reunion visit: a story that had nothing to do with me, with my history with him, with our nameless relationship, and had not been used in the fictional scene. He'd told me that in the recent past, he'd been in a bicycle accident, had hit his head and lost consciousness and been ambulanced to a hospital. The scratchy voice was residual from intubation. That fact alone indicates a level of medical seriousness. But he also told me he'd lost a lot of his memory for names and incidents; and what he did recall of his years at the university had no sense of chronology. And yet . . . his memory of the girl who'd tried to lure him into teenaged marriage was lucid. Long-term versus short-term memory. At the dementia-care facility where I take my dog for therapy, a woman tells me the details of her eighty-pound dog scaring her neighbor three times every visit . . . but she doesn't recall ever seeing my dog last week.

> Depending on the nature of the [head] injury, its severity, treatment received, and many other factors, a head wound *can* result in permanent brain damage that causes an impairment lasting the rest of your natural life.
>
> Some long-term side effects caused by a head injury may worsen. This could be due to the slow degradation of brain cells over time.
>
> —"What Is a Head Injury," Spinalcord.com, 2020

Among the symptoms of long-term effects of traumatic head injury, from multiple sources: memory loss, mood swings, impaired
cognitive function, and other degenerative brain conditions.
Among the symptoms of degenerative brain conditions is psychosis.
Among the symptoms of psychosis are delusions, hallucinations,
depression, even late-onset schizophrenia-spectrum disorders, all
of which can display in "disorganized thoughts . . . saying or thinking things that seem illogical or bizarre to others" (Kernisan).
Research also led me to a lesser-known form of dementia called
frontotemporal degeneration (FTD), "a form of dementia centered
in the brain's frontal lobe. Unlike Alzheimer's disease, which at-
tacks the brain's memory centers, FTD causes atrophy in the part
of the brain that controls judgment, behavior and executive function. People with FTD are often described as apathetic, lacking in
empathy and exhibiting an *impaired social filter* [emphasis mine]"
(Kevyn Burger, *Next Avenue*, 2018). So add loss of inhibition to the
list of symptoms. Our relationship couldn't still (if it ever was) be
one where he would, in his third sentence, tell me his deepest fears.

Crunching the cause and effect is easy, especially if you're desperate for an answer. Impaired cognition + (forms of) psychosis +
paranoia + lowered inhibition = an *excuse.*

It's *possibly* true, *may* be the reason, *could* be what has befallen
him.

There are some factors that would tend to go against my hypothesis, like that his wife might also be endorsing these strange
views (I had only an abridged view of her social media to judge
this). What can't be denied is that finding an explanation was important . . . for me. In fact, my search for a rationalization for his
belief in condom races for five-year-olds is in itself proving that
"once beliefs are formed the brain begins to look for and find confirmatory evidence in support of those beliefs, which accelerates
the process of reinforcing them, and round and round the process
goes in a positive-feedback loop of belief confirmation." My mom
entered Publishers Clearing House *because* of . . . and my mentor
ran for office as a Tea Partier, *needed* to make sure Hilary Clinton
didn't become president, and believed a conspiracy theory no one
else ever heard about *because* of . . . brain damage.

The Orphaned Brain

Is mine the first generation to feel set adrift, pushed from the nest, at sixty? Or is it an upshot of me being childless, so there's only one parent-child relationship in my life, the first one, which inevitably ends? It wasn't as though I lost a lifetime of essential influential parenting; I can remember many nonmalicious but still injurious parental missteps but little, if any, cogent wisdom. My mother gave the lesson of *example*: how to live fully in every moment—recognized, appreciated, idealized, if not followed. But as far as imparting wisdom: I had never, going back to teenaged years, asked her advice or told her of my sorrows or dilemmas. Still, with her passing was the basic loss of someone who cared. When my father followed two years later, the loss became the complete removal of scaffolding, or the sun's gravity. It had been several years since the last time he'd dispensed advice or opinion, but almost everything I did (except writing) included a background question of what he/they would think of it.

If *being* a parent helps to dull the loss of orbit when parents pass, could *being* a mentor do the same when mentors fall from grace? If so, the comparative flimsiness of the female mentor is another topic to be plumbed, the first stop being studies that show college students more often use the words "genius," "wise," or "inspiring" for male professors, while words chosen more often for female professors are "nice" and "friendly," or "strict" and "bossy." Not qualities that develop into durable or profound mentorships. Perhaps, as well, there was a desire lacking in this particular female professor who's now cogitating the subject, not enough of a gut tug to *become* a mentor, or too much residual identity of being the *mentee* to allow for any effective reversal.

Recently, in a cursory communiqué for a practical reason, a former student—male—who had not kept contact with me and likely had read none of my books, even when he was a student, told me that a former undergrad of his—female—was doing a master's project on all four of his novels. *Must be nice*, I almost replied. The irony of his boast apparently lost on him.

My mentor was in a different field, a life coach, not a career adviser. Without analyzing what might have been lacking in my relationship with my parents, and if possible putting undeniable gender contrasts aside, I was apparently in enough dire need of a life coach to become addicted to the rapport, plus seemingly so inadequately or incompletely coached that I never stepped up to pay it forward. Truly alone in a self-made vacuum.

Here is where I should return to the mentor's precarious career situation at the time I worked for him, how young he actually was, how his professional (and then personal) life was destabilized by the monster—ostensibly in a position to be *his* mentor. How unhealthy the whole milieu was for everyone. And still he tried . . . to manage it, to ease it, to help *me* understand and escape.

As he tries, now, to stop five-year-olds from being forced to run condom relays.

Nothing to Offer

2019

In order to embark, as so many of these #MeToo narratives do, in graduate school, this account will have to launch in the middle. We can agree the beginning of a narrative isn't always the ignition of the story. In these explorations, *that* moment we may never find. My best shot will be to look [as] simultaneously [as possible] backward and forward from the middle, examining more various men who missed the cut when the probing for answers was a novel.

1981

The friendship started because we were both from California. After that, and our ambitions to write fiction, and our relative ages, there wasn't much similarity between us. Except our genders. She sought me out as a potential compatriot when we entered the graduate program, and I, a habitual wallflower, was grateful she did. More like a wall weed, because there wasn't much about me beautiful to the senses of sweet-seeking insects nor human males. I was pretty sure of that; I was sure I'd already managed to locate the only one on earth who saw my androgyny as an appropriate package deal with the whole person.

In this venture of graduate school, one significant difference between me and my friend was revealed in the genial East Coast weather and evening light of September, when she urged me to accompany her after class for "drinks" with the professor of our folklore seminar. How long did it take me to realize the professor had asked *her*, and she'd dragged me along as a shield? More than a minute, less than an hour.

My friend—from here on *Student-A*—may have had a few additional invitations from the folklore professor. He disappears now; he is not *Professor-A*—one of our mentors in the writing program who would guide our work and development.

> He was her graduate advisor. I don't know what he advised her in. He read her poems, analyzed her paintings, critiqued her plays, studied her clothing designs, discussed her photography technique, suggested good books and movies, played her songs on his piano?
>
> And he started calling her and visiting her in her windy one-room apartment where she served herb tea that tasted like dirt or perfume.
>
> —Cris Mazza, "Former Virgin" (1991)

See, I've written about this, all these things, before. Never quite satisfying the need to solidify some kind of conclusion because I could never look my twisted perception in the eye.

At some point in 1982, I became aware of the *special* connection between Student-A and Professor-A. *Special*: exclusive, private, unique, superior. I could have chosen any of these words. And at the time, I did. I chose all of them, and more. As well as their antonyms that therefore must apply to me: *not* special (unnoteworthy), not interesting (mundane), doesn't stand out [in this cluster of other burgeoning writers].

Professor-A seemed distracted in our one-on-one tutorial sessions, seemed to have not read my work thoroughly. He made remarks that—when I inquired *why* or *how*—he then backed away from, only to not be able to replace the first observation with another. I remember a specific frustrating session when his greater interest/fascination/enthusiasm/stimulation—that is, Student-A—was squarely in my consciousness as the reason for his listlessness. So I wasn't just sensing a disinterested professor; I was reminding myself what caused it.

Wasn't a professor who was energized by what *you* had to offer, your talent, your execution, your particular way of expressing your perception—wasn't he (sadly, for us, usually a *he*) a crucial cog in your eventual success? Might he not be a key figure in that thing called "connections"? I had heard all about "being at the right parties," and dreaded ever having to make the choice, *go* or *stay home*, if/when I ever received the crucial/alarming invitation, because I knew the tug of *stay home* would easily win. So my whirring thoughts about Professor-A's attentiveness to Student-A might have also determined that she would not have as much need for the chaos of those "necessary" (and elusive) parties, for which the invitations never came.

Basically, my worth/value/potential to succeed as a writer was being called into question by my not earning the most or "best" attention from the professors. I immediately concluded this situation involving Student-A meant *I must not be as interesting or talented. In order to succeed, I'm going to have to get their attention . . .*

But I did not think: *I'd better get sexual attention from my mentors in order to succeed.* That is, my thoughts made no conscious link. The suggestion of that link might have been there anyway: *any* attention meant my potential as a writer would be included. So "that kind of attention" did help; it was snarled up with the need for validation of aptitude and merit. And [any] attention was needed to boost my immergence into a writing career because I was completely without the ability to "go to the right parties," which, essentially, meant the same thing. In more ways than one.

The convergence of these unrelated notions might have been bolstered by the fact that my friend Student-A was no Barbie-gets-all-the-breaks. If so, if I had been seeing a "classically" beautiful (i.e., fashion model) young woman get the "best" attention of the male professors, I might have made different (subconscious) conclusions, including a gross assumption that *that* kind of beauty came with an airhead. (A common cultural prejudice in the 1980s.) Student-A was not conventionally "pretty," and wasn't particularly well endowed in bra size, but was enormously well read and informed in off-the-beaten-path philosophies, culture, and literature. Before entering the program she had (for reasons I never bothered to ask) shaved her head, so her hair was growing in, a soft half inch when we met. She preferred to wear her sweaters backward, sometimes inside out. She carried an oiled parasol instead of an umbrella. One of her outfits was a black military parachutist's jacket worn like a dress over black tights. Her wide mouth, always with red lipstick, could produce an entrancing smile. (Note: I don't use the words "beguiling," "alluring," or "enticing." Her smile may have been all of these, but that would suggest she was "prowling" for the attention. I can't say that she was or wasn't.) Her voice was quiet, sincere, her laugh piping but gentle, comfortable. The exact opposite of the current in-vogue vocal-fry.

Student-A was awarded the outstanding student designation in our cohort, despite her record still bearing an incomplete in a literature course. Perhaps she had written a brilliant comprehensive exam; I'm sure mine was basically adequate. Within a year following our graduation, her thesis novel was accepted for publication by the independent press co-run by Professor-A. To this date, Student-A has not published another book. This may have something or everything to do with the aftermath of her "situation" with Professor-A, but that is her story to tell. My story has to do with the ripple effect of her experience with Professor-A on those others in her sphere, or at least me. As well as I can remember, the amorous attention given her only proved to me that she must be more interesting, deeper, more substantial as a writer. Driven, ambitious, and, yes, competitive—a way of measuring my "success"—I left that degree program with acute disappointment, which I could only direct at myself for not being profound enough.

So I *did* equate Student-A's magnetism—evidenced with more than one professor—as a positive indicator of her total worth that must include her ideas and writing. Therefore, the equation attention = potential = *deserved* career boost (her book publication) was throwing its shadow onto my path as a writer ... including a tacit notion that my worth/value as a writer was integrated with my worth/value as a female?

But, really, that "equivalence" hadn't *started* there, in my twenties, at graduate school.

How often, in how many essays, do I have to use this Erica Jong quote from *Fear of Flying*: "Growing up female in America, what a liability"? We already know how advertising bombarded us with what was required to be attractive, to be desirable, to manage to not end up alone, a state in which a woman was "unfulfilled" as well as less valuable. Putting aside the still-almost-absolute condition of gender inequality that persisted when I finished high school and began college—that I had exactly one female professor as an undergraduate, that we read exactly zero female novelists in high school—it was a small miracle that I didn't have a notion that I should not be pursuing the course I was on, toward calling myself a novelist. Of course that path had started with journalism, veered into secondary teaching, and, having vacated both of those, then went (back) to the only thing I knew I could do. And I was wholly encouraged by male mentors and professors. How I may have subliminally thought I didn't fit, however, shows up, in forty-plus-year hindsight, in the first fiction (if you can forgive the clichés) I wrote as an undergrad, and the first where the main character was not male:

> When most people think of a female star, they expect, and usually see Miss America walk onto the stage or screen; a blond-haired five-foot-eight beauty with legs that start at her shoulders. She'd have blue eyes, daintily sculptured cheekbones, a small thin chin, a cute pug nose, and a sweet red mouth which never says anything wrong, but never really says anything smart either. If that was a "star" I was either a mistake or an exception. . . . They would see a five-foot Italian with a short mop of hair and brown eyes which aren't dark enough to look like a foreign beauty, but are more the color of dirty water. I have glasses I don't like to wear, thick eyebrows I don't like to pluck, and fairly short limbs which don't move with liquid agility.
>
> —Cris Mazza, nineteen years old

Simplistic ideas present in 1975: I was not beautiful, but an odd-looking girl like me could have talent and substance that made her of value; *and* pretty girls were hollow, devoid of idea, their talent only to be beautiful. "Don't hate me because I'm beautiful," they begged in advertising, tired of unfair assumptions like mine. I didn't hate them. I *thought* I was rising above what they had to offer.

After all, in junior high, I'd been told by "cool boys" that I "had nothing to offer." That didn't prevent two other boys from trying to find something, as they pursued me in and among the deserted auditorium curtains (where we were supposed to be practicing our violas and cello), pinned me immobile so that they could grasp and feel parts of my body that might have been changing. And I, not yet "the mistake or exception" in my college novella, actually thought, *They like me.* Maybe those cool boys were wrong; I did have *something to offer.* Thus, although I was trying to escape those groping boys in the auditorium, I'd gotten culture's message: I never told a teacher nor simply left the backstage area for the sanctity of a restroom.

It's thought that girls get the message as young as the toddler stage. In one recent study, "'We found that fathers are using more language about the body with girls than with boys, and the differences appear with children who are just one to three years old,' [Jennifer] Mascaro[, an assistant professor of family and preventive medicine at Emory University, Atlanta,] said" of one study. The study further showed that "[parents] with daughters ... used ... words ... , such as 'belly,' 'cheek,' 'face,' 'fat' and 'feet,' and the scientists raised the possibility of a link between these innocent interactions and body image problems that are far more common in adolescent girls than boys" (Hannah Devlin, *Guardian*, 2017).

Another "study ... has revealed that half of girls feel stifled by gender stereotyping, with children as young as seven believing they are valued more for their appearance than for their achievements or character.... Furthermore, constraining stereotypes have a negative impact on girls' mental health, convincing them first that an ever more demanding paradigm of physical 'perfection' must be met with apparent effortlessness and then that being 'popular'—meek yet sociable—sexy but not 'slutty,' sporty in a narrow, feminine parameter (not 'too muscular') are imperatives" (Natasha Devon, *Guardian*, 2017).

It's not possible to know what my parents said about my body, and while it's true my mother dressed me like this (1), she also dressed me like this (2), and I started high school (the year dress codes were eliminated) dressed like this (3).

It's not a stretch, though, to see that if girls are made aware of the importance of being pretty, they're also aware of the "rewards" when they "succeed." Attention. *They like me.*

From academic to tabloid sources, spanning ten years, some seem willing to look at this possibility without flinching (too much):

> My experience is that some young women come from familial, so-cial, and economic environments where this is the way women relate to men; if they have a request, they "use their bodies" as Ruby Payne states in her book on generational poverty. These fe-male students may have grown up learning that the way they behave is how women are supposed to behave toward men, even ones older than they, and there is a chance they may not even be aware how their behavior is perceived.
>
> —Anonymous, *Chronicle of Higher Education* forum, 2006

> I've always dressed with the express intention to please and grat-ify my male bosses in the workplace.... I am university educated,

reasonably intelligent and, so I've been told, attractive. . . . I use
it to my advantage every single day. Before you roll your eyes in
disgust . . . consider this. By the age of 30 I had . . . a generous six-
figure salary and a high-ranking position in my chosen industry.

—Samantha Brick, *Daily Mail*, 2011

If she's beautiful, a new study says, there is often a hidden selfish
streak. She's lucky and she knows it, and she will consciously—or
subconsciously—use her looks to her advantage any way she can.

—Dale Archer, *Psychology Today*, 2012

I find running a business in a man's world to be a huge advantage.
I wear bright colors, yank up my skirt + get attention. . . . When I
was building my business, I would walk into a room of 600 men
. . . and [if] I dress like a guy in a nice pant suit, no one would say
hi to me, no one would entertain me. The minute I started wearing bright suits and have a nice length skirt on, I would just roll
up . . . into that room, everyone paid attention to me.

—Barbara Corcoran, *Access Hollywood*, 2016

Heresy. Yet I have to admit: I've had this opinion about certain
women I've encountered. Just not about Student-A. And not about
myself, a few years later, when I—

But wait. First, moving backward chronologically, who *was* the
person who went east for graduate work and had a ringside seat
for Professor-A's habitual (it turns out) behavior seeking a coed du
jour?

1979–1981

In a first graduate degree, conferred mere months before I went
east for the second, my committee was three men. West Coast
professors will be named numerically. Only Professor-1 and Pro-
fessor-2 will appear here. (The third member of my committee, my
actual *writing* mentor, was an obscure experimentalist, one of the
first graduates of Iowa, who did nothing but show me how my fiction worked, was the one to direct me to the second grad program,
and whose last words to me, in the late 1980s, were *don't quit*.)

West Coast Professor-2, the mentor in this book's previous

essay, already relentlessly dissected in most of my fiction for reasons beyond this topic—and despite our relationship being all dialogue, occasionally written, often theoretical even when about emotions, or even sex—is *not* a nonplayer here. For reasons I don't remember, he told me a story about someone he knew, a professor of music, who "grabbed a girl after class and physically told her how he felt. They were married in about three months."

I wrote it down word for word in my college journal the same day it happened, so, shaped only by my youthfully sharp short-term memory but emotionally teeming adolescent perspective at the time, our dialogue after the story went like this:

ME: She fell for that?

HIM: I guess she felt the same way, was waiting or hoping he would do that.

ME: (*wanting to remain skeptical*) Still . . .

HIM: She kicked him out three years later. He grabbed another girl in another class, and she—his wife—didn't like that. He said he should have that right, to follow honest impulses.

ME: And he had a double-standard?

HIM: Maybe. He said he didn't. He said she could do the same. She just didn't want to. Her father—

ME: If she was brought up like that, why wouldn't she be scared when he first grabbed her?

HIM: She probably was, but she liked it. She might have been hoping for it. If she didn't know those impulses by then . . .

IMPLIED: (*and heard by me*) . . . something's wrong with her.

Classic predator behavior, narrated to me as "honest impulses," "telling her how he felt," and "she liked it." Need this be picked apart any further?

During this same time, I participated in a drama-department production of *Cabaret*, as a member of the nightclub band. Connoisseurs of *Cabaret* remember that the all-girl band is usually portrayed as men in drag. Not a casting requirement because only men can play the music—it was part of the depiction/characterization of the time/place milieu. But our director thought it would be interesting to have the band actually *be* all girls, dressed as sexy (or

in this case whorish) as possible. At the time I thought his "update" was innovative. Now I think having men in drag on stage at a public university might have caused too much controversy.

As a girl who played trombone, no longer unique but still unusual, I was recruited for the *Cabaret* band. So by day looked like a graduate-student writer, and at night like this (amateurish stage makeup self-applied).

Professor-1 came to a performance. I do recall telling him beforehand about my participation. I do not recall if I supplied his tickets. If there were free guest tickets to cast members, wouldn't my parents have gotten those? Why is this important? If there was an invitation from me, versus if attending was his initiative—it seems significant.

Afterward, the next time I saw Professor-1, he said, "Cris . . . Wow . . . I never would've thought . . . There's a whole other side to the quiet girl who never said anything in class. I mean, *really*, Cris . . ."

I thought it good to show this "other" side to *in-the-background Cris*. After all, I'd performed the *Cabaret* music on stage, live. I was proud of that.

1979

We'll return to Professor-1 later. A step further back, and I'm in my secondary-education program finishing a teaching credential in English that, like the journalism degree before it, I abandoned. Explored at length in two novels, this experience is where I encountered the textbook case of powerful male mentor sexual harassment. Except for two things: (a) Title IX existed but sexual harassment had not yet been identified by an appeals court, and (b) I was devastated when his frank, overt, but *pre*-sexual-contact attention was withdrawn when he was warned that others were "watching." It was not, however, the progressing-then-withdrawn sexual attention that made me unable to be a high-school teacher (which would have been one definition of sexual harassment). Perhaps the sexual attention had made me care less about it? But I wonder how *anything* could have made me feel more anxious, depressed, and desperate over the prospect of having to teach high school? Still, I *was* demoralized over the end of the attention from my supervising teacher. It amounted to asking: *What's wrong with me?*

Was that ground zero for my take on how sex should play in my future career or achievements? I could continue to move chronologically backward, through androgynous wallflower teen years interlaced with instances of sexual discrimination hidden in plain sight. There were other boys who (with my consent) used my body to "practice" before they felt up their first girlfriends (and, again, my conclusion *he likes me*). There was believing when I was told by a man with his hand up my shirt that there was something wrong with me for not wanting "more," when I didn't even "want" *that* from him either.

1981

Yet the other significant alteration in my development during the grad-school era was that, six months before going east, I got married. Seems an incongruity in this self-depiction. But the foreshadow appears in my first paragraph: *the only one on earth who saw my androgyny as an appropriate package deal with the whole person* (since then, this has been proved untrue by Mark). With my first husband, I lost my physical virginity, although not to great sensual or ecstatic fanfare.

Being newly married, albeit with the groom still in California, might have been anybody's explanation as to why the prowling professors in the East Coast program did not "choose" me. Or anybody's explanation but mine. My conclusion was that I wasn't interesting or smart enough. Being not smart had already been implied by my B in literary theory, which I discovered much later was a mark of shame, infamy. And being *uninteresting* would be a direct comment on my writing. These two characteristics together could certainly render me invisible to those whose jobs might be to discover and nurture writing talent.

Twenty-four years old—questionable as to whether the brain had finished developing. Questionable as to whether it ever does. Or if what passed for *development* had been inexorably distorted by culture. *He likes me*: attention = potential.

2019

Before I follow that duped and disappointed girl into her post-graduate-school future, I need to pause in the present—okay, a month ago. I ran into another graduate of my eastern alma mater. She—Student-C—came to a reading where, by sheer happenstance, I read "Former Virgin," which I'd written thirty-plus years ago and had been incited by my disillusionment over Professor-A's conduct, although in the story I made the professor's interest in his student profound and the student's reaction coolly detached; *his* was the disappointment. (I'm sure my alterations to the story can be psychologically sussed out. I had the professor telling the story to an even more desolate female character with her own parallel story.)

Student-C and I had not been in the same cohort. She followed me by a few years. But I asked her if she recognized Professor-A in the story I'd just read aloud. Because of my fictionally flipping the disorientation onto him, she had not made a connection. After my brief summary of what I'd observed as a grad student, she said, "He did the same with someone in my cohort, and it really messed her up for a long time. Mine was with Professor-B, but I never wanted to talk about it, bring it up in this current moment, because . . . Well, *I* know how *I* acted."

1983

Sometimes connections are only made by zigzagging through time, so backward again to the 1980s, after I'd returned to California with my degree and my discouragement and my determination.

Student-A's thesis novel was scheduled for publication at the press housed at our alma mater and run by Professor-A. Production time was lengthy, so her book had not yet appeared when my thesis won a national award for an unpublished fiction manuscript. The prize was money but did not include publication of the winning manuscript. But the awards ceremony would *have* to be one of "all the right parties," and by virtue of being there to accept an award, being noticed would be fail-safe; I wouldn't be responsible for *making* myself visible. I used some of the prize money to fly east again, even knowing how sick I got on airplanes and how the nausea could linger for days afterward.

Student-A housed me during my short stay, and Professor-A and Professor-B arranged to meet me for a meal while I was there. Had they expressed pleasure over a recent graduate winning this award? I assume so. So much about that short reunion was lost to the haze of queasiness. But what remains, what I do remember, has related relevance. First, looking sick as I felt, feeling as off as I looked, still did not prevent one of the three judges—the only one I'd never heard of—to ask me if I'd like to go for a drink after the ceremony's reception. Here it was: being at the "right party," making a "connection," my fateful moment. But how could I drink or eat anything the way my stomach still roiled? I didn't go. If there was a thought beyond that, it doesn't remain. (Maybe if I'd heard of him . . . so possibly my ignorance saved me.)

The second pertinent memory from the award-acceptance trip should have been another piece to the puzzle, to constructing some kind of perception that might have spared me my jarring choices a few years later. By virtue of the award given my novel manuscript, Professor-A arranged a meeting between me and his agent. I assumed he knew the day and time of that meeting, but perhaps it wasn't important enough for him to keep track of. I don't even remember whether I ever had any kind of working relationship with his agent, or whether she was one of a long list to ask to see the award-winning manuscript, only to tell me it wasn't commercially viable. In fact, this is all I remember about my meeting with her: The phone rang and she took the call. Somehow she informed me it was Professor-A. With me still seated across her desk, she accepted a date with Professor-A to attend a professional tennis event. Maybe another area of ignorance: I didn't realize that while it could go vice versa, authors don't usually invite their agents on social outings. I went back to where I was staying in Student-A's loft, and in the course of the early evening, while recounting my day's activity, I told her about the phone call that had interrupted my meeting. I don't remember what she said or what dialogue we had following the disclosure. I don't think I intended to be a shitster—stirring up trouble with an unsolicited offering of private information. But I do recall that after I was tucked into sheets on her futon, I could hear her howling anguish behind the partition of her bedroom.

The only "realization" I carried home from my award-acceptance trip, besides passing up an invitation to "make connections," was that the relationship between Professor-A and Student-A must have still been continuing, but probably would not (and did not) continue after my visit. Student-A, while eventually successful as an editor, has not published another book. But it was too soon, then, to know that.

So I continued on in the wake of the award—rejected by every corporate publisher who asked to see the winning manuscript—as unenlightened as I'd ever been. Student-A's book was published. In another year my award-winning manuscript was rejected by that same independent press—the one with Professor-A's indelible fingerprints. And here's a bit of lingering ignorance: it just occurred to me that my inadvertent intervention in the situation with Professor-A, his agent, and Student-A is perhaps also what stopped any arrangement between me and the agent, as well as ended my book's chance with that press.

Among the things I didn't know or hadn't become aware of at the time the "award-winning novel" was being rejected: In less than ten years I would be an assistant professor listening to senior (male) professors speak cynically (but was the irony veiled wistfulness?) about the era (1960s–70s) when well-known (male) writers were frequent esteemed guests at other universities, and always expected to be granted access to coeds who might want to be impressed by their greatness. I didn't know that on one visit to my West Coast alma mater in 1976, a visiting writer chased one of my peers—his assigned chauffeur—around her sofa after he'd convinced her to take him to her apartment to "rest" before his reading. And *who* was the hosting professor for these (lurking male) writers who had visited my West Coast university and provided them the (ingenuous female) student escort? None other than Professor-1, from my committee of mentors, from the audience of *Cabaret*.

1984–1987

In the few years after my manuscript won its award, when I found myself mentorless for the first time in a decade, I turned to Professor-1 in an attempt to have him (re)fill that role. During this time, he told me a story, and likely gave me sketchy details at best, about a female grad student who'd been hounding him. I don't think he used the word "stalking." I do believe the university did somehow become involved in an official way, and that he may have had "administrative leave" for a semester. I surmise all that because the story he told me became the fodder for one of my most notable stories, "Is It Sexual Harassment Yet?" finished in 1988. I am 100 percent positive I "allowed" (actually invited) him to read the story when it was in a late draft; I believe the last changes I made to the story, to further confuse whether the "she said" or the "he said" was more credible, were done after I—.

> Later that year she would sit naked in a hot tub—at a former downtown motel remodeled to rent out dayrooms with saunas and Jacuzzis—beside a supervisor from the bank. She kept washing her mouth out with the chlorinated water between the times she went down on him, because there wasn't a lot of information on whether oral sex was safe. She wanted to be promoted from teller.
>
> —Cris Mazza, "Change the World" (2006)

It's almost as though I don't know how to begin to re-narrate this scene. Only used once in my work (the above), and at that time rendered that concisely, that one-dimensionally.

It wasn't quid pro quo. It was a desperate need to be *interesting enough* . . . to Professor-1. Interesting enough that he would take note of my work, include my work in any of the books of criticism and interviews with contemporary writers he was having published at the time. If not that, perhaps he'd talk to someone with influence at a major literary journal. My name would come up because my work was different, cutting-edge, provocative. And, in fact, my fiction had become infused with graphic, sometimes deviant, sexual scenes (the above minimalist quote is from long after that phase). There were other psychological (compensating for reality) reasons for my seeking the mantle of fearlessly sexual in my writing. But Professor-1's proclivity for such writing (which I learned later had an aberration of its own), his use of like books and writers in class, his choice of them for his interviews with contemporary writers, could not have had *no* effect on my writing, from the time I was an undergrad to those years just after my second graduate degree and the sack of warped perceptions I'd carried home and added to the others I'd been hoarding.

My award-winning manuscript was foundering in the submission cycle. I was immersed in writing the stories that would eventually make up my first two collections, *Animal Acts* and *Is It Sexual Harassment Yet?* I was audaciously asking him to read manuscripts because I still couldn't tell when a draft was finished. I would walk to his house to deliver pages through the mail slot. And when he made time to talk to me, I went to his house, or to a bar where he facetiously held his English department "office hours."

I think I recall the sly way he said he had an idea for me. Did he say I needed to loosen up? Or did he just suggest it was something I needed? Why do I want to remember the word "need"? He might've said it if my fiction were prim and cool, but it wasn't. Maybe he sensed the pretense in my sexual writing. If so, no one else ever would.

Whatever the reason, his idea was that we would go to a place near that bar where an old motel had been converted into sauna and spa rooms for rent by the hour. He knew I was married. So was he. He knew I knew his wife. Somehow, just like at my East Coast alma mater, this thing he'd suggested didn't have anything to do with wedlock.

Professor-1 supplied the encounter with cocaine and pot. Maybe if I'd opted for the coke, I'd have a whole different memory and perspective on the scene, which now I can only describe with words like mortification, humiliation, degradation . . .

This was maybe six to eight years after AIDS hit the scene—and "bathhouses" had early on been spotlighted as part of the problem. That, and my knowledge of Professor-1's possible peccadilloes, plus my well-underway sexual dysfunction . . . There wasn't much chance the marijuana was going to break through to rid me of inhibition. At any time I could have said, *Wait, no, I've changed my mind.*

But *had* I changed my mind, despite feelings of odium, shame, disgust . . . picturing myself an orange segment turned inside out with a grunting, writhing creature scouring away at the pulp with his teeth and tongue? (An enduring image likely supplied by the pot.)

Besides, was it fair to change my mind after "my turn" on a hard, wet bench in the sauna portion of the cubicle, with, needless to reveal, nothing even close to excitement, let alone orgasm? Wordlessly (really?) we shifted into the hot tub for his shot. That's when I tried to sterilize my mouth with the chlorinated tub water, trusting that this seedy place would have bothered to maintain disinfected water, even knowing that it would only possibly be antibiotic, not an anti*viral*, and no HIV prophylactic had been developed except condoms. He never suggested or produced one.

Oral sex had long been my tactic to compensate for my sexual dysfunction that made intercourse painful and fruitless (for both parties). But that day I made up for nothing with nothing. Was it his use of cocaine? My obvious lack of "response"? My mouth-washing-out "technique"? It seemed to last forever, but it was never finished. Eventually, somehow, and without saying as much, we simultaneously gave up. It must have been me stopping. And he, likely embarrassed, might have said, *Thank you.* Trying to re-create it in this amount of detail feels grisly. So I'll stop here, too, without climax.

It's no story denouement that, although I have a vague memory that he did perform an interview with me, the interview remained on cassette tape, never published, never even transcribed, now somewhere in his archives, which he donated with public fanfare to my West Coast alma mater. I wonder what I had to say to his possibly allusive accomplice questions.

2019

And where does this fit in this current era's wide-angle picture emerging from the shadows—in particular in the world where my career exists—of men, mentors of young writers in the 1970s,

1980s, and 1990s, exposed as pillagers of naïve young woman? It's our brand of naïveté that is more problematic than one might assume (or admit). Especially as Title IX became stronger and sexual harassment was defined and tested in court (*after* most of my experiences). Weren't these predators sensing some skewed implicit notions on our parts? Not just a "weak" female's longing for "love," but a distorted, even deranged definition of our comprehensive value thrust at us, which somehow we bought? What I witnessed happening during my grad-school experience in the East, what I'd serendipitously dodged at the award ceremony when I was too airsick to "capitalize" on a go-out-for-drinks connection . . . is what I returned home and *chose*: In order for him to respect my work, first he had to *like* me. I had to have something to offer.

I Work, Therefore I Am

A(n Incomplete) Conversation about
Identity (with Footnoted Asides)

2019

A retriever retrieves. In fact, he's not fully comfortable without something in his mouth, and bigger is better. Although it's easy to wonder "What are you thinking?" as he calms his stress with a mouthful of stuffed toy (called his "baby"), his lack of a complete cerebral cortex tells me whatever his "thoughts," they're *not* "I am a retriever."

The act of defining oneself is decisively human.

He has a pedigree.[1] It's a sideways tree and he is the final limb. A glance can determine if he is the son, grandson, and generational descendant of champions and/or performance masters. The number of breed championships behind him *might* cause him to conclude, "I'm a beautiful representation of my breed." Or a retriever with no hunting-titled antecedents *should* wonder, "*Am* I a retriever?" Again, without that cerebral cortex, he probably isn't even wondering, "When is my next opportunity to be the retriever that I am?" He has never read, asked about, or worried over his

---

1. He is not Tommy. He was adopted at three years old a year after I said goodbye to Tommy. But his identity was never "not Tommy," the way I may have perceived mine was often to my parents, rightly or wrongly, "not Sibling X."

pedigree and wouldn't recognize his mother. His life unadorned by the need for *identity*.

I have a pedigree too. Mine has blanks.

Identity 1.0 Name and Ancestors

What am I looking for?

It began as a gift for my father, to make a basic family tree, and it started with a simple problem: he didn't remember his grandmother's name. She had died before he was born.

But maybe it originated before that: when my mother gave me a Xerox of the ancestry project of her maternal family researched by one of her cousins, whose venture was a quest to prove a relationship with the Earl of Mar. So my mother's maternal ancestry was already well developed, complete with a heady story involving the earl's bastard son facing accusations of treason in England and escaping to the New World before the Revolution. Followed by generations of seafaring or Civil War exploits, Maine lighthouse keepers, and the expected involvement in lighthouse legends like a baby thrown from a sinking vessel who washed ashore between two featherbeds to be adopted by the Marr lightkeeper on shore, who'd built a bonfire of hope for those going down into the tumultuous sea. Researching, fitting legends into known history, imagining combined possibilities were fodder for a novel, *Waterbaby*.

In the novel, the ancestry quest was complicated by a character's desire to find the source of her own epilepsy (and lifelong self-determined identity as "disabled"), not even being aware her older brother was diagnosed with schizophrenia in his early twenties. The character's fantasized story makes the adopted shipwrecked baby the one who brought epilepsy's aura into the family. She learns, as an aside, that her father died of an epileptic seizure, and thus what she was seeking was on the other side of her family tree.

Schizophrenia made no appearance in the novel character's imagined story of lighthouse lore, perhaps because I already knew it was in *my* father's family—that broken tree that couldn't even name my great-grandmother, while my maternal/great-maternal tree went into the 1700s, including births, deaths, lives, legends . . . a playground for living vicariously in history.

Maybe I perceived my father wanted to see the same grand lineage done for his family. And so I embarked via computer, which my mother's cousin couldn't have used. Similarly, I discovered research already done—but on my father's maternal side. Again, via a cousin . . . this one had married into the Mormon Church, so on the ancestry site run by the Latter-Day Saints, the immigrant Caprigliones stretched back into Italy to the 1840s before Italian databases gave out.

The paternal-paternal Mazzas, a more common Italian surname, were still the stunted part of my tree, but I persisted until my first modest quest was reached: my great-grandmother listed on a ship manifest with her husband and children, their name misspelled, but not in immigration-lore manner where a gatekeeper at Ellis Island gives the family a new name. In fact, according to Alicia Ault in *Smithsonian Magazine*, immigration inspectors were not the ones changing people's names; instead, errors and changes likely happened before arrival at Ellis Island. Simply an error in a handwritten entry on the manifest when the scribe heard Marza instead of Mazza. The error was discoverable partially due to the particular list of children's names fitting my father's list of aunts and uncles—except my father wasn't aware that all three of his aunts had the first name Maria. Their *middle* names fit the information he'd given me, and matched the versions steadily becoming Americanized on subsequent census documents. But the ship's records also had a typed list of "aliens held for medical clearance," which included all the *Mazza*s, with the same first and middle names. The fact that my father's grandmother was listed with the surname Mazza did not cause a question. She was married. The ship would list her that way. So although in the practice of genealogy women are listed with their original surnames, Fortunata Mazza went into my tree with her husband's name. I didn't find record of her death after arriving in New York in 1910, and I left genealogy research for a few years.

What called me back was an inquiry from someone who shared my surname and was researching her genealogy. She had come across my incomplete tree. What allowed her inquiry to return me into the obsession was the ever-present need to escape daily reality, which had made me a novelist in the first place and had become more poignant after 2016.

My new genealogy partner proved more skilled than me at cross-checking other sources, including her willingness to call and contact individuals for verbal evidence. With her help, we discovered not only that my father had not known (or failed to remember) the existence of his oldest paternal uncle (who'd immigrated in advance, thus was not on the ship manifest), but also that two of his aunts had married the same first cousin[2] (one aunt died young, thus the second marriage), *and* that my father's grandmother Fortunata didn't need a maiden name on the genealogy because she was originally a Mazza as well. We've not yet determined exactly how she was related to her husband.

None of which answers what *I* might be looking for, other than the next target, the next important birth or death date, and on to the next generation. Narrowly focused attention that has possibly kept my cuticles from being bloodied by my teeth. No longer doing it for my father, who passed away after my first venture, when I found the "three Marias" and his grandmother's evocative name—none of it had elicited the exclamation of thrill/appreciation I'd craved. But I was now making discoveries the rest of my family, at the twig ends of the growing tree, might appreciate. Except I've decided not to share . . . yet.

> Therapy as a Status Symbol: U.S. Health System Creating Culture of Mental Health Haves and Have Nots. The mental health landscape caters to the "worried well" who can pay $400 an hour and not to those who are actually struggling with a serious mental health issue, one expert says.
>
> —California Healthline Daily Edition, May 24, 2016

---

2. First-cousin marriages are not uncommon before the middle of the twentieth century, and are still legal in some U.S. states. Prior to 1900 such marriages could be a means of keeping property and power within a family. Some researchers believe laws against cousin marriages were a means to prevent consolidation of influence and assets.

Certain of my family members, fully aware of our aunt Marie, her entire life spent in a mental hospital, actually *crave* [self-]diagnosis of mental illness, using these serious afflictions (if actually diagnosed by a reputable psychiatrist who seeks to do more than collect insurance payments) to justify rude or selfish behavior, to allow them to take their dogs everywhere, to explain (and get drugs for) the pressure and fear that are a natural part of life in this explosive century (or human life in general), and even to excuse failures and disappointments among deceased ancestors—pursuing a diagnosis for *him* to explain why *we* were afraid of our grandfather.[3] There is no way I'm going to add fuel to those embers by exposing multiple first-cousin marriages (some of which don't even touch our exact bloodline).[4]

What, besides the misuse of service animals (and I've even considered doing this myself, only to be able to bring my separation-anxious dog with me for *his* emotional needs),[5] or minimizing our aunt's unadulterated life experience, does it hurt to play along with their desire to be diagnosed? Besides the homogenization and

3. Scary grandpa: Did he hit his wife? Maybe, at one time. Did he hit his children? No one has said so. Did he hit us? No. If we cried at his Italian-accented loud gruffness, he said, "I'll give nickel if you cry." Which made getting that nickel strangely difficult.

4. *Reputable* dog breeders don't have to be scientists to know that breeding in the same line (cousins with cousins, uncles with nieces, etc.) doesn't *cause* illness or mutation. Genetic maladies are more likely to be expressed if both sides carry the disorder. From allergies to cancer predisposition, from structural deficits to eye degeneration, genetic health problems do exist, and if "doubled" are more probable. But they have to be there in the first place. They don't pop into existence because the parents are cousins. Breeders try to test dogs for every known genetic health problem. Should we maybe test human couples? Instead, we just assume if they're not related, they won't both carry a dangerous gene.

5. "The United States Dog Registry will certify any dog as a . . . 'therapy dog' for $58, and an outfit called ESA of America [Easy Service Animal?] will happily certify your pet rat, hamster, or iguana as an 'emotional support animal.' . . . If you need an official looking letter to the airlines from a 'mental health professional' indicating that your dog, cat, iguana or goldfish qualifies as an 'emotional support animal,' for 168 dollars, they will diagnose your psychological problems over the internet." Hal Herzog PhD, "Service Animal Scams: A Growing Problem," *Psychology Today*, June 11, 2014

attenuation of the severe actualities of mental illness, it's part of pervasive victim culture, which is part of a larger cultural jostling: a cry of "let me be considered unique by joining this mass chorus," a fad desire to be special and distinctive by joining styles of language, dress, and (mostly) *identity* until there's not a thing special or exceptional about it.

Identity 2.0 Fitting In and Standing Out

In funny photos of dogs being shamed with signs for their naughtiness—eating their own poop, ripping a whole room to shreds, secretly stealing their pack mate's food until found out by obesity— the charges range from antisocial, deranged, narcissistic . . . to abused, anxious, traumatized . . . but truly, none of these diagnoses are included in the identity of *canine*. In a pack, one stands out by surviving. One fits in by . . . surviving. The reward for standing out or fitting in: *surviving*. Is that what's going on in social media?[6]

Besides the number of people not only willing, but in a rush to post news about doctor visits, diagnoses, hospital stays, often with photos during the medical event—and we can only presume their motives circle various forms of sought-after attention, from sympathy to congratulations and more complex forms in between—I've also observed the following:

- Someone who spent several posts sharing a quest to be diagnosed with a learning disability. The person is an accomplished writer, PhD, professor . . . but seems to yearn to publicly attach some kind of diagnoses to that identity.

6. Cultural "research" on social media groups is problematic from the outset. One person may have a blend of family, extended family, old "school friends," colleagues from former employment, new friends from hobbies . . . in other words, a cross-section population. Whereas I've chosen to limit my social media "living room" to other writers, writing-program professors, editors, critics, and a slight outer circle of a few artists, photographers, and politically likeminded family. While I feel completely justified in deciding whom I invite into (and restrict from) my digital coffee klatches, observing cultural changes among this group might not be the best scientific method.

- *"I have been unwell for nearly twenty years, particularly lately, and I feel I have a responsibility and a need* [note this word] *to say why. Fifteen years ago I had a nervous breakdown, left my career, and was declared chronically disabled."* (Followed by 214 comments, well over 400 hearts/tears.) This one fell conveniently into my feed this morning so that I don't have to try to summarize/characterize all the frequent confessions-of-mental-illness posts.
- Posts that recount all the "unfair" challenges imposed on the posters' lives [= every life], such as elderly parents passing, illnesses and injuries, and all manner of financial or emotional fallout stemming from both individual adult decisions and grinding gears of recent history. Posts that have as their aim . . . *what* exactly? Sympathy, of course. Because to be challenged in these universal life passages now means . . . *what* exactly? Or is it just to count the five hundred other someones sending hearts and agreement . . . about *what* exactly? That the poster [= all of us] is therefore more deserving of achievement, success, or triumph?
- In a private email: *Three students failed the midterm and through tears told me the "reason"—anxiety and depression. "Anxiety and depression" have become the new "ADHD"—the former excuse for all bad performance, lack of responsibility, etc. But every time a student just doesn't do their work, it's because they are suffering from "anxiety and depression." Yesterday I said to all four of them, "Yes, I understand: anxiety and depression: we all have it. We're all on drugs for it. We still have to do our work."*

When I read this kind of sharing, I can't help but ponder my cousin's "episode" in his thirties, in the 1970s. The only specific I was privy to: that he'd piled all his belongings outside his house and was currently in a hospital.

But I remember the milieu of that week my aunt stayed with us in the 1970s; her face drawn and pale, so unlike her usual flamboyance, after her daily hospital visit to her son. The tacit worry she and my father must have shared based on their own sister having been committed permanently to a state mental hospital in the 1930s, when she was twelve, for bizarre behavior that blossomed into paranoid schizophrenia (and flash forward: culminated in her becoming comatose within a frozen snarled body for years before she died).[7] Her [probable] lobotomy and sterilization surgeries, and no one in the family was seeking Aristotle's mark of "superiority" for artists and intellects.

> Many . . . melancholics and neurasthenics of the past would be diagnosed as depressed today. . . . Sometime in the eighteenth century, doctors and philosophers stopped blaming exhaustion on the weakness of the individual and started blaming it on changes in society. . . . But . . . many . . . frame exhaustion as a mark of distinction. This idea dates back at least to Aristotle. "Why is it that all men who have become outstanding in philosophy, statesmanship, poetry or the arts are melancholic?" he wonders in *Problemata*.
>
> Small wonder that neurasthenia became such a topic of fascination, promising superiority to those who could detect it in themselves.
>
> —Hannah Rosefield, *New Republic*, July 2016

> In short, with the rise of the psychiatric profession, sadness, a perfectly normal quality of humans . . . came to be seen as a medical condition that needed cure and management by physicians.
>
> —Lenard J. Davis, *The End of Normal: Identity in a Biocultural Era* (2014)

Now (retired and caring for his mother), my cousin did "do his work." And what he did—milling custom doors, as well as his virtuosity at lathe turning wooden vases, as well as his love of fishing—became *his* identity, without a footnote of his diagnosis.

---

7. Compare, to our navel-gazing, our grandmother's response to her child's lifetime of hospitalization and loss of lucidity: "I'm thankful all my children turned out good except one." The reality of her world. That "one"—not a human life but a number—might not make it out of childhood, and that's a decent ratio. Did it cause Nana anxiety and depression? She never stopped visiting.

Identity 3.0 —ERs, —ORs, —ISTs, etc.

Writer, dog trainer, professor, gardener, novelist . . .

I once had a landlady who was a realtor. But it always amused/annoyed me when she would say *I'm a cabinet maker*, and *I'm an organic gardener*. She did those as hobbies. I don't think she even made cabinets for the crummy little house she was renting to me. Those are real professions requiring training, practice, knowledge, and I didn't think a hobbyist should usurp the identity.[8] Consider "photographer." We all have cameras; we even had cameras before smartphones. But we weren't "photographers" unless we strived for our own gallery exhibits or were hired by a newspaper or portrait studio or other professional venues that need images. How often at literary-event gatherings will a guest (with —ER, —OR, or —IST of "banker," "doctor," or "therapist") say to the author "I plan to write a book," or "*I'm* writing a book," or even "I'm a writer too"? Once I grumbled to a photographer, "Everybody's going to write a book 'in their spare time.' That's when I'm planning to do brain surgery," he said, "How d'you think it feels to have a Fotomat on every corner?" This "feeling" has, of course, mutated to vaster dimensions, as newspapers eliminate photographers in favor of reporters with smartphones . . . and the images included in this book have no bylines.

I was even uncomfortable referring to myself as "a writer" until after my first two books, collections of stories, and wouldn't use "novelist" until two of *those* were on a bookshelf. Perhaps it was more comforting for those words to remain in the future: "I'm becoming a writer. I plan to be a novelist." Well aware of the —ER and —IST I'd failed to earn: "secondary teachER" and "journalIST."

---

8. Even after over thirty-five years of training and showing my own dogs, I don't appropriate the "dog-trainer" identity. I say, "I train and show my dogs."

Identity 3.1 The Economics of Identity

> In the highly competitive race for ultimate victimhood, contempo-
> rary feminism is already fractured along lines of class, race, sexual
> orientation, disability and more. Everyone is shouting from their
> own ever-shrinking islands, so obsessed with the particular form
> of oppression they experience that they can't hear anything but the
> sound of their own voices.
>
> —Fionola Meredith, "Feminism Has Become Obsessed
> with Victimhood," *Irish Times*, March 8, 2018

> No, this is not my sisterhood. For me at least, breast cancer will
> never be a source of identity or pride.
>
> —Barbara Ehrenreich, "Welcome to
> Cancerland: A Mammogram Leads to a
> Cult of Pink Kitsch," *Harpers*, 2001

Even though I helped create a few anthologies, I do not merit the
identity of "editor." But back in the nineties, when I edited the two
Chick-Lit anthologies (whose titles predated the rise of books in
that subgenre), the introduction I wrote for the second of those
anthologies of "alternative" fiction by women suggested: "Perhaps with the growth of publicity-via-confessional, on talk shows,
tabloid news and other media . . . a prevailing type of theme anthology [has been] a victim theme." I noted that this trend was a
sales ploy: identify a group whose members could have personal
interest in the book's theme, and you've found potential buyers.
I argued that a publisher of nonmainstream fiction producing a
book of "alternative" writing should not follow a commercial mar-
keting gimmick; thus, in furtherance of the "alternative" nature of
the book, the anthology's theme would be "No Victims."

Another of my justifications for this theme had to do with what
constituted "drama" in fiction. I had become aware, by reading
four-hundred-plus submissions for a previous anthology, that an
übermajority of fiction by women used victimization for dramatic
action. I surface speculated (i.e., without research) that this trend
was not only borne of the attention celebrities were gaining with

confessions of abusive parents, drug addiction, etc., but that a troubled publishing industry was pushing writers to continue to use what was already proving to be successful. How about, I wrote, just for this book, instead of a fiction's drama beginning and developing because of something that—through fate or a fucked-up society—randomly happens *to* someone, let's consider "fiction by and about women where the movement or tension or intensity stems primarily from who the character is, what she wants, and what she decides or *does*."

My minimovement failed to attract attention to the swelling victim culture; instead, these anthologies actually incited another fad called "chick lit," taken from the anthologies' titles and co-opted into something even more commercial than victim fiction: urban-working-girls-looking-for-love-weight-loss-and-fashion fiction. And the victim culture I'd almost idly noticed with some frustration in the mid-1990s (and forgot with the onslaught of the chick-lit movement that stole the title and so drastically changed the mission) has now grown to such fanatical proportions it's like spoofy TV spy shows with the walls of a room gradually closing in to squish us.

Was the advent, or onslaught, of victim fiction overall a bad thing? No, having the formerly silent start to speak out could never be undesirable, even though the rise of the memoir soon overtook fiction's dwindling ability to tackle—with any real results—society's afflictions and injustices. At first, I thought victim fiction's negative impact was only in the limiting of possibilities for what could be considered dramatic action (i.e., a good plot) for women characters, continuing the representation of female lack of agency. But, as memoir took over and fiction has had to emulate it to stay relevant (or even alive), something else happened: victimhood became "status," victimhood became evidence that the writer was truly an artist, victimhood signaled attention worthiness for a writer's work. And, as well, the varieties of what people could claim as their victimhood *identity* increased (or splintered).

It's difficult to understand how or why a person would want an identity—the essence of who one is—based on an unintentional event, episode, or experience, congenital accident, or chromosomal outcome. We can call the perpetrator in a rape "a rapist," because the perpetrator has chosen to act; the act comes from what he or she chooses to do based on who he or she is or has become, so it *is* an identity. But does the casualty want a permanent identity based on being a victim? To always be known as "the raped"? (Or "the sick," "the abused," "the discriminated-against," etc.?) Those identities aren't what these people *do*, believe, strive for, achieve, or accomplish.

Identity 2.0 Reprise: Standing Out

> He has come of age in an era when nothing he could have done or said would have made him look more interesting than being attacked on the basis of his color and sexual orientation. . . . The role of victim as a form of status . . . It can also be handy, in a fashion quite unexpected to anyone who was on the front lines of race activism 50 years ago, as a road to stardom.
>
> —John McWhorter, "What the Jussie Smollett Story Reveals: It Shows a Peculiar Aspect of 21st-Century America: Victimhood Chic," *Atlantic*, February 20, 2019

My second memoir, *Something Wrong with Her*—seemingly titled for a victim identity[9]—revealed my lifetime sexual dysfunction, for which I honestly tried to find my own complicity, since there weren't societally recognized victim signposts to explain why I'd had no normal "sexualization," why I was a teenager and twentysomething terrified of sex and resisted despite knowing I was "supposed to like it." During postpublication interviews, someone brought up asexuality, which I had not considered or pondered while writing the book. Then an independent filmmaker selected the book to be the basis for a film project, one that would not "re-enact" the book, but be a sequel to the book. A *fictional* sequel to

---

9. Would I have used it if I could've? How far would I have gone? How far did I ever go? How far did any of my books' publicists go? What was gained? And what lost? A single anecdote can't answer everything.

a memoir. Naturally the "background" of the film's story would be the memoir (i.e., nonfiction), and that material was included through filmed monologues, sometimes in voice-over, but also docudrama-style: my talking head, half-shadowed, appearing in the film. The film's story was the fiction, with me as the actor (another —OR identity I would never claim). In that story, the "character" of me is introduced to asexuality in a fictionalized context. But it's part of the story, not all of it. The rest of the film was not a "learn to enjoy life by accepting my asexuality" story. The realities of making a (very) low-budget film required that most plot elements—committed to film before fully understanding what the real story was (a beneficial process afforded me in writing but not, I learned, in filmmaking)—would have to remain in the film and be "worked into" whatever story I was discovering. Simply, the story therefore didn't conform to a "my misunderstood identity and how I've come to embrace it" plot formula. The film's producer-director decided he would try to promote the film by sending it to leaders of a national asexual advocacy group, getting their endorsement, and thereby finding an identified group who would be interested in the film, would include it in blogs, would recommend it on group social media, etc. He told me it would help if I researched and joined groups of this sort and started contributing, and from there [self-]promote the film. I didn't exactly agree to do this. But I also didn't rail against it as a form of "I *am*, therefore I am also my art." Instead, I stalled. Stalled long enough for the leader of the asexual group to say that the film wasn't enough of a story about triumph against culture's lack of acknowledgment, lack of empathy, or whatever other lack one might feel the need to triumph against. I'd been released from a decision to participate in fraudulent self-promotion by an accurate criticism of the film's messy message.[10]

---

10. Do I not think people who are asexual would be happier if their identity were recognized, understood, and accepted? Yes, of course. Does culture make this difficult? You *bet*. These are places I wish I'd found my way to before committing to the first minute of film.

Identity 1.2 You Are Not Your Parents

Words that negate can be inaudible and invisible.

Naturally (= by *nature*) there's no "I am not normal" in canine "thoughts" (= sensory perception synapses), despite his damaging anxiety over guarding his resources (= food, toys, and bones). His *normal* is . . . his life. If he eats a hole in his leg, that's just what life is. If he has to be dressed in contrived clothing to let those spots heal . . . that also becomes his life; he can still hunt squirrels out the window. But if I say, "There's no squirrel!" he hears "there's" [= excitement; likewise "where's," to him the same word] and "squirrel" [= any small animal]. "It's not suppertime" only means "*suppertime!*" Dog commands need to be actions, not the absence of actions. A command for "don't run in the house" would be "down" or "settle," a different behavior, not the removal of one.

In 1988, Oldsmobile, facing a dire sales slide, changed its advertising slogan to "Not Your Father's Oldsmobile." Disaster. Perhaps the beginning of the end of Oldsmobile. We only heard "Your Father's Oldsmobile." David Kile in "Panic in Detroit" (1993), *Adweek*, explained: "The theme violated a basic tenet of [ad] writing by telling consumers what an Oldsmobile is not, without telling them what it [is]."

Lately, among Boomers and Gen X alike, the joke is "I'm becoming my parents." The meaning not a commendation but *I'm thinking and behaving in ways I used to disparage in them*. From assuming what we ate for dinner is news, to publicly sharing ailments and medications.

Our parents' character qualities, their actual identities, are (probably) not genetic. And even traits one might assume by osmosis may be minimized by our conscious attempts to avoid "becoming our parents." Whatever the reason, I am not (or can't be) *her*:

A joyful person, delighting in children, friends, family events, travel, food, games and athletics, camping, hiking, hunting, fishing, canning jams, crocheting bedspreads, bridge parties, watercolor classes . . . a typical, even cliché obituary. Somehow forgotten when obituary writing landed on my desk: that she hitchhiked with a girl buddy in the 1940s to go skiing, that she majored in phys ed at an all-female college in 1944 with no means of turning her education into a MRS degree, that she protested her college's policy of housing the two African American students separately. But, yes, her edge softened: She stopped protesting civil rights. She "studied" art, but it was night school for seniors. She wanted her watercolor landscapes to be realistic. Despite earning an English degree in middle age, her preferred reading was serial sagas and mysteries until comprehending just a page might take a half hour. Her TV watching—mostly *Who Wants to Be a Millionaire*—ended when she could no longer understand the questions. But she would not claim "brain damaged" as her identity. She would not refer to herself as a "stroke victim." It had happened by no act of her beliefs, interests, pursuits, or talents. Yet, contrary to my views about the range of dramatic action available to female characters *besides* victimhood, I was unable to contemplate much about her in writing because I couldn't find a conflict to shape a story. Until her stroke.[11]

On the other hand, *his* mother is a *real* bitch, one whose someday obituary will glow with her status as one of the highest-ranked national champions in her performance events. Without that cerebral cortex, he can't write a memoir searching for whoever victimized him into being unlikely to reach the bar set by his dam. But if he could understand, *would* I tell him . . . ? About his first owner, who had aspirations to shape his instinctive drive into an equally high-performing champion but who made monstrous mistakes, teaching him that the world wasn't as he assumed, even that he shouldn't have the dog identity he was born with. A burning e-collar told him proximity to humans—especially those who were cooing and encouraging him to visit them—was hot. Told him anyone approaching his crate lair was hot. Told him even his alpha partner (now me) reaching to touch him was hot. Nearly two years later, while his original golden-retriever joy in working

---

11. While I'm satisfied with "Tell Me," I'm not proud that she had to be a victim before I could plumb her life experience in narrative. Thankfully, I did move beyond victim status in future written expeditions into her identity beyond "Mom."

with a human partner is intact, while his devotion to me is fanatical, his innate desire to be approved of and fawned over by *other*
people is still a snarl of conflict. His response to the proximity of
unwanted attention, after a round of approach and retreat, is to
gather a stuffed "baby" in his forearms and "nurse," although it's
more a pulsating grind. Occasionally he might also leave a spat-
ter of urine in his wake. Then he moved on to licking and chewing
his skin on one foot until "pants" were required to facilitate heal-
ing of the repeatedly reopened wound. I may have increased his
stress when I began bringing him to training facilities where other
dogs or people might dare to look at him (or his toy or his food reward, the anguish of resource guarding combined with his fear).
His means of expressing this to me, besides continually reopen-
ing the raw meat on his leg, is to growl. Not at me. Sometimes,
when another dog or person enters his very large personal space,
his growl is something I can only feel while he's standing up against
me, front legs encircling my waist, pressing his face under my arm,
hiding his eyes.

> Compulsive disorders and displacement behaviors arise from sit-
> uations of either conflict or frustration. When an animal may be
> motivated to perform two or more behaviors that are in conflict
> with each other (e.g. approach-withdrawal, greeting but with fear
> of being punished) . . . In dogs, compulsive behaviors include acral
> lick dermatitis, flank sucking, pacing, circling, incessant or rhyth-
> mic barking, fly snapping or chasing unseen objects, excessive
> drinking, sucking, licking, or chewing on objects.
>
> —Debra Horwitz, DVM, DACVB, and
> Gary Landsberg, DVM, DACVB, VCA, Hospitals.com

I conceded my quest to prove that consistent fair treatment
would return him to a stable canine identity. His doctor prescribed
amitriptyline for canine OCD.

*Yes, I understand: anxiety and depression: we all have it. We're all
on drugs for it. We still have to do our work.*

Dark Money

2020–2021

In the months before the pandemic was declared official, a raccoon lost its life while devastating my car's cooling system in predawn beyond-rural Indiana. A week later Mark's car was totaled by an uninsured enormous SUV whose bumper aligned with his car's hatchback. Still January, our home furnace spewed carbon monoxide and had to be replaced. Cataclysms that come in threes. And not even counting the pandemic.

In May, our twenty-year-old Jeep Wrangler—used to tow our boats from the fishing cabin in the Upper Peninsula to the lakes where we fish, and despite having well under seventy thousand miles—was deemed "unsafe to drive" by the mechanic who always did the annual oil change.

A Jeep is built on a frame of steel pipes. Our Jeep had routinely traversed unpaved roads where mud splashed into the steel-pipe frame via ventilation holes. Strangely, these air holes were located higher than the lowest plane of the frame, so the moisture never drained. Instead, the steel rusted from the inside, and the mechanic warned us the Jeep could fall apart at any time. Repairing this damage might be more than the twenty-year-old Jeep was worth, so the mechanic offered to buy it for $2,000 (he also charged us for the oil change). The $2,000 went to ex-husband and fishing-cabin partner Jim, who had bought the Jeep in the first place. Mark and I saw it sitting in the mechanic's lot, in various different parking places, the rest of the summer, which evoked very real sensations of grief. Once, feeling some doubt (*denial*, the first stage of grief) that we'd made the right decision, we told the mechanic that if he didn't know what to do with the Jeep, we would buy it back (*bargaining*, the third stage of grief). He told us he didn't know whether he would sell its parts to other Jeep enthusiasts or fix it for his son to drive to college. We called this repair shop "the place that stole our Jeep."

So Mark and I faced the reality that we would have to enter the fraught used-vehicle market to replace our means of towing boats. Jeep Wranglers, despite the rusting-frame design flaw, had become so trendy that even used ones were now beyond our budget. So in January 2021 we began looking for a small pickup truck. Used-vehicle inventory was low and prices spiraling upward. We accepted the lack of wisdom in our timing. Still, we found a ten-year-old Nissan Frontier with under sixty thousand miles. The advertised price for the truck, what they call the "internet price," was $15,500 from a new-car dealer of a certain other brand. When we called about the truck, the dealer said it had just come in and wasn't ready to be displayed on the lot, but we could test-drive it. By the time we traveled the fifty miles to get there, the internet price was $16.5k.

After our test-drive, we went home to mull the decision, as the truck hadn't yet been cleared to sell. So we told the salesman we were interested and to call us when the truck was finished being prepared. He never called, but we did, several times, until finally a week later we were told that it was almost ready, but that the dealer had had other inquiries.

Still January, during one of Chicagoland's polar-vortex periods, and the height of a bad winter '21 COVID surge, we went back to the dealer on a (poorly chosen) Saturday. We call this "the dealership to be [not] named later."

The showroom was mobbed, and most of the young male salespeople were wearing their masks either below their noses or below their chins. Most of the customers wore no masks at all. As we waited for our salesman to be able to meet with us, we stood as far as possible from two maskless customers at a desk, a woman and a man who could have been her father, the man hacking a wet cough into his hands. Possibly because I'd backed myself into a corner, someone (perhaps the manager) asked if we needed help, and I blurted "Could you make them wear their masks?" gesturing to a knot of young salespersons with their faces exposed. The boss-person yelled, "Get your masks on."

One of the reasons we weren't yet seated at our salesman's desk was that we'd asked to go speak with the mechanic who we'd been told was, as we waited, working on the truck. We did get back into the garage to see it and speak to the mechanic. The truck was, as it had been at the first test-drive, dull with dust and spattered with winter slush. We asked for a list of what the mechanic was going to do and were told we could get that after the mechanic made his statement. It turns out that's not something car dealers do, but upon our insistence, they did give us an "audit copy" of a repair invoice that listed over $1,000 for oil change, rubber mats, wheel alignment, wiper blades, four tire sensors, and a "protective coating." Maybe this thin, partially cosmetic list would have cost $1k anywhere, but we noted how it did not include new hoses or belts.

I admit to being rattled beyond the usual for large purchases. It was the rampaging pandemic at its highest death rate; the mask-less people crowded into a small, hot showroom; the fact that I was normally insulated, always either at home or on a university campus that demanded mask wearing and vaccinations of everyone. I'm sure they smelled my agitation like a fishing lake chummed with dog food.

What followed next was a dance of interchangeable young men coming in and out as though the salesman's cubicle was a stage, and we, on one side of the desk, its audience. Was it choreographed? The thought didn't occur to me at the time. They came and went bearing personal stories of where they fished and their best-remembered fishing story; that they were waiting for a phone call from Arlington National Cemetery to see about getting a parent interred there; and that they had children (or cousins or siblings) who play drums (or guitar) in jazz combos. Yes, from waiting-for-the-sales-manager chitchat they already knew what we needed the truck for, and that Mark plays saxophone. But did they know my father was buried at Miramar National Cemetery? That algorithm is a step too far for even me to believe, even after the whole parade of young men was over, even after my stunned horror at what I'd allowed to happen, even after I rallied my forces (or previously benumbed faculties) and counterattacked.

Eventually one of the similar-looking young men with one of the similar-sounding job titles who told one of the swirling personal stories put an unlined sheet of printer paper in front of me. It contained a handwritten list with corresponding numbers. These, then, were going to be the "plus title, tax and doc fees" small print on every auto advertisement. I'd prepared enough to know that these might add 8 to 10 percent to the advertised price, but in shocking lack of preparedness actually thought "doc fees" were "dock fees," not "document fees." I clearly recall one of the handwritten items was "Gov't," and, pointing at it, the young man said, "This is what's required by the government." But I can't conjure the rest of the list, which ended at a new total, called the "out-the-door price," of over $21.5k. I was asked to sign at the bottom of the handwritten list, so, hot and gasping for air, I did, hoping it would all be over soon, thinking my budgeted amount of $20k had only missed by $1k, and maybe that was due to the tempestuous used-vehicle market.

The truck, when we picked it up the following Monday, was transformed to shiny liquid-black outside; the dashboard, controls, and interior doors with the sheen of Armor All; new floor mats bearing the dealer's name; and a pungent, sweet smell comparable, most closely, with grape jelly. I was almost proud that we'd maneuvered this transaction and come away with such a nice truck. Until I was telling the story to Jim—*this* story, but it turns out it was being told by a less experienced narrator—and heard myself giving the final price. And I stopped.

"*Wait a minute* . . . I think we got robbed."

"Calm down," Jim said, "they're a big-name dealership, they can't be outright cheating customers. Don't you have the sales receipt that explains all the parts of the final price?"

Yes, I did. But what I didn't have, in that manila envelope they'd handed me in the parking lot along with the keys, was that handwritten list of price add-ons that they'd had me sign. What *was* in the folder was a CARFAX Report (which I'd had to ask twice for), the mechanic's "audit copy," a state-required sales-tax transaction form, and the official "Illinois Buyer's Order." *That* document showed, on the top line, a "price of vehicle" of $19.5k. Below that, the only supplementary line items on the invoice were the "big three" of added fees: registration and license, sales tax, and dealer document fees. Those totaled around $2,000, and the bottom line was the same out-the-door price of $21.5k. So somehow the original "internet price" of $16.5k had risen by $3,000 even *before* the standard added costs of tax, license, and doc fees were added. Had I gotten the most expensive car wash and detailing in history?

Thus began an agonizing version of buyer's remorse, starring me as the doofus who got taken. Distress like that could be (a) accepted as daily torment, or (b) unsuccessfully combated with an equally distressing reaction like trying to cut enough out of our monthly expenses that I could recoup the amount I'd lost as a chump. But we'd already stopped going to movies, eating in restaurants, and I'd never been one to buy clothes; no weekly housekeeper, no yard service, so there was little to cut except future plans for minor home upgrades or even new fishing tackle.

Another method to assuage my torment was to attempt to tell myself my perception was wrong; a big-name dealer can't afford to engage in outright cheating. The damage to reputation would be worse than the money they'd eked out of me; and doing something illegal would not benefit them in any way. Just as I'd also tried convincing myself that a successful auto-repair facility wouldn't risk lying in order to steal a Jeep.

So I started to research. First, the Wrangler, it turns out, did have a documented problem with the steel frame rotting away. Someone (unnamed) on LegacyMechanics.com said, "A common problem with older Wranglers is frame rust. Even the best cared for Jeeps are still prone to rust, because of how difficult it can be to completely clean out the frame rails, and most rust issues start from the inside and work their way out." From CARFAX: "If the rusting process goes on too long, it can eat right through the metal, causing holes and allowing body panels to fall to pieces." So, with this last step in the stages of grief, *acceptance*, the Place-That-Stole-Our-Jeep was set aside.

Turning my angst back toward the dealer who sold us the truck, it was when I called the salesman to try to get a copy of that handwritten list of added costs that my agency found a higher gear. After I described to the salesman what I wanted, he said, "We never keep those worksheets."

"But you had me *sign* it. I would think I'd be given a copy of anything I signed."

"No, sorry."

So, finally, a few months late, I educated myself via the Illinois General Assembly Home Page on any laws that govern the sales of cars. "The maximum . . . base documentary fee beginning January 1, 2020, [is] $300, which shall be subject to an annual rate adjustment equal to the percentage of change in the Bureau of Labor Statistics Consumer Price Index." The current max had been adjusted to $303. On the same website, costs for the "Gov't" fees—title and registration—were $151 and $150 respectively. So the "title, registration and doc fees" had to max at around $600. The sales tax, provided on the state tax form st-556, was $1,431 based on a "sales price" of $19,738. All this added up to a rough $2k that *legally* would added to the "sales price." The mystery still remained: how that "sales price" climbed *$3,000* from the advertised $16.5k to $19.5k even before these legal $2,000 in added costs. Additionally, I'd paid a sales tax on the inflated sales price, not the original advertised price.

With this clarified information, I thought of going to a consumer help segment of a newscast or newspaper. Then I recalled I'd once reported an unfair bill from a pest company. Employees had been swarming through the neighborhood, well-dressed young people going door-to-door to "inform" all neighbors that carpenter ants had been discovered eating the frame of a nearby house, and that "your neighbors are signing up to eradicate them." I signed up.

The contract required I pay for service six times a year for two years. I began regretting this when I could not direct the technician to any particular problem, and I didn't want any pollinators killed. So when the technician showed up one day just after the two years were up, I said "I'm canceling this service," and sent him away. I received a bill for that last service and informed the company I had canceled my commitment. They said, No, you didn't; it wasn't in writing. So I sent this story, as condensed as I could, to the state attorney general's office of consumer complaint. Effect: the last pest-service bill was eliminated.

Now the consumer-complaint form is easily found online, although I chose to print and mail it because I wanted hard copies of my support documents—the internet ad with the $16,500 price, the "Illinois Buyer's Order" showing the "sales price" had jumped to $19,500, plus my extra page of explanation—to be spread out on a desk, not buried in attachments.

The complaint form did not tell me I had a word limit, but I knew the limitations of a person tasked with reading what thousands of consumers of varying degrees of writing experience would send, daily or weekly. I got down to 217 words, probably could have gone lower but my ire called me to stress that $3,000 overcharge.

Mailing these items to the state's consumer-complaint office in early February 2021, two weeks after the truck had taken residence on my driveway, allowed me to put the fury and humiliation of being conned into the background of daily consciousness. Way into the background by the second week of April, when the mailbox yielded an envelope with the car dealer's return address, and inside a check for the mystifying amount of $1,242.

Two months after that, an attorney from the consumer-complaint division emailed to ask me if she could close the case if the dealer sent me the amount contained in an email exchange with her that she was attaching. The attached email thread between the attorney and the dealer also contained a few interoffice communications between the dealer's management and its finance department: "Haven't we already handled this matter?" and "I can cut a check for $918.76 [another baffling amount] and mail it to the address in our records." I told the consumer-complaint attorney that if I received that additional amount, I would consider the case closed. Conjecture says that the first check came as a result of the attorney's first communication with the dealership, but since I hadn't been copied or received any instruction to notify the attorney that I'd received reimbursement, the attorney had contacted the dealer a second time. Thus my apparent silence on the matter caused them to open the checkbook again. The strange amounts, down to the penny . . . ? Curiouser and curiouser.

So the combined amount of refund neared $2,000. The outstanding $1,000 of the overcharge was almost exactly what the mechanic's "audit copy" had said his work would invoice for. That was a concrete and credible (even if overpriced) "dealer cost" I could have accepted in the first place, because it was tangibly proved.

What does remain mysterious, besides the peculiar dollar amounts of the checks—and despite the reality that this experience should actually be *no* enigma—is this: Who or what had they seen walking into their crowded petri-dish of a showroom? Not a college professor, not a novelist, but a five-foot female in her sixties, masked from chin to eyes so that only crow's-feet and gray hair showed, wearing a twenty-year-old winter parka whose zipper no longer worked, monstrous gloves reaching out from the pockets, clutching a folder of printed-from-the-internet used trucks for sale. When I voiced this to Mark, he wondered, "Then what the hell did they see walking in behind you? Your loyal Saint Bernard, who couldn't rescue a turtle trying to cross a quiet street?"

We call our truck "Dark Money."

The Summer of Letting Things Go

2018

Before I left for California, four months after Dad died, I stood beside the prairie garden I'd begun and nurtured beyond my backyard, out by the pond. With the "prairie" part of the name used only in aspiration. It was overwhelmed with black-eyed Susan and bee balm; the grasses were cultivators and not the natives that would have spread instead of staying in clumps. The daisies were large nonnative Shastas. There was not enough coneflower, and creeping Charlie had crowded out the false dragonhead. I would be gone during two of the wettest, fastest-growing weeks, too many Queen Anne's lace, wild aster, and goldenrod would choke the sundrops, and I would not be able to do battle with the invading Bermuda grass and ground ivy. I would have to let it go.

What I would be doing instead was helping to clear out my parents' home of fifty-five years—where I'd lived from age seven to twenty-four—and assisting in the work to prepare the property to be listed for sale. Another type of cultivation altogether, but a backward one. We were uncultivating a home, turning it back into a house.

Feeding Time

1965

The table was set with all seven dishes stacked at the head of the table where my father sat. Everyday stoneware for weekdays, china on Sundays. Hot pads—to protect the plastic tablecloth that protected the vinyl table covers that protected the wood surface—likewise were only in front of his place. When the serving dishes (very seldom a pot straight from the stove) were put on the table, we were all already seated, three on one side, two on the other, and Mom at the other end. Dad dished the food onto each plate, starting with the youngest. For any solid meat other than pork chops or chicken, he would have to carve it first, right there at the table, then he put portions onto each plate, one at a time. Even steak was sliced and doled out, followed by the vegetable (often exotic ones like eggplant, artichoke, or squash flowers), and potato or rice. He passed each plate to the nearest of us, who passed it along to its intended.

Usually he would say the name of whosever plate it was when he first passed it, even though it seemed to always go youngest to

author
eclipsed by
brother's head

oldest so that he could keep track of portions. It's not supposed to sound like a scene from Charles Dickens. We were allowed to talk, even ask for another serving. We also had our manners corrected; sometimes our opinions too. After the main course came salad, which he tossed—adding the oil and vinegar—and served the same way he had the meal. With both the main meal and the salad, but more the salad because it was always tossed, he had to be aware of which parts some of us would not eat, and decide if the battle was worth waging. He'd long stopped trying to get me to eat liver or fresh tomato. Dessert might be served in the kitchen (usually ice cream) and brought in by our mother. But a few times a year, we had a whole fresh coconut for dessert. My father asked the closest one of us to hold the coconut steady while he used a hand-crank wood drill to bore two holes through the shell, in the natural indentations that seemed made for this purpose. He poured the milk directly from the coconut into seven little dishes. Mysterious how he knew how much milk the coconut would hold, but it never ran dry before the seventh dish received its portion. Then, holding the coconut in one hand, he wielded a hammer to break the shell like an egg. From the two halves, he used a long knife to pry out jagged, irregular selections of white meat lined on one side with the brown casing of the shell. He put these pieces into the dishes with the milk and passed them around. Silverware had all been cleared from the table after the salad. We crunched the coconut and sipped the milk directly from the dishes. Then Dad pried additional pieces from the shell and offered them to whoever wanted more, reaching down the table with glistening white coconut meat speared on the end of his knife. We plucked chunks off the blade with our fingers.

Touched

1963

When my younger brothers were between two and five and my mother read to them, I was seven and still liked to get in on the stories. I don't recall if she ever read to just me, alone. There's reason for me to believe she didn't because there was always another interested listener: when I was two, three, or five, my older sisters were still part of a leaning clump of bodies on the sofa, trying to get close to the book in Mom's lap. But those memories are gone, even though I can remember most of the books she read over the years—including A. A. Milne's Winnie-the-Pooh books, Jean de Brunhoff's Babar the Elephant series, Rudyard Kipling's *Just-So Stories*, Charles Kingsley's *The Water Babies*, and more.

Yet I do have one *specific* memory of a particular story time. In this single particular memory, my two brothers were on one side of my mother and I was on the other side. Perhaps my youngest brother was directly on her lap. The pile of arms, legs, and shoulders was warm and soft, and I leaned in without reserve. After a few minutes, my mother's body—the bedrock of so much—shifted like a small earthquake, then her elbow pushed out toward me, moving me away while she said, "You're heavy, don't lean on me."

I kept this floating memory in an e-document folder of stray vignettes, images, scenes, and memory moments, using it more than once in this book, and in others before this. And this next much more recent memory segment was likewise one of the strays in the "future nonfiction" folder:

I was at a dog show. Indoors at a fairgrounds, it was the usual din and chaos and hours of waiting around for my ten minutes to be judged performing with my dog. Exhibitors routinely set up a camp chair beside a cloth dog crate, but most of us hardly ever sit in our chairs. Instead, we stand in clusters of two or three, watching a rival exhibitor or discussing results from previous shows, recent dog illnesses or injuries, and which of the longtime exhibitors we only know through these weekend rituals is now dead or dying.

In an unusual moment of repose, I glanced to the end of the row of empty chairs. A woman I knew had brought her eight-year-old daughter and husband, but of course the woman was off somewhere, gossiping and kibitzing. The little girl was not a particularly beautiful child. Cute, in a gangly, grubby, natural way: thin, stringy hair, knobby knees, one front tooth missing, the other a new too-large adult tooth. She was sitting on her father's lap, facing forward, leaning against his chest, her legs dangling down between his, looking down at a game she was playing on her mother's cell phone. One of the man's arms was around her. As I watched, he stroked her hair once, lifting his chin as though her hair had been tickling his face. Then, his eyes still on whatever he was watching in the dog-show ring in front of him, he leaned forward and kissed the back of her head. She was utterly absorbed in her game. Didn't respond in any way to his (familiar and expected) gesture.

The moment memorized, translated into language, stored, without bafflement as to why, only in what context it would reappear.

2014

In the year or two after the dog-show vignette was stored away, I visited the family homestead—my parents' house for over half a century. The story-time scene occurred there in one of the first years, between 1963 and '68. On this more contemporary visit, my father was ninety-four. His time in the gardens had been reduced by his ruined back, his cracked-then-healed pelvis; and since my mother no longer managed her daily communal tasks, he was doing the laundry and trying to prepare meals. The situation rose to crisis as soon as I arrived. Mom was sleeping on the sofa. Woke to greet me, but didn't want to get up, slumped into sleep again. She ate a few bites of a meal I prepared, but abruptly left the table to return to the sofa, then to her bed.

My father said, "Go help your mother." I don't believe he'd ever said this sentence to me during the sixteen years I lived in this house, when it was expected and routine that my sisters and I vacuumed, cleaned the kitchen after meals, cleaned our bathroom, and changed our beds on weekends, in addition to helping him weed, lug yard debris, paint, and mix cement.

I got pajamas from her bureau and assisted the shedding of clothing and then dressing in flannel, winter white with tiny crimson cardinals. It was March in California. I hadn't ever seen my mother's nude body. Helping her thread her arms into the pajama shirt, my fingers brushed her upper arm. Her skin was satiny soft. I remembered when I was seven—the approximate age of the story-time memory—a hole in her pillow revealed an astonishing piece of flesh-colored foam rubber, which to us looked like our mother's arm. We called it "the Mother." She must have hugged me with her arms, but I didn't remember ever reaching with my hand and touching her bare arm.

Mom sat up for the process of re-dressing, then immediately collapsed onto her side. She said she was dizzy. I straightened the rumples and twists in the pajamas. Then my hand remained on her back and stroked her slowly. I thought I heard her say, "Feels good."

The next morning we were back at the emergency room— her third trip in five days. This time they decided the congestion around her heart was enough to admit her. Those were two never-ending, taxing days, for all three of us. Four days later my two sisters and two brothers had arrived, nurses and a physical therapist had visited, two home-assistance companies came for interviews. In the evenings Mom had played a card game, watched a slide show, and worked on a jigsaw puzzle. She was bewildered by the blizzard of visitors and phone calls and our travel itineraries, but she could count the tricks in her hand of cards. She was apprehensive about the three-day-a-week home helper we'd engaged, and she was tired. So was I. I stood in the kitchen with my packed suitcase, waiting for my sister to take me to the airport, my mother sitting on one of the kitchen stools beside me. The tall stool put her shoulder just below my head. Somebody was talking. I'm not sure who. It wasn't me and wasn't my mother. I think my father was talking with my sister while she stirred a marinara sauce on the stove. "Tired" isn't the right word. "Spent." But I was leaving, going back to a different "real" life. My mother could not escape to some other life. I slouched a little, tipped my head and laid it on my mother's shoulder. I felt her shift. Slowly, she raised her arm and put her hand on the outside side of my face.

Plumbing

2005

Before falling asleep in high school and college, through my pillow I heard the constant drone of a small motor and the rolling rattle of stones in my father's rock tumbler in the basement below my bedroom. Pieces of rose quartz, speckled granite, obsidian, and brown agate tumbled together in water for weeks, maybe months, and came out as rounded and smooth as if they'd been polished by a Sierra creek for centuries.

Last month, in my parents' house, after falling exhausted into the same bed in the same bedroom, the same noise rumbled beneath me. It had been ten years since I'd slept there, twenty since I'd moved out. Was my father, at almost eighty-five years old, in the aftermath of my mother's heart-bypass surgery and subsequent stroke, still polishing stones in the basement in his rock tumbler? Later in the night, after my mother used the bathroom, the plumbing shrieked like an air-raid siren. Toward morning a different rattle and vibration kicked into motion somewhere beneath my bed. One of the eight-to-twelve automatic sprinkling systems, my father told me later in the kitchen, their controls lined up just inside the cellar door. The main water pipes aren't buried but exposed under the floorboards, in rafters of the basement, no secure earth to hold them still when the blast of water comes through, no layer of loam to muffle the whine of vibration. I didn't ask him to explain the phantom sound of the rock tumbler.

2014

It appears I wrote the previous segment almost ten years ago, as my father is now ninety-four. When I visit there's little time to write paragraph snippets of aural, visual, or olfactory sensations that evoke reveries of childhood or the young adulthood that stayed there too long.

Dad recovered from a cracked pelvis in his eighties, but over the next ten years his spine compressed, and he lost four inches of height. This puts him down to my level, five feet. He works in his garden an hour in the morning, maybe another hour in the evening, unless my mother has a doctor or hair appointment, or there's shopping needed, or house chores my mother used to do.

My mother has stopped going outside, driving, playing bridge with friends, doing laundry, cooking, or checking her email. All voluntarily. On the sofa most of the day, she plays solitaire or bridge on an iPad, and sleeps between rubbers. Dad calls the iPad "her game." But he tries to get her to get up from the sofa and do her indoor walking exercises with some kind of loud logic: "When you went to college, why did you major in athletics?"

She looks up, clearly mystified by his inquiry. "I liked it."

Dad stands at the dining-room picture window and looks at his gardens. What is he thinking?

Visits from me or my siblings still include evening card games at the dining table, during which my father will bring out a box or can of candy. A puzzle is always in process on the bridge table, for frequent time-outs during the day. Otherwise we siblings are cleaning out cupboards and closets (making trips to a donation center), doing laundry, and cooking meals. And we're trimming the trees Dad can no longer reach (he's not allowed on ladders) or weeding the garden beds Dad can't get finished in the time allotted to him by either his corroding body or the other responsibilities he's now taken on inside the house. We were well trained: Saturday mornings in elementary school and junior high, before we were free to play or roam to friends' houses, we were assigned a half day of work, either weeding in the yard with Dad or helping Mom vacuum, dust, and fold laundry.

In my old bedroom for a week, just before retiring, I opened a window and pinned aside the heavy curtain with a paper clip—to alleviate the eighty-degree thermostat setting. Then put the clicking clock into a drawer, took my diphenhydramine, or two, to ensure a dead eight hours. Because underneath me, the plumbing, the pipes, the timers, the furnace, they're keeping their itinerary. There are stones to smooth into pebbles.

Still Early

2010

In the same room where he called us to watch *The Wonderful World of Disney*, Perry Como Christmas specials, and men walking on the moon—my father sat in front of a purported news broadcast listening to his trusted familiar faces tell him that the new healthcare law would have death panels to decide when medical care should be withdrawn from elderly people, like him. Not many years later, my mother lay chronically asleep in a hospital bed in the big room at the end of the hall where we, as children, played, practiced our instruments, read, hammered typewritten diary entries, and dreamed. The scars where we taped posters to the wallpaper still remain. What's invisible are stretch marks from growing up in a family haven, like wolves raised in a natural-environment refuge, taught to group hunt, to share and protect, to live in the pack, but not how to evolve.

2014

The yearlong crumple into end-stage congestive heart failure cold stopped my mother's usual activity, extinguished any desire or impulse to try to make a meal or do laundry, to write a note card or check her email. She began sitting on a love seat all day, playing card games on an iPad and falling asleep. Every two or three weeks—without the energy to get out of bed, or suddenly laying her head on the dinner table to sleep, or falling on her way to the bathroom—there would be an ambulance trip to the ER. Occasionally she was admitted for a night or two in the hospital. Each discharge was supplemented with a pile of brochures and flyers, and one or two home visits from a nurse with a new thick loose-leaf notebook of after-hospitalization care information and records; charts to record daily weight and how much liquid to intake; and a new list of what medications were to be stopped, which doses changed, which new medicines started. All of which was undertaken, of course, by my father.

My torpid mother listened to the nurse, or seemed to, then went to the sofa to sleep over her iPad. We were confounded by Mom's inability or unwillingness (or inability to be willing) to do the seated exercises recommended by the physical therapist, the growing frequency of her soiling the bed or the sofa, the withdrawal from watching a ball game or going out to a buffet restaurant, or the longer and longer naps. Meanwhile the staples in the pantry were invaded by moths, the three-day-a-week cook/companion we engaged was fired by our father after two weeks for not putting tomatoes into beef stew, then the Meals on Wheels discontinued because the food was too processed and bland to encourage either of them to eat.

Three weeks into home-based hospice, on the last day of my last visit, Mom didn't want to wake up for her tiny breakfast. The day before, our cousins had arrived, and as each came to the bedside, her eyes gleamed, her smile flowered, she reached for hugs; she mouthed, occasionally whispered, "I know you." The next morning, utter fatigue. My sister played her violin. We sang Girl Scout songs. Mom didn't open her eyes. She moved a little, fussed when the care worker tried to rouse her for breakfast by stroking her face. I was the only one leaving that day, so my brother and his wife took my father out of the room "to give me my time" (but strangely still accompanied by my sister's violin, a milieu that had always engorged my sense of my comparable dullness). I sat on the bed near my mother's knees and stretched one leg alongside her body. She moved her arm over and placed a hand on my shin. I sat there listening to a folk-song melody, feeling the warmth of her hand. The last words she had previously spoken just to me had come the day before: in the morning before the visitors, when I told her she looked more awake today, she said, "It's early." I sat there wondering how those words might become significant.

For most of the past five decades, when a migraine or bout of vertigo put me into a ball of writhing nausea on the floor beside my toilet, my slurred moans of "why" and "oh please" still also included "*Mommy . . .*" Just this past year I've let that whimper mutate, only slightly, to *"Tommy . . ."* My dog. This has never been bewildering. I have never silently cried *"Dad"* (can't even fathom *"Daddy"*) in any private moment of wretchedness. This makes sense as well.

It seems an offspring identity is difficult to annul. I've watched, as docilely as reading a narrative, as my father shows me the moth traps he put into his pantry, makes schedules with the home-care company, calls the numbers in my mother's phone book to notify her old friends she is in hospice care . . . and never guessed his head might be spinning, his joints rusted, his kidneys gasping, his muscles half-starved.

As always, he pays the household bills and arranges for maintenance of the house where we (supposedly) grew up. (We're completing *that* process elsewhere, and in stages.) Overlapping with our juvenile and young-adulthood eras, over the course of his first forty years at the homestead, Dad used natural volcanic rock blasted out of the hillside to erect rock-wall terraces, filled them with soil, and there established his fruit and vegetable gardens, a place to raise rabbits, and another spot for the chicken coop. The livestock has been gone for over two decades, but up until this year he has maintained most of the seasonal terraced beds, the ones that aren't the permanent home of fruit trees. He had to let a few areas go fallow more recently, as the four hours a day he could work outside became reduced to three then two then barely one. But two years ago he was still grafting new trees onto hardier root trunks, a process that won't bear fruit for maybe another three years. He had time, as long as my mother was able to help make jam. That ended in 2012, according to the last jars still in my pantry in Illinois.

He was ninety-four, now five feet tall—down a full four inches. We stood eye to eye. A retired community-college physics professor who'd gotten almost thirty years out of his pension. Conservative talk media had recently taught him that anyone getting a public pension these days was draining the taxpayer.

What did he think about my two-course load as a Research 1 university professor? I never asked. Still too vivid in my memory: the time in the 1970s when my sister ran crying from the dinner table after she tried to defend Zero Population Growth. Instead, Dad and I talked about gardening and rainfall (but not about climate change).

When Dad was in his seventies, I learned that he hadn't been in the hospital since his stint in the military in the '40s when he was sick, so sick he thought he was going to die. He doesn't know or doesn't remember what the diagnosis was, but during my childhood and young adulthood, well into my middle age, he was never sick beyond colds, the flu, and hurting his back in the garden a time or two too many. He never complained, never milked his minor ailments, which could have been more significant than anyone suspected.

There were ways to not be completely insensitive to the fact that he was no longer forty and impervious, like the time he helped me to build a raised garden in his sixties. At the hardware store, he explained to the young male employee that he ordinarily would load the railroad timbers himself, but had hurt his back. In his seventies he stopped using a campsite in favor of a cabin in the Sierras, and hiked for the last time to the lakes at ten thousand feet. In his mideighties, while visiting my summerhouse in the Upper Peninsula, during long days of exploration by car and fishing in a canoe, my dad hardly ever had to use any of the outhouses my ex-husband was always searching for to relieve his own prostate-crowded bladder. In Dad's later eighties, a bout of his lifelong occasional nemesis vertigo toppled him from a ladder while picking persimmons, and he cracked his pelvis. *This is the end of the house and rock-terraced gardens and the tall fruit trees,* we all thought. But it wasn't. We siblings and our spouses—some of us only during visits from other states—began helping with the annual tree trimming, with fruit harvest, with weeding, pruning, soil cultivation, and construction of bird nets.

We worried about the upkeep of those terraced gardens, the areas of the property where junk had amassed, the fifty years of storage of "possibly useful items" hoarded in the basement. He had finally been able to relegate the lawn and hedge upkeep to a landscape service, but that's as far as he would trust them. There'd been a minor heart attack, pacemaker and stents inserted at some point after the cracked pelvis. We didn't really believe he was invincible, indomitable, immortal. But there must have been a latent conviction from childhood that our five-foot-four, 130-pound patriarch was interminable.

In my forties I tried to mark the end of childhood—and the last chapter in a memoir titled *Indigenous: Growing Up Californian*—with my mother's brain attack. The stroke, following open-heart surgery, damaged the language-processing part of her brain and launched the inevitable parent-child role reversal. That last chapter, "Tell Me," focused on her struggle to regain language but also exposed the part of our relationship that had never developed—mother-daughter confidences. At that point any opportunity to remedy the lack was gone forever.

A part of that story I didn't dwell on, for reasons I didn't want to examine, was the time I made my father cry. That's how he defined it afterward. Actually it was just an uncharacteristically raw moment. Soon after the stroke, I reached my father by phone, and my throat tightened, my words wobbled, my voice broke. Then my father sobbed.

While there have been circumstances, places, and situations in my life where crying was far too often my answer to my own drama, family circumstance was never one of those times. This lack was not consciously chosen, but observed after the fact, especially lately. Now looking back at that occasion with my father, I must have sealed the pact with myself. I must have been roiling: hot, ashamed, confused, horrified, guilt laden, displaced, sent into anguished orbit. The patriarch was supposed to be such strength and stability, hysterics weren't an option. I displayed enough of them with and for a list of other older men, supposed advisers, longed-for mentors, miscarried lovers. So, a tacit promise: not here, not again.

Over the ten to twelve months of my mother's final decline, Dad lost thirty pounds. His vertigo was a more frequent companion, so he'd voluntarily stopped driving farther away than the grocery store. Tinnitus began and became unyielding. He'd lost the use of one of his arms, likely during one of his attempts to help my mother up from a fall. His once camel-like bladder had started waking him two or three times at night, in addition to the times he was roused by my mother. He was relentlessly exhausted, probably malnourished.

He did not report any of this to me. He told me about the first night one of the care workers stayed over and my mother became frantic, wailing for the woman to go home, calling out for my father, but mostly erupting into long strings of *no-no-no-no, go away.* She could only be calmed when he got in bed with her and held her. About himself, he said nothing. And I didn't ask.

When the four paternal cousins visited, they noticed. The eldest, a registered dietitian and recently retired medical-facility food-service consultant, sat on the floor across the coffee table from me and said, "I needed to come say goodbye to your Mom, she meant a lot to me. But I'm worried we're going to lose your dad. I've called him for gardening advice all these years, but not lately. I haven't come to see him for a while, and now he's skin and bones."

I told my cousin about the home-visit cook and companion we'd scheduled six months before, a girl barely out of her teens who couldn't cook the way Dad liked. "Beef stew without tomatoes. He couldn't forgive it, let alone forget." Then the Meals on Wheels started, and who could blame him for stopping that after two weeks—packaged processed microwave meals and white-bread rolls? "We try to make extra frozen meals when we visit, put them in individual containers in the freezer. Most of them from the last visit are still in there with the last Meals on Wheels."

"I'm going to become your dad's personal chef," he said. "Who's the leader among you guys?"

I paused and set aside the obvious answer, *my dad.* "Leader?"

"Making decisions about your parents, how do you make decisions, is there one of you taking charge?"

"I don't think we work that way. We each do what we can that is helpful. You might have noticed we, or at least me . . . I'm a little . . . passive?"

"Ya think?"

2015

My father—during his ninety-fifth year of life, while his eighty-nine-year-old wife was in and out of the ER and under what seemed to be constant (if chaotic) medical supervision—thought the warnings from his favorite pundits had materialized: the death panel had met, and his HMO's protocol for caring for patients of *his* age was to stop all treatments and not interrupt "the dying process." His perception was compounded by a primary care physician in a vast HMO who seemed to behave in kind. I wonder if he had ever seen a popular bumper sticker in 2010: *Our healthcare system already has death panels. They're called insurance companies.*

My father's conclusion about his own healthcare in 2014 would not have given him new appreciation for the inherent wrong in making healthcare a for-profit business or financial gamble against longevity. His pattern is to refrain from personal complaint, and for over nine decades he had demonstrated what can only be called hearty resilience. Now it has been precisely his fortitude that took the hit. Repeatedly hearing from media spokespeople he respected that the depraved healthcare law was forcing his HMO to let him die, he might have simply decided his experience meant his favorite pundits were being proved right. He did not fight back; maybe didn't know he was allowed to or that someone might listen.

He might have thought his weight loss was routine, this level of muscle atrophy standard for his age, more frequent trips to the bathroom an inevitable progression, sleep deficiency something to be endured under the circumstances, likewise the screaming tinnitus. One thing he did mention was the pain in his incapacitated shoulder. His arm down to his elbow stayed fused to his ribs. Even eating was difficult, so how was he maintaining personal hygiene, not to mention preparing his meals or changing his clothes?

I didn't ask those specifics—only "Did you tell your doctor?"

"He says he can't do anything about it."

Those might not have been the doctor's exact words. Perhaps an evasion for a condition that can only be fixed with surgery. My father's translation generalized whatever the doctor had said into the death panel's decree. It never occurred to me, however, to say, "Let me call them; let's get you a different doctor." It never would have occurred to either of us that someone else should take over. It was no longer still early.

The day in late December 2014 when my siblings left me alone with Mom before my departure, she replaced the previous last thing she had said to me alone. She was neatly, freshly tucked in by her caregiver, who sat across the room making notes in a chart, trained to not be listening, or to appear not to be. Still, I was halfway on the bed, once again a leg stretched flat beside Mom's body, her hand on my ankle. I didn't speak first. Her skin was so silky; I must have been stroking her arm. Then she said, with faint voice and great effort to form words, the last she said to me, "Time for you to go . . . home."

The first five words were similar to what I'd heard suggested that *I* should convey to *her* at this moment. I told her I'd be back in December. And I was, a week after she died.

The Summer of Letting Things Go

2018

So many episodes or situations that could be, and at one time I thought would be, dramatized here: The long-distance debates on the most cost-effective yet classy way to raze and replace Mom's kitchen that had, for all its unstylishness, still managed to produce our holiday, wedding, birthday, reunion, and everyday meal rituals. Then the actual modernization rehab of Mom's kitchen for the real estate market just months after a plumbing calamity flooded it and three other rooms now under repair as well. (And no kitchen facilities for those of us gathered there for the household purging.) Five siblings with five separate piles of (and five separate priorities for) what we would keep from our parents' lifetime possessions that were being summarily jettisoned. The hundreds of photographs taken of our last views of Dad's amazing maze of hand-built rock-wall terraces turning his one-third acre into a family-sustaining minifarm, even though now the garden beds were fallow, cleared, arid and brown as the California landscape. Add a last (and predictable) skirmish based on festering sibling resentment. All of which should have been, could have been, part of the necessary *letting go*. But of what?

What does "letting go" even mean? Allowing rabbits to nest in the firepit even though it means protecting them from the dogs who share their yard? Allowing a neighbor to accuse me of teaching my dogs racism and challenge us to fights because I really don't know what life has felt like to him? Allowing a dying dog an overdose of barbiturate? Allowing the guidance of former mentors to be diminished by the reality of their fallibility? Allowing physical intimacy to dwindle because doing nothing is better than feeling nothing? Allowing the sound of a violin to reduce me to drab irrelevance because you're not the center of the universe to anyone but yourself? Allowing a parent to be aware she is dying? Allowing a tended garden to be overwhelmed with noxious weeds?

Once, when Mom was wistfully imagining living in a senior residence with bridge games and puzzles available in a sunny, social
great room, I said, "How could you stand turning this place over
to someone else?"

"It's time for another family to be raised here." She said it so easily, even through her language-impaired brain damage.

She never got her dream of a return to dorm living in the last
part of her life. She didn't leave home on her own terms, like the
rest of us did. Even Dad had made his own decision to leave, although the "terms" of not being able to care for himself weren't
what he would have chosen. Still, he didn't have to wake up to
broken plumbing pouring water into his house one December
morning.

Turns out that flood gave us the exigency needed to do this crucial work before pain of letting it go could paralyze us.

In dispensing with silly, childish questions, Mom used to give silly
answers. Was she trying to get us to think for ourselves? Was she
just too busy to give us nonessential information? Was she protecting us? It would seem, from my examples, a little of each:

#1. Bending forward over the Pontiac station-wagon bench seat:
"Mommy, what color is Dad's hair?"

Quick turn of head: "Blue."

After resuming usual position the back seat, whispered clarifica-
tion from one sibling to another: "It's so dark blue it looks black."

#2. Finding an object in a utensil drawer: "Mommy, what's
this?"

"A thing." Busy Mom passing through the room.

Enlightenment from one sibling to another: "That's a *real* thing.
Anything else called a thing is really something else."

#3. Looking out the picture windows to the valley below, where
surplus World War II military searchlights marked the locations
of car lot sales or shopping center hoopla: "Mommy, why are they
called searchlights? What are they searching for?"

"Lost children."

Looking again at the spotlights crisscrossing in the clouds. "How do they find lost children up in the sky?" Did I ask aloud? Did she answer? Nobody else was there to create an answer, not even an explanation I could give myself.

Perhaps searching for lost childhood.

It's not lost if you know where you left it.

Day of Reckoning

2022

An Ambition Is Born

He called me Barbra, that one time. He brought out one of his albums, *My Name Is Barbra*. Her childhood photo on the cover. How much did it resemble me at five? He thought it did.

I'm spending too long trying to figure out why this uncle thought I had *ever* resembled Barbra Streisand. Will I need to characterize him? A bachelor in his midthirties when I was five, elementary-school principal and independent-bookstore owner—wads of cash from the store register on the floor of his . . . Thunderbird? Danced boogie-woogie with our feet on his shoes and frequently sang Dean Martin's rendition of "Volaré," including Italian verses. Resembled Sammy Davis Jr. and preferred music of that era, including Sinatra, Tony Bennett, Perry Como, and, undoubtedly, Streisand's first popular albums.

My parents agreed with the choice in music: my first birthday-gifted album was *Barbra Streisand's Greatest Hits* in 1971 (the album was released in 1970, which surprises me). I had a lot to take in, having been primed to believe I once looked like her. Certainly not conventionally pretty; I thought her mesmerizing, exotic, outlandishly charismatic. The fact that instead of conforming, she had made herself even more offbeat, which contributed to her getting her first toehold: the talon-like fingernails so that she wouldn't have to learn to type, the Egyptian winged eyeliner, the beehive-pixie hairstyle with a side-parted curtain of bangs covering one eye. Yet I didn't spend teen years emulating these.

It was the lyrics.

I don't remember exactly when I acquired *Je M'appelle Barbra* and started listening to "I've Been Here," and its French Berlin Wall double. It was decidedly *not* when *Je M'apelle Barbra* was freshly released in 1966. After being birthday gifted the first *Greatest Hits* album in 1971, I started acquiring more Streisand albums whenever my teenaged budget could do so, not only those that came out later in the '70s, but the twelve albums from the '60s pictured on the back of *Greatest Hits*, one of them *Je M'apelle Barbra*.

The renowned French songwriter Charles Dumont wrote "Le Mur" for Edith Piaf, but she had rejected it. Then Streisand became interested. Dumont refused to let any French singers have it until Streisand made her decision (album notes from *Je M'appelle Barbra*, 1966). He did let a German singer record it in 1965.

"Le Mur," lyrics by Michel Vaucaire, was a song about the Berlin Wall, metaphorically described as "the color of boredom." Streisand recorded it in French on *Je M'appelle Barbra*. (Following the English-titled *My Name Is Barbra* and *My Name Is Barbra, Two*, sandwiched between *Color Me Barbra* and *Simply Streisand*. Repeated assertions of her name.) The building bolero style of "Le Mur"—no verse-verse-refrain, simply a grinding melodic build to a rallentando, crescendo finale—probably called out for an English version. But the same song sung in English at the end of the album's B side, was not a translation; it was not about a wall. Its new title was "I've Been Here." And with those words, it ended.

Streisand didn't write her lyrics. She didn't have to. Her you-can't-not-notice-me image was a conduit . . . but, no . . . Her instrument was a voice so perfect, so clear, so magnificently immense, an immature brain engorged itself with endorphins.

Could I have just as easily become stirred to motivation by Roslyn Kind? Born almost exactly five years before me, four off-Broadway credits, ten television guest spots, small roles in four films, four (now-unfindable) solo albums . . . She was determined, dogged . . . I guess. I don't really know. She is Streisand's half sister. Attempting to build a career in the same or similar world, to be assessed and appreciated without comparison, having headlines about her performances like "Streisand's Sister Has 'Come to Terms' with Superstar's Shadow." It could have been *my* ambition's mantra. But I didn't want to be Streisand's sister. I wanted to be Streisand. For the world to know I'd been here.

A Mistake Is Born

> There's . . . more to maleness and femaleness than X or Y chromosomes. About one in 20,000 men has no Y chromosome, instead having two Xs.
> For these 15,000 or more individuals in the U.S. . . . , their chromosomes are irrelevant. It is the total complement of their genes along with their life experiences (physical, mental, social) that makes them who they are.
>
> —Intersex Society of North America website

The adrenaline of certain songs wasn't the only factor in the particular tone of my aspiration. It certainly fed off something the opposite of uplifting, something that had been festering, largely unnoticed, for years. Mom's repeated mistake.

Mom can't be blamed for the "error" of only supplying an X chromosome. Although chromosomes aren't the be-all of gender, and likely no biological "error" happened at my conception, I'm confident that for at least a moment, maybe more, my father bemoaned this turn of events as at least a disappointment, if not a cruel blooper, for a man who already had two daughters. And at the time of my birth, no one knew that one of those two older daughters was endowed with a concoction of brilliance. Of personality, of energy, of intellect, of talent.

Mom also cannot be blamed for her maternal pride, nor for the series of "mistakes" it allowed to happen. Nor can I claim that my feelings should have been enough for her to end the practice of gathering extended family to listen to my gifted sister play her violin. Besides the memories of sitting there feeling like a lump of nothing—a dull, talentless, ugly nobody—while she performed, it started to seem that almost everything about me, from quirks and personality traits to goals and dreams, was compared to my sister (and not only by Mom) in a way where I was the diluted, less interesting version.

> Research shows that the impact of a child's *perception* [emphasis added] of differential treatment is greater than the impact of the love and attention she receives directly from her mother.
>
> —Peg Streep, "Unloved Daughters and Their Siblings: Five Common Patterns," *Psychology Today* online, June 10, 2015

By this time my father had gotten his sons—two of them, younger than me. I don't know how these family concerts affected them (perhaps they were too young, or not expected to sit still indoors for the music). I don't know if it affected my eldest sister. Years later, as an adult, she had feelings of being irrelevant and swept aside by the same uncle who'd called me Barbra. I can only make claims about how *I* felt, and the possible lifelong results: difficulty being a truly supportive friend to other writers, perceptions of being valued less than colleagues, and (the opposite of the leading adult symptom of "unfavored" children) ambition to be renowned in my field.

> The middle child is . . . subject to constant comparisons. This child's individual uniqueness is often undervalued. In essence, they are never enough and are made to feel that they are always lacking something.[Likewise] unfavored children are . . . often viewed as the "lesser" child while the other child is viewed as the more intelligent, athletic, agreeable, etc. . . . In addition to feeling insufficient, they are made to feel as if they have no identity.
>
> —Grace Marguerite Williams, "How to Understand the Unfavored Child in the Family," Owlcation, July 19, 2018

> Unfavored children are more likely to exhibit . . . inappropriate social behavior that makes it difficult for them to make friends. . . .

Giving and receiving love requires vulnerability, and children who grew up unfavored often develop defenses against true vulnerability.

—Sarah Cocchimiglio, BetterHelp, November 19, 2021, medically reviewed by April Brewer, DBH, LPC

The nature of the human brain is to look for evidence that supports what we already believe. But I didn't start any of this thinking and searching until almost two years ago, listening to a call-in advice show as entertainment during my hour-long commute. The host is a licensed marriage, family, and child counselor. She stresses character, responsibility, accountability. Answers are often general because, more than guiding one person with a dilemma, she is helping a thousand others recognize something in their own life or behavior. For example: *You have a crocodile in your house. Why are you hoping it'll turn into a puppy?* But every once in a while, she seemingly abruptly changes the subject and asks, "What was life like in your house when you were eight?"

That day, the jump-to-childhood call went something like this (recreated):

Caller: I have a really hard time being happy for my friends when they have successes or good news.
Therapist: Can you give me an example?
Caller: One of my friends got a promotion, it's not even in the same field as mine, but I felt punched in the stomach. I'm sure she could tell my reaction was . . . weird. I know I wanted to get away as quickly as possible.

It could have been at this point the therapist made her sudden request for details on "life when you were eight."

Most people have trouble with this question, phrased so as not to be leading. Usually they give answers like *My parents were divorced*; or *A big, close family, lots of aunts, uncles, and cousins*; or *My dad traveled for work, so we didn't see him much.* So the moderator did have to help and specifically asked the caller about siblings. Yes, there were siblings. The moderator helped again: Were any of them very accomplished and maybe frequently praised for it?

Yes, my sister . . . And of course the caller's details flew out my car window. I had my own details, whether factual, only in my own perception, or (in actuality) a combination. I'd heard what I needed to hear. It has settled, cold and unwieldly, in my guts for a while now.

People

> *Around people I don't know, I'm totally at a loss.*
> —Barbra Streisand

The lyrics for "People" always left me cold. "People who need people . . . are the luckiest people in the world." What was *that* about, anyway? So it's not my quest for serenity but that I'm *unlucky* that I want to live in the woods with my closest neighbor no nearer than a mile? "Nobody, no no-*body* . . . is gonna rain . . . on my parade." Except a parade isn't solo, and there wasn't a Streisand song that extolled isolation (except in irony, as in "Free Again" or "Lullaby for Myself").

But I did need my mother, and I wasn't necessarily deprived of her. I wasn't left out of family card games, archery, or croquette, singing around a campfire, hiking the John Muir Trail. Mom was my Girl Scout leader in junior high. She taught us to make fire starters from cardboard egg cartons with sawdust and paraffin, how to build a fire, to cook over a fire, to bank a fire, to put a fire out. I also joined her life passion of swimming lessons and earning Red Cross swimming badges—Mom was a Water Safety Instructor (WSI)—but I was the first of her daughters to only make it as far as *junior* lifesaver. I tried out for and didn't make the high-school swim team that both my sisters helped originate. At Scout camp one year, where Mom was the swimming counselor, I lined up with my peers for a race across the short side of the pool, sure my heritage would lead me to win; belly flopped into the water and churned my limbs in the splashing and backwash of the other kids, most of whom outweighed me; and got to the other side among the last. It was as though our parents' genes were getting diluted as she had more female children (the two boys had different pursuits and successes for earning parental pride).

I also needed my siblings, and maybe especially my gifted sister. Although only two and a half years older, she was four grades ahead of me due to starting early, then skipping a grade. So it was possible for her to play with me through her eighth grade (until she started high school at twelve years old). Sure, we fought, but we also laughed (she apparently laughed harder, sometimes until she threw up). She had the real Barbie and Ken; I had Barbie's red-haired best friend (and her red-haired boyfriend). I accepted my sister's handed-down clothes eagerly because they must be better than what I already had, until I became taller than her, in which case I felt ungainly, clunky, a monster at five feet, compared with her. Even my flaws and ticks were chalked up to just copying my sister: thumb-sucking, lisping, nail biting.

More than once a teacher would recognize my last name and express her expectation at how well I would do. "You'll be a good reader," one proclaimed. Then in order to stay in the top "reading group," I had to cheat on my self-guided SRA reading tests. How could I *not* read well?

> SRA Reading Laboratory worked by color-coding reading materials according to the reading ability level required. It emphasizes the role of the student in directing his own learning, assessing his own skills as he works his way up through the levels. The age range runs from kindergarten age through to grade 12 and beyond.
>
> —Don H. Parker, inventor of SRA,
> *Reading Laboratories 1C Kit*

> Where you started depended on your past work and your teacher's heuristic assessment of your abilities.
>
> —"11 Tiers of Frustration: What the SRA Reading Levels
> Really Meant," Medium.com/omigods, May 21, 2019

My sister had taught me by reading to me, then handing me the book, and I looked at the words that represented the story I clearly remembered. I was pretending to read. I became a slow reader with trouble getting my eyes to go all the way, left to right, across a line, and some dyslexia thrown in. One elementary year I fell behind in everything, not even realizing there were assignments to complete and someone was keeping track. Instead I spent considerable time sweeping the classroom with one of those big T-shaped dry mops. I was revealed, and was in turn astonished at Mom's utter astonishment.

I began piano lessons at eight and quit at ten when my sister, on her own without lessons, became better than me. Then I started playing cello because my sister played violin; I auditioned for the youth orchestra because she was first violin there. I only made the "training youth orchestra." After my audition, the director, who knew damn well who my sister was, said, "Well, you're not much of a cello player." I begged my sister to audition for a local summer-program production of *Fiddler on the Roof* where *she* could play the haunting violin solo, even though I had zero chance of making that pit orchestra myself on either the cello or my new instrument, trombone. But at least I would be associated with a star.

In high school, after abandoning careers of chicken farmer and then archeologist, when I told Mom that I wanted to be a writer, she simply blurted the first thought that came to her mind: "Oh, [Sister] was always a good writer!" (Flash forward: When this sister told me she'd written a poem that she'd considered reading at our dad's funeral, my heart seized, my brain froze and broke in pieces around my feet. To her credit, she didn't read it, so neither of us had to find out how badly I might have reacted if she had.)

Probably the most telling incident is one that does have photo proof, and yet no one saw the tacit cry for ... (*What did I want?*) Maybe the story can convey that I either didn't have what it takes or didn't know how to be a good student. Maybe due to my not learning to read the best way; maybe my pitiful teen torment got the largest portion of my focus and energy; maybe because my growing-busier parents hadn't ever directed me (after guiding their two eldest children) on how to sit and do homework (or that activity called "studying"); or because it was hopeless to even try to measure up to my skipped-a-grade sister's aptitude. My grades were enough to graduate, enough for the public university we three girls were given as our only choice, not nearly good enough for any kind of scholarship (the only way to have another choice). And, although my "essay" on the identity of the high school won a contest to be printed in my senior-year yearbook, I was not in the school's top fifty GPAs in a class of five hundred. I might have been in the next ten or twenty. Somehow close enough that I took my sister's thick yellow cord from when she, at sixteen, had graduated the year prior with honor-roll distinction, and I wore it to graduation. Despite my sister not knowing, and neither my parents nor anyone else noticing, there is perhaps no other single instance that illustrates the complex relationship my ego has had with her.

> Xuan Zhao, a research scientist at Stanford University's SPARQ (Social Psychological Answers to Real-World Questions), . . . [said,] "According to self-verification theory, it feels nice to be seen and be appreciated for who you are, especially when other people see you the way you want to be seen." She [added] that in terms of interpersonal relationships, we have a fundamental need for relatedness: "Signs of others' positive regard, appreciation, or warmth . . . create strong positive emotions, just as satisfying as other biological needs." And it feels especially nice when the compliment comes from a relationship that is important or meaningful to you.
>
> —Ieva Gailiūtė and Mantas Kačerauskas,
> "Rare Compliments," Bored Panda, January 10, 2022

Did I do nothing as well as my siblings? I did triumph at the junior-high science fair, doing experiments on honeybee color preferences using my father's hives. I'm not sure which of my family members were there the night of the fair. Would my sisters have left their homework and practicing on a weeknight? Would my parents want my younger brothers darting around a buzzing auditorium? Wouldn't my dad, a college physics professor, have given up *Gunsmoke* or *Hawaii Five-O* for junior-high *science*?

My father was an enigma for us all, his approval elusive and tenuous. He didn't pay much attention to what I did, tacitly accepted the assistance that was required of me when he slaughtered and dressed the rabbits we raised for meat. He went to the high-school guidance counselor to make sure my eldest sister was placed into chemistry, not home economics, but his only comment on my courses was to threaten to take me out of band if my grades (mostly Bs, some Cs) didn't improve; and he once tried to talk to (but actually yelled at) me for "separating myself from the family." By then, at high school I was the trombone section leader; at home, musical instrument practicing was reserved for the violin. I typed. And more than once someone would call down the hall, "Stop typing!"

> *My mother told me I should be a secretary. [She] never really thought I could become anything.*
> —Barbra Streisand

Yet it's impossible to say that family homelife wasn't sheltered, nonthreatening, reliable, rich, warm, and fun enough to be nostalgic about; not as much as some families, way more than others. But hard as I try, nothing, so far, alleviates the memory of those extended-family violin concerts, or the comparisons where I wasn't the one who prevailed. All innocently perpetrated, without malice, but I invented neither the fact that they happened, nor my perception of what the sum said about me. Nor have I imagined the all-too-real result in my personal and professional relationships to this day.

Stony End

Wasn't I born from love? I know my parents were crazy about each other. I also know they wanted a boy. The pre-conception climax for them must have been like millennial fireworks. But time didn't stop there. And this isn't the end.

Today, I needed to talk to a comrade, a peer, a friend, and had no resources. The few on my list have demanding jobs (one will require a name, "Diane"). Plus no one wants to entertain a devolvement into throat-choked whimpering. And the event—not a tidal wave, more like dribbles from a leaky ceiling—that led me to this state: a student dropping my graduate workshop, then signing up for a different workshop. First response, always: people don't like me. A boomerang problem; I need to talk to someone about my underlying fear that people don't like me; I don't have a friend available to talk to . . . because people don't like me? Because I don't have the tools to be a friend? Because I have developed "defenses against true vulnerability" and therefore have "exhibited inappropriate social behavior that makes it difficult to make friends"?

What do I need to say about *defenses against vulnerability* and *inappropriate social behavior*? Give examples? Like never saying "How are you?" when meeting other faculty in a social situation? (Diane called me out for that one over thirty years ago. Which helped put a two-decade pause on one of the very few true friendships I have now; besides the humiliation, I thought she must not like me enough to stay in touch.) Like responding to a friend's (again Diane's) major life choice with incredulity instead of support because it wouldn't have suited *my* life trajectory? (Remarkable, and to *her* credit, that we are so close now.)

Like starting a writers group and engaging in a prolonged argument with a member who thought people with poor moral standards could not be successful characters? Like accepting invitations to readings or book-launch parties and then finding excuses to not go? Like sending an editor who'd taken a serious interest in my work a two-page single-spaced letter that must have contained persecution-complex scenarios and/or anxiety-laced fears of rejection/failure (so that years later this editor asked my agent if I was "dangerous")? Like sending an email to two other NEA grant recipients (who had contacted me to form a discussion group) that I thought was jovial and friendly but must have contained something lamentable because I never heard from either of them again? Like being relieved my mother-in-law was in the hospital at the same time as a big writing conference so that I could use her as an excuse to not attend? Like when I did go to the conference other years, but attended zero events or readings? Like telling a friend you haven't read her new book yet because it too clearly reminds you that you're writing outside the topic boundaries that larger publishers have decided are what's worthy? Like, therefore (perhaps rightfully), not having any close friendships at my university English department job?—all but one or two no more than an acquaintance? Like being able to count on one hand the former PhD students who have kept in (meaningful) touch? Like seeing that many people keep good friendships with those they knew in college, even high school, but I haven't done so? Like the paranoid conclusion from many different bits of "data" (including, like an apprehensive sixteen-year-old, being stricken at how so many people never acknowledge my comments on their social media posts) that, in general, most people just don't like me?

> "More times than not, [envy is] a reflection on ourselves . . . ," Vernessa Roberts, Psy.D., L.M.F.T explains. "It could be reflecting what we're feeling about ourselves at the time, where we think we are in life, and where we think we should be."
>
> —Patia Braithwaite, "If Envy and Jealousy Are Impacting Your Friendships," *Self*, November 13, 2020

One conclusion, besides the negative rating as viable friend, that could be examined is a certain degree of paranoia. Still, I've had trouble applying that to many of my (unreliable?) examples:

With multiple colleagues with whom I thought friendship could grow, one or more of the following would happen: We'd get together once, then, unless I reentered the campaign of trying to make another date, I never heard from them again. Usually after I did restart the scheduling drill, after they were not able to find a date for getting together (more than once they forgot to even check a calendar and answer me), I decided to stop trying and just wait until it was their idea, which it never was. [Conclusion: the spouse really didn't like me.]

A PhD student whom I'd chosen to present in our student-plus-guest-writer reading series, quietly removed me from her dissertation committee and then defended without so much as a polite notification. An email to her asking if I inadvertently said anything that caused this went unanswered. [Conclusion: she and/ or her dissertation director didn't like me or thought my participation a negative sum.]

At another PhD student's Zoom oral exam—with a committee of five professors, three in literary studies, two novelists, all who know one another—during a discussion thread having to do with current novels and the presumptions made by readers about the novelist's private life, one of the professors, in introducing his take, began by side addressing *one* of the novelists present: "You would know how this happens, Lew . . ." The "other" novelist on the committee was not acknowledged. [Conclusion: as a novelist, I am (have now become) invisible, even to my colleagues.]

How much does decades-past history *cause* me to perceive that many to most social or professional encounters exist on a spectrum from ignoring me to disliking me, with a lot of disrespect in between? And even if perception is (proved) wrong, the initial emotional (brain chemical) reaction *was* actual. And sometimes the resultant behavior is all too real as well.

The weekend after the fearful (and, turns out, incorrect) presumption about why a student dropped my course, which led to an interior catalog of many similar assumptions, awakening me (yet again) to my dearth of friendship, I lost (another) day to a crippling headache. Then I found in my newsfeed a suggestion that some troubling emotional and physical symptoms and behavior might be the result of repressed anger.

Anger . . . ? Is that what was behind the persistent Gatling-gun sound of the typewriter in my teenaged and early twenties bedroom? A bundle of frustration and rage?

Specific symptoms from this list (see next page) not already admitted into evidence:

- Ten days after the last headache, including ten days of not writing a word in this narrative, another headache, another useless day.
- Remaining the epitome of dogged practicality as we cleaned out our parents' house, never crying once, changing the subject if need be, which provoked the more emotive, ardent (and talented) sibling.
- Never once sitting beside my garden to contemplate the sensuality of flowers, herbs, and vegetables; always weeding, pruning, hand watering, inspecting for pests.
- It didn't take a pandemic to get me to avoid literary galas, but certainly gave me an excuse to forgo any struggle to make an attempt.

- Like slamming things when I knock part of my body against
something or bump my head; sudden ire over having to repeat
myself; burying the head of a hammer in the ground over and
over if I miss the stake I'm pounding?

The impact of repressed anger can include the following [note:
strike-throughs are those I can't assign to myself]:

- Psychosomatic symptoms and physical ailments such as
headaches, chronic cough and digestive issues
- Emotional numbness
- ~~Lethargy~~
- dysthymia: a mood condition indicated by low-grade de-
pression and/or irritability often accompanied by sleep
disruptions, fatigue, and poor self-esteem
- Lack of motivation, ~~chronic procrastination~~
- ~~Urges to hurt oneself~~
- ~~The inability to stand up for oneself, and thus let others take advantage . . .~~
- ~~Having unreasonably high and unrelenting standards~~
- Having a harsh inner critic
- Inability to relax or have pleasure in life
- Confused sense of self & identity
- Being ~~abused~~ or used by others due to inability to assert
boundaries
- ~~Co-dependency~~
- Paranoia and ~~intense~~ anxiety
- The tendency to judge others
- Alienation and social isolation
- Self-sabotaging behaviors
- Sudden outbursts that surprise others
- Lack of satisfaction in relationships and friendships
- Broken relationships, affairs, & divorce

Imi Lo, "What Repressed Anger Looks Like," *Psychology Today*, January 11, 2022

What? Me, (still) angry?

Angry at being assigned female in a world made for men. Angry that they started to let girls play Little League Baseball many years too late for me. Angry at being ugly in a society that rewards (females) for beauty. Angry at being neurotypical in a culture that has grown to venerate bipolarism and ADHD. Angry at being asexual and anorgasmic in a sexualized era. Angry that at one time I bought into my worth as a writer being connected to my sexual attractiveness. Angry for apparently not working hard enough, for not having the "right" things to write about, for scaring away the best support I ever had from corporate publishing. Angry at one of my first publishers, whose mission included never letting books go out of print, but who let my books go out of print. Angry at my workplace in academia that bafflingly joins the rest of the mainstream culture in rewarding authors who make more money with perks, honors, and basic acknowledgment. Angry at being never as special, as funny, as smart, as spirited, as talented, as visible . . . as a sibling . . . to whom the anger cannot be directed, nor at the parents.

Who else is there?

Stony End

Not yet.

> There's a part of you that always remains a child, no matter how mature you get, how sophisticated or weary.
>
> —Barbra Streisand

Back to Barbra

Streisand might also have reasons to be angry. That she was never nominated for best director even when one of her films was nominated for best picture? That she was deemed *difficult* while men are *discerning perfectionists*; *aggressive* when men are *committed*; *vain* (to direct as well as act) when men are *multifaceted* and *multitalented*. Her interview doesn't mention women being *pushy* and *selfish* when men are *ambitious*. (That was Reese Witherspoon.)

Had I been saved from the worst of this by my chosen androgynous name? Or had I ever faced a similar double standard for my own difficult ambition? And, really, what was the *difficulty* of it? That it never achieved what I hoped? What I wanted? Or what I *needed*? That not achieving those levels came with such perceived invisibility and/or disregard? Am I going in circles? Am I finished here?

Spurred out of stasis by another call to the radio therapist that takes an uncanny jump to childhood:

Caller is a sixty-eight-year-old woman who recognizes that all her adult life she has been seeking to get approval from others and assuming she never gets it. "What does seeking or trying to gain approval look like?" the therapist asks.

"I think I try to be how they want me to be." (Or how she assumes they want her to be, therapist points out.)

This is where the therapist makes her gearshift: "So which of your parents didn't approve of you?" [This caller is sixty-eight years old!]

Barely a hesitation. "My mom." Voice throttled. [This woman is sixty-eight years old!]

The maternal disapproval she detailed (without any strain to recall) was borderline abuse, and not anything I ever experienced. The reverberations were: a sixty-eight-year-old woman . . . dogged by disapproval from sixty years ago.

The therapist said (something she has said to many others), "You're hanging on to old hurts from forty, fifty, sixty years ago; it's become part of who you are. You say 'I want to get past this,' but you actually don't because if you ever did, life would change in really uncomfortable ways. You wouldn't know what to do without it to define you."

Not an immediate parallel. While the lack of approval from my father—which I think was equally distributed among his offspring, although with differing levels of his (dis)interest—should never be disregarded, for now it's only a bedrock underneath the *can't-compare-to-exceptional-sibling* form of lack of approval I perceived. The substratum of my fractious ambition.

The radio is still on; someone else is calling. Parents who dislike their son-in-law; they list his negative characteristics and traits . . . This couldn't have anything to do with me, until . . .

Therapist's response: "Your daughter *picked* him. Ask yourself why. You've known your daughter for twenty-five years; what lack does he fill for her? What problem was *he* the answer for? Girls often pick a man to marry because he answers something they need. Family dynamics mean a lot to how a girl chooses a guy."

The man I "picked" when I was twenty-four was a member of the same orchestra where my sister had started her professional career as a musician. But he was one step "better"—not a member of a multivoiced "chorus" like the violins, but a brass player, a soloist on his parts. What lack did he answer for me? An easier question for me than it would have been for my parents: I became "attached"—like atoms that bond to form a particular molecule—to someone seemingly of equal or higher performable talent than my sister.

Thirty-five years later, two husbands down, I tried to arrange for Mark to play that role too; begged him to bring his clarinet (his saxophone was too large) for family Christmas carol concerts, plus had him improvise, show off his special jazz chops . . . only to discover that my sister could improvise on her violin as well. When Mark told me he didn't like doing this—his clarinet playing was rusty, he felt like he was horning in (that is, *intruding*; the *horn* pun not intended)—I realized what I was doing and stopped asking him.

Stony End

We're still not there yet. Maybe we should be. But we're not.

The Way I Was (My Name Is Cris)

I started changing my name in college. For the first time, I had my own room, and was no longer sharing bedroom and bathroom with hours of violin practicing. The violin and its master were three thousand miles away at grad school. The incessant typing coming from my room was at least half spent on letters to my sister—letters which, if they'd survived, would be better than a detailed journal of my nineteenth and twentieth years, when adolescent anguish was still aflame.

I finished changing my name in my late thirties, when I finally told my family this was now my only name.

I took my name from my grandfather's—a frequent name in my extended genealogy, Crescendo (v. increase in loudness.) He went by Cris. I thought my writing career would a crescendo. It was for a while. The decrescendo began in earnest during perimenopause. But by then the name was mine.

It wasn't exactly my George Eliot move; more that I hated my girly (nick)name. I was aware of, but never considered the parallel of, Streisand dropping the middle *a* from Barbara because she disliked her name. It was the foundation of my (in my twenties purely instinctive, not articulated) objective to be appraised without (female) gender clouding or clogging or choking perceptions (of my writing). Then many of my characters made a similar passage: Veronica to Ronnie, Tamara to Tam, Corinne to Erin. Some did not have a mother, some were without a father, most did not have siblings. I didn't do this because Streisand had lost her father when she was one year old, or because of her siblings (whom I was unaware of). And being told she was too ugly to be successful stirred something in me, but it didn't feel analogous. I wasn't necessarily surprised nor disillusioned when she never answered a letter I wrote—and I don't recall how old I was, nor the subject of the letter, except that I was no longer (even latent) adolescent. And then I never wrote to Streisand about *Yentl*.

Itzhak Beshevis Singer, author of "Yentl the Yeshiva Boy," envisioned Yentl as "the soul of a man" in a woman's body. Was Singer suggesting a "true female" couldn't long for knowledge and study? I can understand Streisand's impetus to change that idea to a "women are unlimited" theme. But what is the "female soul" Singer imagined women *should* have?

Streisand's *Yentl* was given *female* sexual urges. Female sexuality had/has become hugely essential: crucial that we have it, that we use it, that we be gratified by it, that we publicly share it. It has remained the definition of "female." Of all the definitions of "female" I rejected, this is one I failed at so spectacularly, one would have to wonder how much I'd ever wanted to succeed.

> The radio therapist says that women (in committed relationships with men) who have stopped having sex should pick one: let the man have a girlfriend, let him go to prostitutes, or let him masturbate to porn. I subliminally chose one. And when the explicit adult website contained a ransomware bug that froze his computer, Mark called the fake Microsoft number that popped up and paid to have a fake technician "clean" his computer of evidence that the fake tech told him "proved" he was viewing child porn and would be sent to the FBI. Together we spent weeks getting his charges reversed, changing all our passwords, locking and putting alerts on our accounts. And I bought him a new computer, all the while trying to convince him I wasn't in the slightest offended or hurt by what he'd been doing. All this, plus trying to grasp the extent of his fear, ultimately caused by me, has possibly been my biggest day of reckoning.

Unlike in Singer's story, Streisand's film all but forced Yentl to give up the newfound opportunities only open to men, but also wanted her to see *that* as an accomplishment itself. The film's final aria, "A Piece of Sky," is a rousing ambition song—with one of the longest fortissimo notes Streisand's ever held (I measured all the others)—which made me suspect I hadn't been living its message,

"The more I live, the more I know. The more I know the more I realize what's left to learn" (Bergman and Bergman). The final "Papa watch me fly" could have prompted the radio therapist to ask Streisand, "What was life like in your house when you were eight?" Her father had died before she knew him, had been replaced with a stepfather, and it can be said that she spent part of her career (life?) striving to re-create an essence of "father" to be proud of her.

I was known as the kid who had a good voice and no father.

—Barbra Streisand

For me, every book review, every blurb, every interview, every invitation to read or teach . . . was also—even without consciously thinking about those extended-family spotlight violin concerts—a way for relatives I seldom saw to perceive that I was something too. Sure, that family audience had only wanted to listen to pop-music renditions on the violin. And, sure, aunts, uncles, and most cousins never actually saw any of my reviews, never read any of my books, and only asked how much money I made on them. Except that one uncle who had owned a bookstore. He saw Streisand in me.

When he was diagnosed with Alzheimer's but still able to attend family gatherings, he sat across from me at a long outdoor dining table, got my attention (touched my hand? tapped my arm?) and said—with marked spaces between each word, the same way his Italian father (my grandfather and namesake) had spoken English to children or strangers:

"What—is—your—name?"

I faltered. First thought: Was my name now a problem for my family? Next thoughts: Had my name change confused him further? Did he no longer know *any*one at this loud, messy gathering? Or was *I* being singled out as someone he no longer knew? Had I become a stranger? Would each possibility suggest a different response? Would I have to tell him my (chosen) name? Or would I have to help him remember me by using the detested and rejected former name?

True, he probably couldn't remember my name. But he knew who I was. "I have you on my bookshelf," he said, beaming.

Stony End

Perhaps the above should have been the end, a softer landing.

When my parents were gone, gone also was the hope to win the status I'd seen given to (earned by?) a sibling. I've let this essay sit for several weeks. And then it all cycled around:

Because refreshments were impossible at a masks-required grad-student reading, I asked my faculty colleagues to bring eight to ten copies of their published books, and we would have a book giveaway prior to the reading. I brought one copy of six different titles. A cloud of browsing formed around the table of books. The students worked quickly; when everyone finished and returned to their seats, the exposed table revealed that the only remaining books were all six of mine.

That this might happen was the single doubt I'd had about the book giveaway. And then it had actually, and so precisely, happened. But what had made me catastrophize the possibility? This: In 2004 the grad-student reading series was still structured as one professor with two or three students, as it had been since I was hired in 1993. Six readings, and each professor would go once a year. The last year the readings were done that way, 2004, I'd had a new novel released. I did my reading to a very poor turnout of about a quarter of the students and only one other professor. The following month, the grad-student reading featured an older man (possibly older than I am now) who, after decades of not having anything published, had his second book of stories come out in 2003. That event was mobbed, and afterward a cluster of students surrounded to congratulate him. Quite likely I was the only one who noticed the difference between the two events, and I can understand that his years of drought heightened their impulses to support him. Still, that was the first time I grasped that my standing in the very program I directed was more as glorified administrative assistant for their paperwork, and not as a writer whose work meant anything to them. When I took over as director, I changed the series so that no professors ever read in the grad-student series. A decade later, the book giveaway's harsh whisper, *Lest you forget . . .*

But, a few months after the book giveaway, in the morning before a remote faculty meeting, I must've forgotten that warning. I found myself figuratively taking a deep breath before sending an announcement of my new book's release to the department personnel via a listserv email that would include a link to an excerpt just out in a local Chicago monthly magazine—in more honest terms, *fantasizing* about this announcement with a weird and puerile hope. Interrupting my reverie, the department head had just sent a message on the listserv congratulating one of my colleagues for a national writing prize and concurrent publication of a poem in the *New York Times*.

Being published in a citywide monthly was nice, but compared to publication in the *New York Times*, it was like starring in community theater rather than on Broadway. Despite their theoretical protestations about capitalism, English professors tend to align the amount corporate publishing pays writers for their work with the literary value of the work.

But to have actual mood-altering feelings about this, or any that last longer than a moment, is an immaturity I'm forced to realize. As well, an abrupt comprehension: the department head is now the parent, and my colleagues are the relatives at the family violin concert who I presume view me, in comparison with my colleague, as a talentless clod.

At that remote faculty meeting, my square of the expanded Brady Bunch screen held a grim-faced still photo while the rest of me sat off camera staring out the window. When I turned off my computer and went downstairs, I snapped at Mark for not exercising the dogs during the meeting so that I would have to do it now. Did the crisp air and joyful dogs help? There were too many other things at the meeting to raise unease. A decade-long decline in the number of English majors, cryptic comments about deciding what hiring requests the department will make "depending on if we start to lose the top-heavy part of the tenured faculty to retirement." Intuiting their hand-rubbing keenness to begin cutting away the tired, the irrelevant, and those who were hired by a few pensioner-patriarchs three decades ago, those whose career visibility all happened and ended when the now-fortysomething faculty were in high school . . . to be replaced with choices of their own . . .

I didn't descend into absurd bawling until the following morning, after waking from a dream about my college mentor, who did validate my undeveloped attempts at creating literature, and whom I loved and was affected by in ways that can't be defined—although I tried in my 1979 journal: "Although I often wished you would not always read my mind so thoroughly, nothing you ever said to me was wasted." One of the supposedly unwasted things he said was "You're not the center of the universe to anyone but yourself." But ultimately, this too, in fact, was squandered.

At one of my first essential crossroads, when departing the safety of academia for employment as either a journalist or high-school teacher had become unthinkable—even though I was being ushered out by both a completed master's degree and a not-so-secret plan to separate me from my employment in his office—my mentor brought with him from home an enormous beer mug, clear with big red letters reading, *I Bet You Can't.* He said it had been given to him by a friend when he was on the brink of a major life decision, and now it was time for him to pass it on to me. That one-gallon beer mug has resided on the top shelf of my office at a university where I have been a professor for three decades. It's past time I find the right situation to pass the mug on, as he did in his thirties, probably because it's obvious he won that bet.

He is now an ultra-right-wing conspiracy theorist.

> Here's a dream: I got to school and met you, and you asked how I was (weird enough!), and if I was over my cold (I never had one!), and while I answered, another you walked past, smiled ever so slightly, but said nothing. I wasn't even amazed. I said, "There's two of you." You said, "This is my Friday self, leaving. That's my Monday self." What finally amazed me was that his Friday self was just leaving on Monday morning.
>
> —Cris Mazza, 1979 college journal

Here's another dream, forty-plus years later:

Why we are together again is, in this dream, unspecified and unquestioned. But it is, by context, a reunion. Not a party, just a coming together after some elapse of time. We were standing near a window, with a countertop running along the wall under the window. I was facing the window. Was it noisy? There must have been a reason I couldn't hear him. This caused him to speak directly into my ear, from a position of standing behind me, the heat of his face touching my cheek, the gust of his voice against my ear.

"I only heard half of what you've said," I protest. Despite never hearing a single word, I do know it was something about making a recording with one of his wind orchestras. He is an instrumental music conductor, not an English professor; this is not a peculiar fact supplied without logic by oneiric brain waves, it *was* his identity, although like all of us, not a complete identity.

With a whoop of joy, he leaped into the air, flipped sideways, and landed on his back on the countertop in front of me. I could tell, I just knew, my powers of perception were biconically acute: He was happy because he thought I'd said I'd heard the recording he'd made with the wind orchestra. His efforts and vision validated; his identity buoyed.

The dream did not allow me to make the mistake of correcting him. I woke.

I didn't sleep again.

In a few hours I wept. What for, I couldn't say.

CRUX, THE GEORGIA SERIES IN LITERARY NONFICTION

DEBRA MONROE, *My Unsentimental Education*

SONJA LIVINGSTON, *Ladies Night at the Dreamland*

JERICHO PARMS, *Lost Wax: Essays*

PRISCILLA LONG, *Fire and Stone: Where Do We Come From? What Are We? Where Are We Going?*

SARAH GORHAM, *Alpine Apprentice*

TRACY DAUGHERTY, *Let Us Build Us a City*

BRIAN DOYLE, *Hoop: A Basketball Life in Ninety-Five Essays*

MICHAEL MARTONE, *Brooding: Arias, Choruses, Lullabies, Follies, Dirges, and a Duet*

ANDREW MENARD, *Learning from Thoreau*

DUSTIN PARSONS, *Exploded View: Essays on Fatherhood, with Diagrams*

CLINTON CROCKETT PETERS, *Pandora's Garden: Kudzu, Cockroaches, and Other Misfits of Ecology*

ANDRÉ JOSEPH GALLANT, *A High Low Tide: The Revival of a Southern Oyster*

JUSTIN GARDINER, *Beneath the Shadow: Legacy and Longing in the Antarctic*

EMILY ARNASON CASEY, *Made Holy: Essays*

SEJAL SHAH, *This Is One Way to Dance: Essays*

LEE GUTKIND, *My Last Eight Thousand Days: An American Male in His Seventies*

CECILE PINEDA, *Entry without Inspection: A Writer's Life in El Norte*

ANJALI ENJETI, *Southbound: Essays on Identity, Inheritance, and Social Change*

CLINTON CROCKETT PETERS, *Mountain Madness: Found and Lost in the Peaks of America and Japan*

STEVE MAJORS, *High Yella: A Modern Family Memoir*

JULIA RIDLEY SMITH, *The Sum of Trifles*

SIÂN GRIFFITHS, *The Sum of Her Parts: Essays*

NED STUCKEY-FRENCH, *One by One, the Stars: Essays*

JOHN GRISWOLD, *The Age of Clear Profit: Collected Essays on Home and the Narrow Road*

DEBRA MONROE, *It Takes a Worried Woman: Essays*

JOSEPH GEHA, *Kitchen Arabic: How My Family Came to America and the Recipes We Brought with Us*

LAWRENCE LENHART, *Backvalley Ferrets: A Rewilding of the Colorado Plateau*

SARAH BETH CHILDERS, *Prodigals: A Sister's Memoir of Appalachia*

JODI VARON, *Your Eyes Will Be My Window: Essays*

SANDRA GAIL LAMBERT, *My Withered Legs and Other Essays*

BROOKE CHAMPAGNE, *Nola Face: Memoirs of a Truth-Telling Latina in the Big Easy*

MADDIE NORRIS, *The Wet Wound: An Elegy in Essays*

CRIS MAZZA, *The Decade of Letting Things Go: A Postmenopause Memoir*

LYDIA PAAR, *The Exit Is the Entrance: Essays on Escape*